A Cumberland Endeavour

A Cumberland Endeavour

Hine Brothers of Maryport:
The People, The Ships and The Town

Ian Hine

To Edna,

With Best Wishes,

Ian Hine

Jan., 2013.

The cover shows
"The Old Harbour, Maryport, 1896",
by William Mitchell of Maryport,
used with the kind permission of Mr Eric Galletly.

Printed and bound in Great Britain by Marston Book Services Ltd, Didcot, Oxon

Dedication

FREDA GRAHAM
1939 - 2002

This book is dedicated to Freda Graham, who undertook a large part of the background research, particularly in respect of Lloyd's Registers of Shipping, where her conscientious, accurate and intelligent work enabled us to produce reliable and informative data about the Hine Bros. fleet. She also worked indefatigably through the archives of the various local newspapers held in microfiche storage in London and produced comprehensive notes and references to the relevant events of the time. These would arrive accompanied by humorous and insightful comments, backed up by her knowledge of the subject and of Cumbrian attitudes and people, and were a joy to read. From a Maryport family herself, and with connections to Hine Bros. (her grandfather was an engineer on one of the steamers), Freda was an enthusiastic colleague and a skilled researcher. I am sorry she did not live to see this book: I hope she would have been proud of it.

Acknowledgements

THIS BOOK HAS BEEN a spare-time interest for me and has been more than twenty years in the making, with irregular bursts of activity interrupted by other more urgent - if not more intriguing - matters. Now that the task is over, I would like to acknowledge the contribution of several people whose help has been vital along the way.

Firstly, my sister Lesley Buswell née Hine, whose inquiries into our 'family tree' revealed the connection with the Hine family in Maryport (we descend from Joseph Jackson Hine, so Wilfrid and Alfred are my great-great-uncles); and cousin Mrs. Patricia Hine of Canberra, whose tireless work on genealogy and Census records has allowed me to sort out relationships in a family with an amazing number of Wilfrids and Alfreds!

My wife has supported my labours throughout, and deserves my thanks for her patience: she is now greatly relieved to be able to reclaim the dining-room table.

Over the years a multitude of people have been kind enough to give me pieces of information, documents, photographs and other memorabilia which have helped in putting the story together. I would particularly like to thank John Whitwell of the Maryport Maritime Museum; Mr. and Mrs. D. Ritchie, Mr. K. Rich and Mr. P. Dulling, Miss C. Dixon and so many others for valuable encouragement.

I am grateful to Gordon Taylor for his skill in re-photographing some of the pictures used in the book. I am grateful also to "Sea Breezes" magazine for consent to include material from their past editions, and am pleased to record my appreciation of the Museum of Monterey, Ca., which allowed me access to the "Allen Knight" and "Capt.Walter F. Lee" collections of historic prints and negatives. The National Maritime Museum, London, and the State Library of South Australia have also given kind permission to reproduce photographs from their archive collections, and I thank them both. Since the introduction of the world wide web the number of sources of material, including historic ship pictures, has mushroomed to the point where many illustrations seem to be 'in the public domain' and reproduced in multiple outlets: if therefore I appear to have omitted an acknowledgement or attribution it is in good faith and not from a desire to deny proper recognition. Finally, I would like to express my particular thanks to Eric Galletly for his kind permission to use the painting of "The Old Harbour, Maryport, 1896", by the famous artist William Mitchell of Maryport, as the cover design for this book, and to Dr Tony Gray of WORDS BY DESIGN, who has moulded the manuscript and pictorial material so skilfully into book form.

While I have made every effort to 'check my sources' and produce an accurate record, I have no doubt that errors or misinterpretations may have crept in. This account is not a comprehensive one: it has been much more difficult to decide what to leave out than what to put in! I should be very pleased to hear from readers who can add to the archive, or put me right where I have got it wrong.

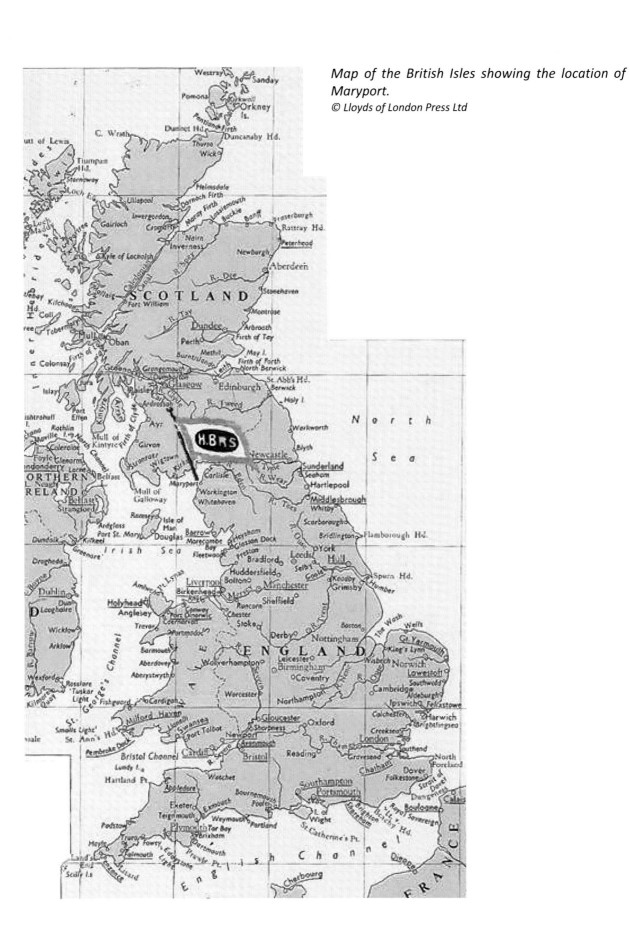

Map of the British Isles showing the location of Maryport.
© Lloyds of London Press Ltd

Contents

Chapter One
The Beginnings

MARYPORT is not deeply rooted in the past. On the outskirts of the present town site lie the remains of a Roman fort and its supporting garrison settlement which once supplemented the defences of the western end of Hadrian's Wall, while nearby are the traces of a twelfth century motte and bailey castle, but the area does not have a noteworthy mediaeval history. There was no significant urban or commercial growth on this stretch of the coast: at Ellenfoot, a small natural harbour at the mouth of the river Ellen, a dozen or so squalid huts were home to a small fishing population and in 1748 there was only one substantial house – a farmhouse called Valentia, built 30 years before. The local manor house, Netherhall, developed from a fourteenth century pele tower: the Middle Ages were turbulent times, with raids by the Scots from across the Solway Firth and by Reivers from the neighbouring border lands.

It was Ellenborough, a little way inland, which was the principal village in the Manor of Netherhall. There is little indication that the Lords of the Manor – the de Sheftling, Eaglesfield and latterly the Senhouse families – had been moved to a higher degree of humanitarian or civic enlightenment than their counterparts elsewhere; indeed, the Senhouses were notorious for their weakness for gambling, which frequently reduced the family fortunes to precarious levels.

In the middle of the eighteenth century, however, things began to change, the stimulus being the exploitation of the coal mined on the Senhouse estate. Coal had been mined by open-cast methods or from primitive shallow shafts since at least 1719, when the Collector of Customs at Whitehaven had reported that:

the coal trade at said creek is carried on mostly by small vessels that belong to Dublin and the north of Ireland... the inhabitants near Ellenfoot not concerning themselves with shipping, only in digging and loading the coal in sacks on horseback to the Harbour.

As Lord of the Manor, Humphrey Senhouse of Netherhall owned most of the land and thus most of the coal. He also owned the harbour, and the ancient right to levy a charge of one shilling for every ship anchoring within it – a right preserved for at least another century by subsequent Acts of Parliament. He must have been aware of the potential value of the natural assets, and that the Lowther family were developing a similar enterprise based upon the nearby port of Whitehaven, because in February 1749 Senhouse petitioned the House of Commons with *"a Bill for Repairing, Enlarging and Preserving the Harbour at Ellenfoot"*. The Bill was passed and development began, and in case it should be thought that Senhouse's motives were merely greed – and a desire to outdo his neighbours – it has to be said that in fact he and his cousins invested considerable sums of money in the operation. By the end of March 1749 new levies were being enforced on coal shipped out through Ellenfoot, and on any incoming cargoes. By May, work had begun on improvements; a harbourmaster was appointed, and the responsibility for the management of the harbour was vested in a body of Commissioners nominated and appointed by the Lord of the Manor. The enterprise was an instant success: within a year the Whitehaven Collector of Customs, who was still responsible for Ellenfoot harbour, had to request that the number of 'searchers' there be trebled to cope with the increase in workload.

With this phenomenal upsurge in trade and employment came the impetus for urban development, and Senhouse set about the task. He was by no means an uncultured man, having a keen interest in the Roman remains in his manor (as had all his ancestors since the mid-sixteenth century) and also in the exciting economic and scientific events heralding the Industrialisation of Britain. It has been suggested that his plan for a new town – a 'gridiron' pattern of straight streets regularly spaced and intersecting at right-angles – was influenced by the area's Roman history. Be that as it may, plots of land were rented, leased or occasionally sold for residential development and the hamlet began to grow into a small industrial town. Progress was such that in 1756 an Act of Parliament conferred upon this new conurbation the name MARYPORT, in honour of Humphrey's wife Mary, daughter of the Bishop of Carlisle. The harbour, however, continued to be known as Ellenfoot in Acts of Parliament up to 1812.

A harbour town naturally attracts maritime businesses, and Maryport was no exception. In 1752 one John Bell fitted out a ship in the harbour, though whether it was actually built there is uncertain: in 1760 the Ritson family, who were later to diversify their interests into shipbuilding and shipowning, set up in business as sailmakers, and in 1765 William Wood moved into town and opened a shipyard. When Pennant published his "Tour" in 1774 he included useful facts and descriptions of the "new creation" of Maryport. About 100 houses had sprung up, and a population of 1,300 *"collected together by the opening of a coal trade on this estate"*. A ropeyard and a skinning business are noted, and the harbour is described as, *"wooden piers with quays on the river Ellen, where ships lie and receive their loading"*. Pennant counted about 70 ships between 30 and 300 tons using the port's facilities, rewarding the Lord of the Manor's enterprise and vision – and replenishing the Senhouse coffers!

Despite the "repairing, enlarging and preserving" envisaged by the 1749 Bill, the harbour at Maryport at this time was still very primitive. Coal was still delivered by the sackload on the backs of pack-animals, so loading a vessel was a painfully slow process. The navigational aids for the ships were also, to put it kindly, rudimentary: the only beacon to guide the mariner to safe haven was a lamp in the shop window of William Curry, a bootmaker in King Street! Incredibly, this state of affairs continued for nearly 50 years, until a permanent light on a wooden post was erected on the quay in 1792. Similarly, for over 70 years all ships intending to enter harbour would have to look out for a flag flying from a mast on Mote Hill, south of the town; for that was the indication of sufficient depth of water in the tidal channel for vessels to reach the quay. (It was not until 1846 that a proper light and signal station were erected on the new South Pier.)

Nevertheless, the ships kept on coming, loading, and going, and the little town's growth and development was able to continue. By 1781 there were 355 houses in Senhouse's grid-iron town: in 1794 Hutchinson's "History of Cumberland" quotes the number of ships belonging to the port as 90, with an average tonnage of 120. Trade from Maryport by now was not just coastal or across to Ireland: some ships were crossing the Atlantic to trade (or had been before the War of Independence) and were also trading with the Baltic ports in timber, flax and iron as well as coal. At this point it is appropriate to mention that there was also an iron foundry in Maryport: the seeds of an industry which would grow and blossom a century later were sown in 1752, but they certainly did not flourish at first and the foundry closed in 1784. It was not all smooth progress in the coal-mining business at that time either: at about the time the foundry failed, the open-cast and shallow diggings became worked out. Fortunately, plentiful seams of coal were discovered in deeper pits which would be sufficient to sustain the industry for more than a century to come.

By 1810, Britten and Brayley's "Description of Cumberland" noted between 90 and 100 ships of up to 250 tons belonging to the port; and Jollie's "Cumberland Guide and Directory", published a year later, tells of *"an iron furnace, shipbuilding, saltworks, a pottery, a glasshouse, a cotton mill, and extensive muslin manufactories"* enhancing the industry of the little town and supporting a growing population. In 1821 the population had risen to 3,500; by 1828 the port was exporting some 40,000 tons of coal each year, and trade was still increasing.

With such an amount of coal to be shipped, older methods of transportation had given way to the horse-drawn cart. Convoys of these would be encountered on the rough roads from the mines at Flimby, Dovenby, Dearham and other inland villages, making for Maryport and its little harbour. For each cartload of coal delivered to a waiting ship the First Mate would issue the carter a token or tally, redeemable at the Colliery Office as payment for haulage.

One of the men earning his living in this way was a carter whose name was Alfred Hine. Alfred's father was of Cumberland stock but after the death of his first wife in 1802 he had married again and set up home in Tyldesley, near Manchester. Alfred, the fourth child of this union, was born in 1808: nothing is known about where he spent his early life, but his wife, Ann Jackson, was a Maryport girl and it is probably because of her that he came to the town. Alfred and Ann set up home in King Street, near the harbour, and it was there that the first of their children were to be born: Ann (Nanny) in 1833, who died in childhood; Mary in 1835, and then the two sons – Wilfrid (1838) and Alfred (1841) – who were to influence so strongly the development of Maryport's character, and who feature so prominently in this history as it unfolds.

The growth of the town continued apace, despite the various epidemics of disease which struck the town. Maryport had outgrown its public utilities: the water and sewerage systems had become inadequate for the demand, with disastrous consequences. There had been a cholera outbreak in 1832, and over the next 20 years the population was exposed to the ravages of dysentery, tuberculosis and typhoid.

Trade increased, however, due to several factors, the first of which was the completion of the Maryport and Carlisle Railway. This transport link, begun in 1840 under the supervision of George Stephenson and completed in 1845, boosted Maryport's importance as a port and distribution centre serving a wide area, and established an advantage over its neighbours; it was not until two years later that Whitehaven achieved a railhead.

Secondly, under the auspices of the new Board of Trustees, enlargement of the dock and improvement of the harbour facilities had taken place. In 1837 the 'New Dock' – now called the Elizabeth Basin – was opened, and in the following year a significant milestone was passed when Maryport became a Port, entitled to register shipping in its own right. It had its own Customs House instead of being merely a subsidiary of Whitehaven, and by 1842 there was enough trade to warrant the establishment of a Bonded Warehouse. In 1843 The Lords Commissioners of the Admiralty ordered a survey of the Solway ports, and Commander Denham, R.N., F.R.S., duly inspected the Maryport scene. As a result of his report, Humphrey Senhouse's local Board found themselves with more work to do; widening and deepening the channel, building a new pier – and finally replacing William Curry's makeshift harbour light!

Significantly, a political change had also occurred. By an Act of Parliament of 1833 control of the affairs of the Harbour and of the town had been transferred to a Board of Trustees, with a constitution altogether different from the Commissioners before them. The Lord of the Manor retained the Chairmanship of the Board and nominated four Trustees personally, but in the new structure a further eight Trustees – a clear majority – were to be elected by secret ballot of the ratepayers of Maryport as representatives of the townspeople and the shipowners. This was an astonishingly advanced and enlightened measure for the times, and raises the question of Humphrey Senhouse's motive in making this change. Did he wish to combine the concept of Maryport's physical layout as a blueprint for future industrial town design with a blueprint for democratic local government? Did he realise that paternalism and the rule of the Lord of the Manor was becoming irrelevant to a bustling, busy town? Or perhaps Senhouse had an inkling of the financial minefield which lay ahead of Maryport and its harbour in the future!

Despite the New Dock and the widening of the channel, trade in the port could not keep pace with the demand for the transport of coal. The railway brought it in from further afield, and local collieries also increased their output yearly: in 1841, 150,000

Maryport in the 1850s

tons of coal were exported, and this rose to 269,000 tons by 1853. Loading facilities worked under greater and greater strain: there were 113 vessels registered to Maryport alone in 1840, and dozens more from other ports visited regularly. The boom was continuing, and bigger and better facilities had to be provided if Maryport was to keep ahead of its competitors – Workington, Whitehaven, Harrington and Millom, to mention those just within a few miles along the coast. Maryport's trump card was to be a 'wet dock' – that is, one which did not empty at low tide leaving vessels immobile on the mud, but maintained a full and even depth of water which allowed ships to be loaded and moved in between tides. The Trustees were confident that the extra income and dues would quickly recoup the costs of construction once the wet dock was in business, so they set about trying to raise the finance necessary.

Money had been a problem for some years: the mortgage debt for the previous works was already £5,000 and although the port was making a profit of over £2,000 per year the Trustees were not in a position to increase their borrowing in the financial market place. An appeal to the public for loans produced £6,000, a considerable sum in those days, and the Trustees were able to pledge the surplus revenue from the harbour to the project. The colliery owners might have been expected to join in – in their own interest if for no other reason – but they were not helpful, and in fact only two even responded to the appeal!

Again the Senhouse family stepped in. They offered a 'pound for pound' arrangement to match contributions by the Trustees; and more importantly still they stood security (along with some of the other Trustees) for a bank loan for the balance of the cost. Work began again, and despite a storm in 1853 which demolished the South Pier, the wet dock was completed in 1857. From the New Dock, access to the new wet dock was via an entrance fitted with a pair of dock gates which were closed between tides to maintain a depth of at least 14ft. of water within the basin. Over a quarter of a mile of extra quayside had been constructed, at a cost of £40,000, and this provided over three acres of safe anchorage. On 20th October 1857, in an atmosphere of public rejoicing, the Elizabeth Dock was opened. The town was decorated overall, illuminated at night, and the people of Maryport must have felt that prosperity was assured.

During this 20 years of progress the fortunes of Alfred and Ann Hine and their family had gradually flourished. Another two children had been born – a daughter Barbara in 1845 and their youngest son, Joseph Jackson Hine in 1850 – and the family had moved from King Street. They now lived in Brow Street, a road which runs up the escarpment north of the harbour from the quayside to High Street. Alfred's business was secure – he appears in the Trade Directory of 1847 as "Alfred Hine, Carrier" and also in the 1851 Census.

In the family's entry for the Census of 1861 it can be seen that Mary and Barbara, aged 26 and 16, were still single and living at home. Joseph J. was 11 years old, and Alfred was 19 years-of-age. His occupation on this occasion is listed as 'draper's apprentice': he was apprenticed to Mr. William Leighton, draper, of Senhouse Street, whom his sister Mary later married !

But what of Wilfrid? In 1857, just three weeks after the opening of the Elizabeth Dock, a small notice had appeared in *Adair's Maryport Advertiser*: *"We are glad to announce that a Grammar Class is at last established in the Mechanics' Institute under the Superintendence of Mr. Wilfrid Hine."* He was 19 years old then, and developing the enterprise and concern for his fellows was to be typical of his future. By 1861 he had left home, moved to Liverpool, and was becoming increasingly involved and skilled in the complexities of shipbrokerage, marine insurance, and other aspects of maritime commerce.

About this time Alfred too moved to Liverpool, to work in the counting-house of a large drapery business. He only stayed there for three months: at Wilfrid's suggestion Alfred gave it up and followed his older brother into his profession. He returned to Maryport and went to work for Westray Fearon, a local marine insurance and ship broker, while Wilfrid remained in Liverpool, in the employ of a firm called R. Nicholson and Company. Wilfrid was evidently a trusted and competent employee, because by 1863 he was the company's signatory on payments made to the crew of a British barque by the Consul in Buenos Aires.

Two years later, on November 9th 1865, Wilfrid and Alfred's father Alfred Hine met his death. The facts cannot be better presented than they were in *Adair's Maryport Advertiser*, and while modern readers may find the eulogistic prose rather pretentious, the appreciation of his worth and worthiness in the local Victorian society comes through sincerely. He was 57 years old.

Melancholy Accident – Death of Mr. Alfred Hine

Yesterday morning about 8 o'clock as Mr. Alfred Hine, carrier, was setting out on his usual journey to Whitehaven, his horse suddenly started on the Railway bridge, the train running under the bridge and throwing up steam having frightened the horse, when Mr. Hine, reaching forward to catch the rein, was thrown to the ground. It is supposed he must have fractured his skull in the fall as there was a deep wound in the temple. He was immediately conveyed to the Station Inn and no time was lost in obtaining medical aid, but although he was living at the time he was never heard to speak and was conveyed back to his home, which he had left only a few minutes before in high spirits, now a mangled corpse. Mr. Hine has been intimately associated with the history of Maryport for the last 30 years as one of her distinguished public characters. Sanguine and enthusiastic, no benevolent scheme was ever set on foot but had his heavy support. But great as were his usefulness and popularity abroad, his enjoyment within his own domestic circle when surrounded by his "household gods" transcended all other enjoyments: and though public societies may miss him and much work that fell to his lot may be left undone, yet it is within the magic circle of home where the cheerful ring of his well known voice, now heard no more, will be most missed, where the golden bowl will be felt to be broken and the silver cord loosened.

Adair's Maryport Advertiser, 10th November 1865

On a happier note, however, just three months earlier the *Advertiser* had carried the announcement of the marriage of the young Alfred (now aged 23, and described as a 'ship broker') on 26th July 1865 at Crosscanonby. His bride was Isabella McLennan, eldest daughter of Mr. McLennan, Her Majesty's Coastguard. Wilfrid had married a few years before and he and his wife Jane were already the parents of a daughter, also called Jane, born in 1864. In 1866 Alfred and Isabella produced their first daughter, Christina, and Wilfrid and Jane's second child – another daughter, Anne – was born in Liverpool in September of the same year. Two years later the sisters-in-law did it again, but this time each delivered a son! Both boys were born in Maryport, and both were christened Alfred (Alfred Hine junior, son of Alfred and Isabella, was born on 19th April, while Alfred Ernest Hine, son of Wilfrid and Jane, appeared on October 14th).

1868 also saw the beginnings of the Hine Brothers' involvement directly with the ships themselves, rather than just their cargoes, voyages and insurance. On Thursday May 21st a fine little barque was launched from Taylor and Scouler's yard in Sunderland, ready for the 'southern trade' – between English ports and Australia, South America and the Pacific. She was built of wood, copper-bottomed; 119 feet long by 27 feet beam, and 327 tons register. She was named the **"Robert Hine"** after one of her part-owners who lived in India and had a family connection through Wilfrid's grandfather's first marriage. Nicholson and Company were the registered owners and Wilfrid was her manager. Her first master was Captain Joseph Wilkinson, and when the fitting-out and loading was completed the "Robert Hine" sailed for Adelaide on 10th July.

In the following year Wilfrid also found himself the manager of the **"Abbey Holme"**, newly built by the famous firm of Blumer of Sunderland and launched on September 16th 1869. She was a fine iron clipper; a three-masted barque of 516 tons register, 157 feet in length, 28 feet in beam, and drawing 17 feet of water. This beautiful ship had many connections with the town of Maryport apart from Wilfrid's involvement, as several local gentlemen were part-owners, and the name "Abbey Holme" refers to a district in Cumberland of that time.

Abbey Holme, c.1875

Once again, Nicholson & Co. of Liverpool were registered as her owners of the "Abbey Holme", and her Captain was to be Wedgewood Robinson, a local master mariner, who for the last five years had captained the **"Humberstone"**, a wooden barque built in Quebec in 1863. Wilfrid soon found cargo and destination for her, as the "Abbey Holme" is recorded to have arrived in Valparaiso, on Chile's Pacific coast, on January 19th 1870 – barely 125 days after her launch!

Alfred's involvement directly with ships and sailors had developed too, but in an entirely different way: he was a Captain of the local rocket brigade. Together with the coastguard service, founded in 1822, and the lifeboat service, organised on a national basis from 1824, the use of mortar and rocket apparatus was established as a means of saving the lives of seafarers in distress – in this case by getting a line aboard a ship in imminent danger of stranding or wrecking on a shore during a storm. A Board of Trade notice of 1866 describes the procedure in detail for the information of masters and crew, and graphic illustrations are included opposite.

During a terrific gale one Sunday night in February 1869, the Maryport Coastguard reported sighting a ship in distress close to the harbour. The rocket crew assembled, and within 20 minutes they had located the vessel and had fired a rocket over her to carry a 'whip line' aboard. Unfortunately the ship's crew do not seem to have read the Board of Trade's guidance notes – or perhaps the master of the "Robert Bruce" of Belfast, with

Plate 1: The Rocket Arranged for Firing

Plate 2: The Rocket Line Carried Over a Wreck

Plate 3: Landing the Crew in the Breeches Buoy

masts and rigging washed away and within sight of shipwreck, was unable to summon up the necessary *"coolness and attention to the rules laid down"*. With commendable persistence and accuracy the rocket brigade put three more lines aboard, but still without response, and the crew did not take the opportunity to haul a stronger rope aboard and escape using a breeches buoy. There was thus no alternative but to launch the lifeboat, which came alongside the "Robert Bruce" and took off the master, Captain Stranny, and his five-man crew without mishap; the ship herself was wrecked north of the town soon afterwards. The Maryport press praised Alfred and his men for their conduct, and roundly criticised the ship's crew for their ignorance! Interestingly, almost exactly two years later the *Maryport Advertiser* describes another three days of terrific gales: on March 9th 1871 the Brigade was called out to a schooner which was being blown past the harbour entrance by the wind. Thirty men, and the rocket equipment drawn by two stout horses, *"dashed along the road by the Tanyard, the surf repeatedly covering them. On reaching Saltpans they found the vessel beached, and without delay fired a rocket over her with a rope attached, by which means all the crew and the Captain's wife were saved"*. No names are included in the report, but Alfred was probably among the 30 – particularly as the schooner concerned was the **"North Branch"**, part-owned by his brother Wilfrid!

The brothers kept in regular contact during these years; indeed, they corresponded almost daily. Some of Alfred's letters to Wilfrid have survived, and from the notes which the methodical Wilfrid made it is clear that he received his brother's letters in Liverpool the morning after they were sent from Maryport – and replied to them the same day. Alfred's letters are not easy to read: he wrote in a fluent hand and used a form of abbreviated shorthand code, not unlike modern 'speedwriting', intermingled in the sentences. For example, on 21st July 1869, he begins:

My dr. Bro,

Rd. yr. v. short but w. ltr. this m.g. & we r. v. v. g. to hear y. r. going to try to be here next wk.

and he always finishes:

I r.
D.W.
Y.A.B.
Alfred

– presumably, "I remain, dear Wilfrid, your affectionate brother, Alfred."

To compound the difficulty, Alfred's habit when one side of the paper was full was to rotate it through 90 degrees and carry on with the sentence, rather than turning the paper over! When the letter was finished it was folded to form a packet of some 8cm by 4cm, sealed with wax, addressed (not in an envelope) and despatched. As no postage stamp was affixed the letters presumably went by private courier or by railway, with other commercial post, to Liverpool.

The letters give a fascinating glimpse into the personal, family and business life of that time. Wilfrid's wife Jane was apparently suffering from a chest infection and pleurisy, and Alfred succeeds in persuading the family to return to Maryport in August 1869 for the good of her health, extolling the virtues of "a change of air and scene" and "nourishing and strengthening food". He sets about arranging accommodation for Wilfrid, Jane and their three young children at his mother's house, and bemoans the lack of room in his own home in High Street: he also undertakes to engage a "little girl from the town" to help care for the children. In another letter he suggests they borrow a pony and trap for a month for family outings; throughout, there is an obvious affection for his kinsfolk and enthusiasm for their visit. The health of the family features in other letters too: on 26th July, Alfred writes: "Isabella's M(other) is very poorly – has spit up a quantity of blood these last 2 or 3 days". The suspicion must be that Mrs. McLennan was suffering from pulmonary tuberculosis, and it may have been that disease which carried off Alfred and Isabella's daughter, little four-year-old Christina, the following year.

Not all the family news was ominous, however. On July 22nd, Alfred reports that 'Josey' – Joseph Jackson Hine, their younger brother – wants his mother and Alfred to join in with him to find the cash to buy a pony and trap from one John Graham, as "it can be got cheap, say £19 or £20." Alfred comments, "If we can raise the money M(other) and I will go for it I think and make money too." Joseph, by this time nearly 20 years old, was helping his mother continue the family business of carting and carrying: *Adair's Maryport Advertiser*, lst October 1869, proclaimed:

FLIMBY LAND-SALE COAL

Mrs. Alfred Hine begs respectfully to inform the inhabitants of Maryport that she has been appointed Agent for the above House Coal. All orders for Coal for the Town and Neighbourhood with which she may be favoured, will have prompt attention.

44 Brow Street

The letters also contain much maritime information and comment, suggesting that the brothers were able to direct business to each other, and that their respective firms had many ventures in common. In one letter Alfred agrees with Wilfrid's decision not to "re-class" (re-register at Lloyd's) the "Humberstone", but find her a cargo to Australia and sell her there. A French company, Curcier & Adet, chartered the barque and Capt. Robinson handed her over to Captain Clark before moving to the new "Abbey Holme".

From Liverpool the "Humberstone" made for Bordeaux and Rochefort where Captain John Smith assumed command; she took on a large cargo of brandy destined for Melbourne and Sydney, and made good time on her voyage. The "Melbourne Argus" of Thursday 21 April, 1870 reads:

For Sale, or Charter (after delivering balance of cargo in Sydney), the barque Humberstone, 322 tons register, built in Quebec in 1863, classed A1 seven years, which expires December 31,1870. Passed half time survey in 1868, when she was opened under the Inspection of Lloyd's, and at a cost of £800 was caulked from keel to combings, and had now pitch pine foremast; this voyage had
now pitch pine main mast, and is now in excellent order; has delivered 500 tons of coal; stands and shifts without ballast; sails well, and delivers her cargoes in good order; is fitted with double topsail yards. Now discharging a general cargo from Bordeaux and Rochefort, at the Victorian Railways Pier, Williamstown, where she can be inspected.

For further particulars, and list of inventory apply to: Captain Smith, on board.

From Sydney the "Humberstone" obtained a charter from Hong Kong to Melbourne, loading a cargo at Foochow, but this enterprise was to have tragic consequences. On 21st October 1870, in ballast on her way to Foochow, she struck a sunken rock S.W. of Formosa and rapidly sank. The ship's one lifeboat was launched and the ship's company climbed on board, but as she went down the sinking "Humberstone" heeled over on top of it, capsizing it. The lifeboat stayed afloat, but only the second mate, Edward Heselton, and four sailors were able to scramble aboard: the first mate, Adam Holliday, was rescued in a half-drowned state but later died. The five survivors endured the horrors of six days without food or fresh water in an open boat before being picked up by a passing junk. The rest of the crew were lost, including Captain Smith; an able and steady mariner, who left a widow and four young children.

In the last of the letters to Wilfrid still in existence there is a rare but important insight into Alfred's personal situation: after eight years as a clerk with Westray Fearon, Alfred had been offered a proposition which was to change his life. Some years before, the local company of Hetherington and Son had set up in Maryport as Ship's Brokers and Chandlers in premises they had built at Custom House Quay: the business had not been a success and the company was about to fold. In August 1869, out of the blue, the owners offered Alfred the option to take over the premises if he wished to set himself up on his own account!

For Alfred, dispirited and frustrated, married and with a young family and no savings from a clerk's salary, the risk involved in this huge challenge needed serious consideration. Presumably in reply to a query from his brother, he writes:

> *Yes there is a lot of work at the office, and I do think a portion would surely fall to my share if I were in business, and really Wilfrid I must be doing something as I can't go on at this rate much longer. It's bad enough to have to work for a man whom you can never respect, but to be labouring without any prospect of being advanced is dismal enough. I asked him today for my wages which were due on Saturday and he coolly told me he had no money by him! We must have a serious talk about matters when you come (D.V.) and see if something can't be arranged, Wilfrid.*

This letter undoubtedly had important consequences. Alfred and his more experienced older brother must have appraised the shipping market in Maryport and its prospects, assessed the possibilities of starting up independently – in competition with his present employer – and decided to grasp the opportunity. The premises were much too large for his needs at first, but he made ends meet by sub-letting parts of the building to other businesses – including, appropriately, the Customs Authority! Within a year, Alfred was his own master, and becoming part of the the local business community: in the press announcement of Christina's death in July 1870, she is described as, *"the daughter of Alfred Hine, ship and insurance broker"*. By 1871 the *Maryport Advertiser* was referring to him as *"Mr. Alfred Hine"*, and his office in Custom House Buildings was often used for the auctions of ships and equipment.

He was also the local agent for the Liverpool Underwriters' Association, and Secretary of the Solway Mutual Marine Insurance Association, known as the 'Solway Club'. In this early co-operative venture the members – local shipowners – contributed to a fund to provide compensation for losses or damage. The premium each was required to pay was determined by the declared value of his own vessels, the total value of all the ships insured, and the claims upon the fund. For example: in 1870 the losses sustained by Association members came to just over £650; the ill-fated "Humberstone",

insured for £500, making up the largest part of the year's claims. In April 1871 Alfred's committee did their calculations and resolved to call upon the members for £2:0:5d (£2.02p) per £100 of insured assets. So Captain John Kendall of Maryport, who had insured his schooner "Perseverance" with the Club for £600 and the "White Star" for £900, was therefore presented with an account for £30:6s:3d – nearly £1,000 today! (The rate chosen, incidentally, suggests that about £32,500 worth of shipping was insured with Solway Mutual Marine: about a million pounds' worth in present day terms and another indication that Maryport's prosperity was still increasing).

Alfred had also taken his first steps as a shipowner in 1872 when he and two friends acquired the wooden barque "Roslyn". One of the co-purchasers was a Mr. Harrison, and the "Roslyn" was re-named the **"Jane Harrison"** after his wife. Their experience of ownership was to be a brief one: the vessel was fitted out and set sail for Valparaiso on what was expected to be a three-year mission, but within a few days the "Jane Harrison" was struck by lightning in a storm and sank! However, the inauspicious beginning of this enterprise led to a long association with Hine Brothers' ships for the third partner, Captain J. Johnstone, who went on to serve the Company in sail and steam for more than 20 years.

In 1871, the town was indeed a hive of industry. The population was now 7,413, supported by shipping, the coal trade and the rebirth of the iron industry. Three years earlier the Maryport Haematite Iron Company had been formed and was running six blast furnaces, while the Solway Iron Company, established in 1870, was in business with another four. This new local demand for coal did reduce the amount available for export, and adversely affected Harbour dues for a time; but supply increased to meet the demand, and cargoes of iron and steel were also being shipped out, to the satisfaction of the Trustees.

In Liverpool, Wilfrid prospered and began to expand his interests. In addition to the "North Branch" he became part owner of four more ships in his own name. In 1872 he bought the "King Arthur", a 422 ton barque of composite construction

"Hazel Holme", c.1874

(that is, the frame of the ship was iron, but the hull and decking were of wood) built two years earlier in Whitby. Wilfrid changed her name to **"Hazel Holme"**, put Capt. W. Clark in command and engaged her in voyages to Mauritius and Australia.

He also acquired the **"Glenfalloch"**, a wooden barque of 449 tons built in Scotland in 1861: under Capt. Johnstone she was employed to trade between Liverpool and the ports of the St. Lawrence River. And for the South American trade, particularly to Valparaiso, Wilfrid purchased another two wooden barques; the **"Aline"**, and the 513 ton **"John Norman"**, built in 1855 by J. Westacott at Barnstable. Westacott's yard, incidentally, was almost unique in that it was roofed over: ships were built under cover protected from the elements, and received higher classification in Lloyd's Register. The "Aline" was a barque of 474 tons gross, built in 1867 by Hardie of Sunderland.

The sixth ship in Wilfrid's enterprise was another wooden barque, the **"Cereal"**, just under 300 tons and built on Wearside in 1859. This fine little ship was part-owned by her master, Capt. James Ritchie, one of the many Cumberland sea captains destined for a long association with Hine ships.

His career as master of the "Cereal", however, was about to come to an abrupt end. What happened is described graphically by Capt. Ritchie's daughter in an article she wrote for "Sea Breezes" in 1927:

In August, 1872, my father left Swansea in command of the barque "Cereal", owned jointly by the late Mr. Wilfrid Hine and my father (the late Captain James Ritchie), both Maryport men. The vessel had a cargo of coal for Santos and all went well till after she crossed the Line, when, one day, the strange antics of the ship's cat attracted attention. As a hatch was left open in the daytime for ventilation the cat was in the habit of going down the hold; but this day, on coming up again, raced about the deck scraping her paws.

Soon afterwards a faint curl of smoke was seen and it was found that the ship was on fire. Matters looked hopeless, but everything possible was done to save the ship, boats were made ready and towed astern in preparation for leaving the vessel quickly if necessity demanded. However, the crew were spared the horrors of a long boat trip, for a vessel hove in sight. To the surprise of all – for many of the crew belonged to Maryport – the vessel proved to be the "John Ritson" of Maryport, commanded by Captain George Curwen, a Maryport man!

By this time the fumes were very bad, so the Cereal's crew transferred to the "John Ritson" before nightfall. The two masters decided to take both ships' crews to the burning ship next morning and endeavour to save her. However, just as they were preparing to set forth the hatches of the "Cereal" blew off and the vessel was quickly enveloped in flames. This was on 28th September 1872, in Lat. 4.30 S., and Long. 27.45 W.

The "John Ritson" was outward bound, so my father (and mother, who was with him at the time), his officers and part of the crew were transferred to the first homeward-bound vessel sighted, and she bore the Cumbrian name of "Portinscale". Surely a chain of Cumbrian coincidences.

The "Portinscale" was returning to Ireland, having rounded the Horn from Pisagua in Chile. She arrived at Queenstown on November 20th with Capt. and Mrs. Ritchie and the mate of the "Cereal", while the "John Ritson" made port in Montevideo with the rest of the crew on the 27th. A postscript to the adventure can be found in the *Maryport News* of May 16th 1873:

Captain George Curwen of the "John Ritson" has been presented with a handsome gold watch by Capt. Ritchie of the "Cereal" for his gallant and humane conduct towards Capt. Ritchie and his crew whom he rescued from the ship when on fire at sea.

On the domestic side, 1872 had seemed to be a fortunate year for the family in Maryport: in August Barbara Hine was married to John Robinson, a local master mariner, while in April Alfred's wife Isabella bore him another son, christened John McLennan Hine.

However, 1873 began tragically with Isabella's untimely death in March at the age of only 30. Alfred was left, at the age of 32, to bring up his two sons – one still a baby, the other only four years old – having lost daughter and wife in rapid succession. His mother and sisters doubtless supported him in this difficult time, and his strong Christian belief would have sustained him: the family's staunch Baptist faith and Alfred's capacity for hard work seem to have kept him going. Perhaps it was this tragedy that decided Wilfrid and Jane to return to Maryport, as on July lst 1873 Wilfrid combined his shipowning and shipbroking business with his brother's insurance and mercantile interests to form **'HINE BROTHERS OF MARYPORT'**, based in Alfred's office in Custom House Building.

Such then were the beginnings. The town – Maryport – entering what was to be the most prosperous and exciting period in its whole history; the age – Victorian England – when men with imagination and the capacity to work hard could turn opportunity into reality; and the brothers – Wilfrid with his commercial experience and contacts in the wider shipping world, Alfred with detailed local knowledge and standing in the community. Wilfrid and Alfred Hine set about combining these ingredients to produce their success story.

Chapter Two
Growth and Development: 1873-1881

THE LAST QUARTER of the nineteenth century was a period almost unique in the history of British merchant shipping. Changes – political, economic, technical and even geographical – began to influence this giant of an industry. The American Civil War ended in 1865 and left Britain's main competitor 'hors de combat', with its merchant fleet in chaos. Civilian shipbuilding was almost at a standstill in the United States at a time when industry and commerce both sides of the Atlantic were crying out for raw materials, manufactured goods and fuel. The Suez Canal, which opened in 1869, sounded the knell for the era of the Tea Clippers and the China trade, consigning the classic "Windjammers" to the history and legend of sail. Just as significantly, the first railway link across the U.S.A. was completed in that same year, as was a road across the Panama isthmus, allowing access to the Western States and the Pacific without having to 'round the Horn'.

Two technical innovations deserve mention: firstly, iron was being used more and more to build sailing ships. Wire rope and iron tackle became standard for standing and running rigging, as did metal winches, windlasses and pumps. Ships thus became more robust, watertight, and efficient in construction.

Secondly, steam propulsion began make a real impact as more and more scientific and practical advances were made. Steamships were more predictable and punctual on voyages, and could therefore reserve berths in ports in advance. They carried a smaller crew, yet thanks to steam-powered winches and donkey engines they could achieve rapid loading and unloading times. However, they had to carry fuel – thus less space for cargo – and they depended on stocks of coal being available in foreign ports. Also, because of their high capital cost, steamships were very expensive items when not productively employed – for instance, if they

"Castle Holme",
c.1880

broke down or could not attract a cargo to transport.

A sailing ship was cheaper to run, but required a larger crew. At about 100 days, the passage time from London to Melbourne by sailing ship was faster than, or at least competitive with, a steamer (and this remained true until the 1930s) – but unfortunately favourable winds could not be guaranteed! Moreover when her cargo-holds were empty a sailing ship was top-heavy and unstable, so she had to load ballast (usually rocks or gravel): the time involved in loading and unloading cargoes and ballast at different ports of call made for delays and lengthy passages.

However, sail and steam could co-exist by meeting different demands – and could flourish, because of the overall expansion of the market. A confident economic climate supported investment in commerce and transport, while the availability of labour and the maritime traditions of towns like Maryport around Britain's coastline ensured that a large merchant marine could be sustained.

By the end of 1872 Wilfrid was the owner or managing owner of five vessels; "Aline", "Glenfalloch", "Hazel Holme", "John Norman" and the little schooner "North Branch", having already lost the "Humberstone" and "Cereal": he was also manager, for Nicholsons of Liverpool, of "Abbey Holme" and "Robert Hine". It had not been an auspicious year for either of those two vessels.

On July 2nd, 1872 at about one o'clock in the morning the "Abbey Holme", outward bound to Brisbane, was off the Isle of Wight when she was involved in what the "Daily Telegraph" called a *"Fearful Collision"* with the "Lapwing", an iron steamer en route for Rotterdam with a general cargo and four passengers. Despite being hailed by the sailing ship the steamer continued to bear down upon her in the darkness, only altering course at the last moment when collision was in any case inevitable. The vessels struck with a terrific crash, and according to the "Daily Telegraph" report apparently *"hugged each other for about five minutes"*. During this time three of the Lapwing's crew – including Alice Foster, a stewardess – jumped aboard "Abbey Holme"; the rest stayed on their own ship, probably reckoning themselves just as safe

where they were. That was a fatally wrong decision: when the two ships separated, it was the "Lapwing" that went down – rapidly, with the loss of 21 lives. Captain Wedgewood Robinson launched his lifeboats to search for survivors, but found none: only four of the remaining crew survived, picked up by passing steamers.

Capt. Robinson set about trying to repair his vessel and continue the voyage, but this proved impossible and the next day a government tug had to tow her into Ventnor for safety. A huge hole could be seen in the starboard bow, which was 'burst' as the press report put it, low down on the waterline. Repairs took several months; but had she not been built in watertight compartments the "Abbey Holme" would have been lost. Eventually she set out again, calling at Adelaide and Brisbane and returning to London in August 1873.

The "Robert Hine", Wilfrid's first ship as manager, had been working efficiently under Captain Wilkinson since her launch in 1868. At the end of 1870 command passed to Captain Edward Ward, but while at Guayaquil in Ecuador in August 1872 he died, and was buried there. To replace him, Wilfrid appointed a young master mariner to bring the barque home. Captain George Brown was born in 1847 in Maryport and had gained his Master's certificate in 1867. The "Robert Hine" was back in London on April 8th 1873, and her new captain began a career with Hine Brothers which would span decades of service: indeed, he and Wedgewood Robinson were destined to become the company's Superintendents of steam and sailing vessels.

One of the first actions of the new Hine Bros. company was to purchase both the "John Norman" and "Abbey Holme", increasing the fleet to seven. They probably used the insurance money from the two lost ships, and the "Abbey Holme" may well have been bought at a bargain price after her accident.

In any case, it was not necessary to be hugely wealthy to be involved in such transactions because of the system (which lasted well into the twentieth century) of ownership of merchant vessels. All ships were divided into 64 equal 'shares' which could be bought and sold, inherited or transferred, just like shares in a company. The names of the owners of shares in a ship had to be registered, and it was not permitted to have more than 32 owners per vessel. Shares in ships changed hands regularly, and shares in new vessels – or even ships commissioned but yet to be built – would be offered at prices reflecting the cost of construction and fitting-out. Many private individuals took the opportunity to invest capital in this way, and the master of a ship commonly owned a share in his vessel. At the end of each voyage, after the ship's accounts had been calculated, any profit made would be divided among the shareholders as return on their investment: of course if the voyage made a loss, or if the ship needed repairs or refitting, they were liable to make up their share of the deficit. The part-owners normally agreed to appoint one person as 'Ship's husband', who was entrusted with the management of the vessel's affairs on their behalf. Certainly Wilfrid and Alfred Hine, who not only had the necessary expertise but also were substantial shareholders in the ships, acted in this capacity as managing owners of their fleet.

The business was soon under way and prospering: Lloyd's shipping lists for the year 1873 record Hine ships crossing oceans in all directions! The "Glenfalloch" was bound for Newfoundland then Brazil; the "Robert Hine' sailed for Valparaiso in June, and the "John Norman" followed in October. This barque met severe weather just after leaving Liverpool, however, and had to put into Queenstown with her rudder gone and making a good deal of water, having had to jettison part of her cargo of coal. The "Aline" too, returning to Liverpool from Tome with a cargo of wheat, had to put in at Valparaiso for repair of a leak and was delayed there a month.

The "Hazel Holme", commanded by Captain Ritchie (late of the "Cereal") hardly saw home waters at all that year: she sailed from Cardiff to Mauritius, and then to Port Chalmers, New Zealand. She returned to Mauritius via Australia, and arrived on March 6th 1874, to take on a cargo for home. Three weeks later the barque was loaded and ready to sail when a hurricane hit the port, creating havoc in the crowded harbour. Nineteen ships were damaged by storm, fire or collision, though it appears that the "Hazel Holme" escaped the worst by shipping her anchor and drifting clear. She went aground, however, and had to unload part of her cargo to be refloated: she was then moved into a dock and divers examined her hull. No leak or serious damage was found, so after repairs to her keel and copper-bottoming she left for London on May 4th.

A month later, on June 3rd 1874, Captain Brown set sail from Liverpool in the "Robert Hine" with a general cargo, bound for Arica in Chile and Mollendo in Peru. This voyage, which eventually took nearly a year, made such an impression on the young mariner that years later he published his account of his "Experience aboard the Barque Robert Hine". Approaching Cape Horn the ship ran into a violent south-easterly gale, which threatened to drive her onto the shore. As the "Robert Hine" tried to tack to change course a heavy sea struck the vessel, carrying away nearly all the rails, bulwarks and stanchions on the starboard side, damaging the crew's quarters and flooding the cabin. Captain Brown laconically remarks, "This would be about midnight". One can only imagine the discomfort, exhaustion and fear of those on board during that night. Daylight revealed more problems – the foremast rigging had been washed away, and the hull had sprung a leak. The ship was obviously in no state to continue a voyage, especially for the ordeal of the Horn, so the captain decided to run for the Falkland Islands for repairs: arriving on September 28th, the ship stayed for six weeks. Captain Brown commented that Stanley Harbour was one of the best he had ever visited, and he noted that the inhabitants

were mostly Scotch carpenters; there would be from 100 to 150 men in the place, but very few ladies, I should say not more than six. Several of the men asked me, should I ever visit their island again, if I would kindly bring them some wives!

Setting sail again, the "Robert Hine" again met a south-easterly gale on approaching Cape Horn; so a course was set through the Nassau Straits, to use the shelter of the islands and channels. This course, however, produced a different cause for concern – that of the native inhabitants of the region, or as Captain Brown called them, the 'Patagonian Savages'. He was so apprehensive about them that he kept his ship under way, without anchoring, while waiting for the gale to abate. He took other measures too, as his story relates:

> Before entering Nassau Straits I gave orders for all guns, cannon and revolvers to be got ready for action, as a precaution, in case the natives attempted to board our ship. We also had a plentiful supply of hot water ready, and the carpenter sharpened all his axes, adzes and other cutting instruments. When all this had been done, I told Mrs. Brown she had better retire to rest. Sleep was out of the question for myself, as I was bound to be on deck until the weather moderated and we were safely through the Straits.
>
> But Mrs. Brown answered, "No, I am not afraid of the savages, but if you will make further preparation for keeping them from boarding the ship I will go to my room." Then she told me that in the storeroom there was a large number of pickle and preserve bottles, which she suggested should be broken upon the deck in case the natives attacked us. This I thought was an excellent plan and was not long in getting the bottles broken, as suggested. We were two nights and days in this place before the gale moderated sufficiently to allow us to go through into open water. Several times when we were passing the small islands we heard the natives shouting and screeching, but no boats came off to us, for which we were very thankful.

A brave and resourceful woman, Mrs. Brown! The Captain was destined to meet the savages, though: on their return journey, foul weather forced the barque to shelter in Good Success Bay, just north of Cape Horn on the Pacific coast. Also anchored there was a small schooner; Captain Brown, fearing it to be a pirate ship, again ordered his defences readied for action (including the

broken bottles!). In fact those aboard were missionaries, who gave the crew a month's supply of free provisions! Captain Brown continues his story:

> I was then asked to accompany them on shore, as they were anxious to learn for themselves what the natives were like. The information that had reached them was to the effect that the people were very wild and treacherous – indeed, perfect savages. I, however, declined the invitation, as the manner in which I had seen people dancing and jumping like madmen around their fires all night convinced me that it was wiser to remain aboard my ship. I also suggested that the best plan for us would be to heave up anchor and clear out. But they were anxious to land, as they were anxious to learn whether they knew the language of the natives or not. If they were ignorant of it, they agreed not to land. With this, I promised to accompany them, providing they did not object to me taking two 'bulldogs' with me. They looked around and asked where I kept the bulldogs? I produced two revolvers, which they said I could take on condition they were only used in self-defence. We then went within 100 yards of the shore in the schooner's boat; from that distance the missionaries hailed the natives in the language they knew, and received from one of the tribe a response in the same tongue. The knowledge that at least one man could understand them was very pleasing to the missionaries.
>
> After a lot of talk the native was asked if it was safe to land. Certainly the prospect was not very inviting, as the people all appeared to be painted ready for war. Not one of them had any clothing on whatever. Men, women and children were all quite naked, although it was freezing hard and exceedingly cold. The man answered back that under the circumstances it was perfectly safe to land, but that it would not have been so had he not been able to act as interpreter. We then

landed, and immediately the natives came crowding round us; they commenced taking hold of our clothes, shaking them vigorously – first our coats, and then every article we had on. I asked the missionary the meaning of this, and he said it was the way they had of expressing their desire to become possessed of our clothing. As we were shivering with cold, of course this was out of the question. After this they sat around fires, first one, then another, going close up to the burning sticks to get warm. I may say these people have no places of shelter whatever, neither houses nor huts; their only comfort is a wood fire and, what appeared very strange to me, they always sat on that side of the fire where the wind was blowing towards them. I asked the reason for this and was told that if they were sheltered by the land it would be draughty and they would be more liable to take cold. During the whole of our visit I hardly took my eyes off the natives, as I feared they might treacherously attack us.

Once I struck a match to light my pipe, and in an instant they were all round me, amazed at the sight; they had never seen a match before and when I gave them one or two their delight was very great. I thought what a good plan it would be to bring all the matches we could spare on shore and barter them for the bows and spears they had, for whilst they carried these I was very uneasy. This was done. For a box of matches they gave me a bow and arrow, and in a short time I had secured all their weapons, which were placed on board so as to be out of their reach.

With contact made, the missionaries showed the natives how to cook food using an old pan they had found. Confidence and trust between European and Patagonian grew. In Captain Brown's words again:

After this we took three of the natives on board the "Robert Hine", for the purpose of showing them over the ship. I went down into the cabin first, our visitors following. The first, who was some distance from the other two,

on reaching the room, almost the first thing he saw was a picture of himself in the mirror upon the stern-post casing. The shock to him was tremendous; he made a terrific leap, nearly through the skylight, and dropping down upon the floor fainted right away. His friends would not venture any further, the reason for their brother's fright being quite incomprehensible to them, and they stood bewildered. After we had brought the fellow round, they became somewhat reassured, and then the fun commenced. First one and then another would peep at the mirror and then give a big jump backwards. This was repeated for at least a dozen times. At length the missionary succeeded in explaining the mystery to the man who acted as interpreter, and was at last able to satisfy them that the persons whom they saw were themselves and none others. Then the sailors let them see through their quarters, and when they came again on deck they were dressed in some of the old clothes belonging to the crew. They were all highly delighted with their costumes, and their exhibitions of joy were amusing to watch. But the greatest fun was after they had returned ashore, indeed, it was a real 'jubilee' occasion amongst them. The next day three of the ladies were dressed in the sailors' clothes, and day by day they were passed on to three fresh persons until they had all enjoyed the new sensation.

1874 was an eventful year at home, too. Wilfrid and Jane had another daughter, christened Isabella after Alfred's late wife. Wilfrid began to make his mark in local society, chairing celebrations at the Baptist Chapel and also delivering an address at the Band of Hope anniversary meetings in the town. Both brothers were staunch Baptists and teetotallers: Wilfrid had been the first member of the Maryport Band of Hope, in 1851 – at the tender age of 13!

The fleet continued to expand with the purchase of a small schooner, the **"Tom Roberts"**. Under Captain E. Hall this little vessel, only 103 tons net and 77 feet long, scurried industriously round the ports of Britain, and the coast of France and Portugal. The brothers also became managing owners of the **"Queen of the Fleet"**, a wooden barque built in Nova Scotia in 1857 and captained by James Tierney. She was engaged in voyages to Canada and the eastern seaboard of the U.S.A. But most significantly of all, 1874 was the year the brothers moved into the steamship age.

The **"Florence Richards"** was launched in February, and at 1051 tons was the largest steamship registered at Maryport at the time. She was owned by a Mr. Sloane Richards of Birmingham and was intended as a bulk carrier. The *Maryport Advertiser* described the new ship as combining speed with carrying capacity, and commented:

We trust to see her often come to her own port laden with ore, and taking away again the manufactured pig-iron, and hope she will be the pioneer of a few more ships of similar class.

Hine Brothers were the ship's managers, and they appointed Joseph Wilkinson (the first captain of the "Robert Hine") as her master. He soon found himself a very busy man: the demand for such ships, and perhaps the skill of Wilfrid and Alfred as brokers and agents, resulted in a full timetable for the "Florence Richards". Consider her first year:

- Maryport to Malaga to Carthagena to Barrow, then back to Maryport.
- Next to Trieste, Porman, Swansea, Cardiff, and to Naples and Carthagena, returning to Middlesborough.
- Then off to Malta, Girgueli, Gibraltar and Liverpool, before making three consecutive trips from Maryport to Rotterdam (on one of these she ran aground).
- Then Maryport to Brouwershaven to Rotterdam, to Newcastle-upon-Tyne, Dublin, and finally home to Maryport in time for Christmas!

The "Florence Richards" was also significant in that she represented the start of a connection between Hine Brothers and the firm of J.L. Thompson, Shipbuilders, of Sunderland which resulted in all but one of the new Hine steamships being commissioned from that yard from then on. The north-east of England was a traditional source of excellence in English shipbuilding, and was where the technology of iron ship construction was most advanced.

The brothers turned to Tyne and Wearside for their new sailing ships, too. In 1874 they commissioned three vessels from Bartram, Haswell and Co. of Sunderland, and the first of these, the barque **"Eden Holme"**, was completed at the end of the year. (The launch had been planned for 21st December 1874, but the brothers had written to Lloyd's Register suggesting that since the vessel would not be fitted out and ready to sail until the new year she should be registered in 1875. Lloyd's wrote back, politely but firmly declining to change their entire system to suit Wilfrid and Alfred, so the launch was delayed until 9th January 1875). The "Eden Holme" was certainly a fine ship in appearance, design and standard of construction, and at 827 gross tons was the largest sailing ship then registered at Maryport. Wedgewood Robinson had supervised her building on behalf of the brothers, and obviously took his new job seriously: in February 1875 the builders wrote apologising for delays in fitting-out which they claimed were due to "your Mr. Robinson" requesting them "to do several things which are not fairly in our specification". It was resolved amicably, however, and Bartrams did their part nobly: on February 14th the new barque left for Gravesend, to pick up a general cargo for Australia. Her captain was John Robinson, a cousin of Wedgewood Robinson and the husband of Barbara Hine.

The maiden voyage, from London to Brisbane, was remarkable for several reasons. Twelve days before "Eden Holme" set sail, the "Glenfalloch" had also left for Brisbane; in her case, from Liverpool. She crossed the Equator on her 25th day and arrived on 29th June; a creditable 111 days' voyage. The next morning, however, the "Eden Holme" appeared, after only 99 days at sea – an excellent time for an untried ship! In fact, Captains Johnstone and Robinson made the two fastest passages to

"Eden Holme",. c. 1878

"Myrtle Holme", 1875
(picture courtesy of Mr. & Mrs. D. Ritchie)

Brisbane that year. There had been one tragic aspect to the voyage: the First Officer, Mr. Clark, fell from the main rigging where he was working and was lost overboard. A lifebuoy was thrown out and the "Eden Holme" went back to search for him, but to no avail. A sailing ship needs time to turn and retrace her steps, and the Bay of Biscay is a cold, rough sea: not many such accidents had a happy outcome. Mr. Clark, described as a native of Maryport and a good officer, left a widow but no family. On a brighter note; Barbara accompanied John Robinson on this voyage, and a possible reason for the Captain's record time comes to light: the announcement of the birth of their second child in Brisbane seven weeks after their arrival! The return journey began three months later, and with wife and baby Alfred Robinson aboard the Captain took a positively leisurely 107 days to get home! Captain J. Randall then took command of "Eden Holme", and was her master for nearly 20 years.

The second Bartram & Haswell vessel was the **"Myrtle Holme"**, launched on 18th June 1875 by Mrs. Ritchie, wife of the master James Ritchie (of the "Cereal' and "Hazel Holme"). The "Myrtle Holme" began life ship-rigged, that is, with square-rigged sails on all three masts, as depicted in the painting commissioned by Capt. Ritchie.

Within three years, however, she is registered as a barque, with fore-and-aft sails on her mizzenmast; perhaps because of the (apocryphal) reputation of Captain Ritchie as a hard driver of ships, but more likely because a barque needed a smaller crew than a full-rigged ship. Whatever the truth of Captain Ritchie's reputation for speed, it can be noted that "Myrtle Holme" left London on September 24th and arrived in Adelaide on January 20th 1876 – another 99 day maiden voyage, but this one 1,000 miles further!

The third and largest of the new Hine clippers was launched on September 16th 1875. Some idea of her size is given by the fact that compared with the "Cutty Sark" she was two feet longer, slightly slimmer, and 75 tons more in displacement. The **"Castle Holme"** also started life as a ship, but was reduced to a barque in 1880. She had local connections to Maryport: her name refers to the part of the town at the base of Castle Hill: her sails were made in Maryport by Robert Ritson & Co., and

"Castle Holme" as a barque

carved in her stern tailboards and cabin woodwork were the arms of the Senhouse family, who had probably invested in shares in her. Captain Wedgewood Robinson, who had supervised the construction, is registered as her master for the first year of her long life.

There are other happy events to record in 1875. Since March Joseph J. Hine, by then 25 years old, had taken over the family business. His publicity was a model of Victorian probity:

> Joseph J. Hine 44 Brown St., Maryport –
> begs to intimate that he is in a position
> to supply on hire Horses with Open or Closed
> Conveyances, Wagonettes, Dog-carts, etc. –
> All orders of pleasure-parties, Weddings,
> Funerals, etc. will receive his prompt attention
> at the above address.

Thus established, Joseph married Miss Elizabeth Temple at the Baptist Church in November 1875 and settled down to family life.

Earlier in the year Alfred Hine had remarried. His second wife was Miss Mary Eaglesfield, six years his junior; their first child, Mary, was born the following July. Wilfrid, meanwhile, found time to engage in a hobby. On a couple of occasions in 1875 his name appears in bowls tournaments results; without conspicuous success, it is true, although he did reach a semi-final once!

In the autumn of the year, Hine Bros. acquired part-ownership of the **"Aikshaw"**, another iron barque newly launched on Wearside – this time at Doxford's yard, Sunderland. She had been built to the order of her new commander, Capt. E.W. Tyson of Maryport, who was the other major shareholder. The *Maryport Advertiser* commented that the vessel was *"... an excellent model, and is expected to be a large carrier and a fast sailer. She is intended for the Valparaiso trade."*

1875 ended dramatically with the loss of the "Queen of the Fleet", which had left Maryport in August carrying only ballast and was en route for Canada. She was in good order and well found, but with a slight leak which required only about ten minutes pumping every watch (four hours) to keep her dry. This inflow increased, however, and after ten days at sea the crew requested Captain Tierney to make for a port, as the ship would not be fit to cross the Atlantic. They proceeded to Belfast, where a surveyor ordered them back to Barrow for repairs: she went into dry dock for the necessary work to be done, and set off again on 22nd September with captain and crew satisfied with the state of their vessel.

After four days "Queen of the Fleet" hit bad weather. First a squall carried away the upper parts of all her masts, together with some sails and rigging. The weather worsened daily, and after three weeks disaster struck: in the midst of a storm the ship began to fall apart! Water began to pour in, and the pumps were manned every watch. The ship's carpenter, Joseph Kendall, described how he went into the hold with the Captain, the second mate, the steward and the cook: *"The plank ends forward were loose, and working from an inch to an inch and a half... they got oakum and the cabin carpet to try to stop the leaks, and nailed a piece of plank against them, but this did no good."* They then looked over the bows, and saw that the planks and copper sheathings of the hull had spread open. Kendall continued, *"They put a sail over the open seams, but it was soon washed away. All this time the pumps were kept going night and day. The captain worked his turn at the pumps."*

Captain Tierney had hoped to sail his ship home, but the crew told him point blank that they could do no more than try to keep her afloat until another vessel came in sight. The sails were taken down, the ship hove to, and the order "All hands to the pumps" was given. For three days and nights they pumped; four hours on, two hours off, watch by watch, until by good fortune the barque "Enchantress", a Canadian ship, appeared and answered their calls. With seven feet of water in the hold, JamesTierney ordered his exhausted men to abandon ship. No lives were lost, though the sextant and chronometer could not be saved and Joseph Kendall's valuable tools went down with his ship.

As in all such cases, a Court of Enquiry followed. The Court assessors, Messrs Senhouse and Ritson, must have been aware of the campaign of Samuel Plimsoll MP. against 'coffin ships' – vessels which were unseaworthy, overloaded and heavily insured against loss by unscrupulous shipowners. (A Royal Commission had produced a report verifying Plimsoll's criticisms that year, and legislation was to follow in 1876.) They enquired in depth into the repair work done at Barrow, and heard testimony from the master mariners who had inspected the repairs that everything had been done "to make her strong and fit for sea". This was attested to by the foreman carpenter of the Barrow yard, who was called as a witness, and confirmed by Joseph Kendall, who stated that Alfred Hine and the Board of Trade inspector had also examined the ship. They also heard that the "Queen of the Fleet" was probably worth nearly twice what she was insured for.

Their judgement exonerated all parties of blame for the loss, and returned his master's certificate to Captain Tierney, but commented unsympathetically that, "had the Captain been willingly supported by his crew... the vessel might have been kept afloat longer and got to a port of safety."

On the day this judgement was announced it happened that the 'Maryport Club' – another of the local Mutual Marine Insurance co-operatives – held its General Meeting and declared its results for 1875. Despite being one of the companies insuring the "Queen of the Fleet", the Club had a good year: the number of ships on its books rose from 97 to 118, while the rate to be paid by members was expected to be just under four per cent, which was less than in previous years.

The town and its maritime traders moved into 1876 in buoyant and confident mood, and Hine Bros. were in the forefront of the expansion. Enthusiastically they bought ships of all types, to diversify the company's activities and provide a comprehensive service. For the coastal and local trade they acquired three small brigantines (two-masted vessels, with square-rigged sails on the foremast and 'fore-and-aft' rig on the mizzen). These were the 185-ton **"Maggie Gross"**, the 167-ton **"Glastry"**, and the 145-ton **"Clara"**.

The "Clara" is of interest in that she was one of the first British ships to pioneer the use of perforated sails. This apparently illogical idea was invented by an Italian shipmaster whose theory was that a cushion of air, or 'dead wind' as he termed it, collected in the belly of the sail and reduced its efficiency by acting as a cushion: he believed that a hole in the centre of the belly of the sail allowed this dead air to escape and the 'true wind' to blow against the sail surface. The positioning of the holes in the sail was important, and the site and number of holes – which were only about six inches in diameter – varied according to whether the sail was rigged square or fore-and aft; topsails had four holes, topgallants and royals only two. Advocates of the system claimed several advantages for perforated sails, and made the point that any wind that did escape through the holes in one sail would be caught up by another – the mizzen to the main, and the main to the foresail – and very little of the driving force of the wind was actually wasted. Basil Lubbock in his book "The Colonial Clippers" states that these sails became quite popular with experienced captains, and details other practical aspects of using them.

The brothers also bought the S.S. "Florence Richards", which they had managed for two years, and no less than five more steamships as well! The **"Earl of Carrick"** was the newest, built in Scotland the previous year; the **"Horatio"** was three years old and constructed in Newcastle; the **"Maitland"** had been built in 1872 in Scotland; the **"Thomas Vaughan"**, five years old, came from Middlesbrough, while the **"Mersey"** was a ten-year-old steamer built in Sunderland and previously owned by Powell & Co.

On April 6th 1876, Capt. John Robinson, freshly returned from Australia with "Eden Holme", became master of the "Mersey". Wilfrid and Alfred probably offered this command to their brother-in-law to allow him more time in his home port with Barbara and the family. The "Eden Holme" would be away for a year at a time, and would be operating from the major docks in London or Liverpool, whereas the "Mersey" would be carrying ore and pig-iron on shorter voyages between the Solway ports and those of northern Europe. And so it was; but not for long.

Barely four months later, on August 11th, the "Mersey" struck a rock off the Pembrokeshire coast in dense fog. The steamer was loaded with pig-iron, and sank like a stone: most of the crew of 17 were below and had no chance of escape. Captain Robinson called to the sailors who were on deck with him to abandon ship and swim for a nearby island: he himself knelt down to pray, and went down with his ship. Only two of the sailors, James Colville and Isaac Burkett, survived. They were picked up from the island later by a passing steamer which was bound for Waterford, so it was two days before any inkling of the tragedy reached Maryport. Moreover many of the crew had been signed on in Barrow on a casual basis, and there was apparently no complete list of who was on board. Of the 15 who drowned, however, four – Captain Robinson, his cousin Charles Robinson the mate, the second engineer and one of the seamen – were Maryport men. The rock on which the steamer met her end is referred to as 'Mersey Rock' in the Pilot manuals to this day.

A relief fund was rapidly set up in the town to aid the nine widows and 20 children of those lost: subscriptions from Maryport citizens came to £24, of which Hine Bros. gave £10, and the total donated was £60. Assuming that Barbara would not have requested aid from the fund, each widow probably received the equivalent of about £300 in modern terms – hardly a huge recompense. Rudimentary benefit schemes for sailors had been in operation in Britain for some years, but payments were low; real hardship, as well as personal loss, was the prospect of those bereaved.

There were happier events to relate in 1876, however: the 6th July was a momentous day for the Company with the launch of their first new steamship, the **"Alne Holme"**. The name Alne refers to the old name of the Ellen River on which Maryport stands, and to the even older Alauna, the Roman settlement above the town.

Captain Joseph Wilkinson had progressed in eight years from being the first commander of the "Robert Hine" back in 1868, and he was now the 'Overlooker of Steam Vessels' for the company. He conducted the maiden voyage of the "Alne Holme" before handing her over to her new master, Captain Richard A. Turney, whose command began with the excitement of a rescue at sea.

On September 30th, off the Portuguese coast, the "Alne Holme" sighted a sailing ship flying distress signals. In Capt. Turney's words:

we bore down upon her, when she proved to be the brig "Brothers" of London from Lisbon – Master reported ship in a sinking state, and asked to be taken on board as brig had six feet of water in her forward hold, foreyards and main topmast gone – took the crew on board consisting of Captain, mate and four seamen and proceeded on.

Within three weeks of this rescue, another Hine steamer was saving lives at sea: the "Florence Richards", now commanded by Capt. John Kay, took on board the crew of the schooner "Two Marys" of Belfast, disabled and sinking after a severe gale in the North Sea.

In October 1876 came another milestone in the company's history with the launch of the **"Brier Holme"**, the last and finest of the clipper barques designed and built for Hine Bros. The commission for this ship had gone to J.L. Thompson rather than Bartram and Haswell, and under Wedgewood Robinson's supervision the shipbuilders surpassed themselves: a local marine surveyor is reported to have declared the "Brier Holme" the best-finished barque ever built on the Wear. Confirmation comes from a source perhaps more objective: the "San Francisco Daily Commercial News" Shipping list of May 4th 1877 states:

San Francisco probably has more new ships arriving during the course of a year than any city in the United States, but it is seldom we find so fine a vessel in port as the new British barque "Brier Holme", which arrived on 30th April. She is a model of strength in every part and is as strong as iron can make her. All her fittings are first-class and she is certainly the best-finished iron vessel which has come to this port for a long time.

Classed as 100 A1 at Lloyd's – the highest grade possible – the barque was 206 feet in length, 33ft 6in beam, and 921 gross registered tonnage. She was designed to carry a complement of five officers

"Brier Holme" in San Francisco Bay, April 1877
(Picture courtesy San Francisco Maritime Museum)

and 13 seamen; and as well as capacious cargo holds there was accommodation for ten saloon passengers who travelled in surroundings of elegant luxury. Capt. J. Johnstone, the master of the "Glenfalloch" since 1872, was given command of this beautiful new addition to the fleet, and he remained with her for nearly 14 years.

1877 was the year in which the Hine brothers began to come to prominence in the public life of Maryport. In many cases it seems to have been Wilfrid who was the more outgoing and ambitious. He had been mentioned the previous year in connection with the activities of the local Liberal Party – as a member of a delegation here, chairing a meeting there – trying to establish West Cumberland as an independent constituency and promoting Sir Wilfrid Lawson as the Whig candidate. 1877 found him proposing a vote of thanks at a meeting supporting votes for women, and he was elected an officer in the Literary and Scientific Society, which met at the Athenaeum in

Maryport to hear lectures and discussion on a wide range of topics. He had not, however, abandoned the religious and social causes he and his brother had espoused: he remained active in the Band of Hope and was prominent in the life of the Maryport Baptist Church.

Alfred seems to have been content to concede the limelight to his elder brother, but was by no means in the background. Temperance was his particular enthusiasm, and in 1877 the local paper frequently recorded his name among the speakers in support of the movement. He was also a Literary and Scientific Society member, and was their delegate to other meetings on many occasions. Their wives, Jane and Mary, supported them loyally in good works in the community: for example, at the end of 1877 a Bazaar was held in aid of the building of a new Sunday School at Grasslot (now a part of Maryport). The enormous sum of £452:10s:3d was raised – about £18,000 today – of which the Hine ladies accounted for nearly a third. Since Mary had given birth to another daughter just six weeks earlier, this was a noble effort!

Business was brisk too, and the Company became Lloyd's agents for the area in 1877. Hine Brothers had agents or offices in all the local ports, and in Swansea and Liverpool. In London their shipping interests were handled by Messrs Devitt and Moore, renowned in their own right as shipowners and brokers.

The increase in the volume of trade, and the gradual change of emphasis from sail to steam, led to a considerable reshuffle of commands among the regular corps of master mariners in the Company's service. The "Maitland", after three months under the command of Capt. Wilkinson, passed to Capt. George Brown of the "Robert Hine", who thereby made the transition from sail to steam.

Plainly, this was meant as a proving period for the young mariner, still not 30 years old, and he must have impressed the brothers because in February 1877 he was given command of their latest acquisition, the **"Esk Holme"**. This was another new J.L. Thompson steamship; 925 tons, and fitted with the latest boilers, engines, steam-driven winches and windlasses – as the *Maryport Advertiser* put it, *"all the modern improvements in marine engineering"*.

Capt. Saul, who had joined the company with the "Glastry", must also have made a good impression. The brothers soon sold the ship to a local shipowner, but retained Capt. Saul and promoted him to replace Capt. Johnstone in the "Glenfalloch". Capt. Holmes, another brigantine master, also achieved his advancement: transferred from the "Maggie Gross" to the "Hazel Holme", he found himself part of the clipper fleet and set off from Gravesend to Hobart, Tasmania.

But promotion may also come about in less happy circumstances. During a voyage from Antwerp to Swansea in July 1877, Capt. John Kay of the "Florence Richards" was lost overboard. At least, that is the presumption: it was at night; no-one saw or heard anything, and as he was not on watch his disappearance was not discovered until the next morning. Captain G. McLeod of the "Clara" – the third of the brigantines – took over. Like Capt. George Brown, he had converted from sail to steam

via a brief command of the "Maitland" the previous year.

Sadly, there was soon another pair of 'dead men's shoes' to be filled. Captain Holmes, returning from Queensland on only his second voyage in charge of the "Hazel Holme", became suddenly ill and died at sea. The burden of command was thrust upon the first officer, a young man who had joined the ship less than a year before. Not the easiest situation; but let the man who found himself unexpectedly in charge of ship and crew take up the story:

The second mate was a bit older in years and experience than I, and our first question was the appointment of a man to take his place. The four apprentices were all first-voyagers. as was also the carpenter; it then remained only for us to choose one of the crew. Three of them had joined in Swansea and made the voyage, but one had deserted in Rockhampton, been caught about a week before sailing, and kept in gaol until we left, when he was put on board by the police.

He was an excellent sailor but just a bit troublesome on the passage out, and wasn't much improved by having to come with us against his will. Still he was the best seaman, so calling all hands aft I said a few words about our loss, and bluntly told them I have selected him to act as second mate.

This was a bit of a surprise to all and had an electric effect upon the man himself. He stepped in front of the men and asked if there were any objections. As none were raised he continued, "Now, men, any complaints you have on this passage tell me, and I will tell the Chief Officer and he will report to the Captain." So then I heard the title applied to me for the first time.

The new Captain was Joseph W. Millican, only 23 years old but with a businesslike air and a maturity beyond his years. In his memoirs written 50 years later he goes on:

Reaching London we berthed in the West India Dock. I went up to the city and found the agents were Messrs Devitt & Moore, who entered the ship and got everything in readiness for paying off the crew. In due course Captain Robinson came on board and the condition of the ship seemed to please him, which was satisfactory to me. Then later the owner came and made many inquiries as to the death of the captain, and having said a few kind words to me, promised that if I passed my examination he would give me command. Words fail to express what I felt that this promise. I, at 24 and looking but 19, with barely ten years' experience, to have command!

But Joseph still had to get his master's ticket; and straight away if he was to take the "Hazel Holme" on her next voyage as her captain. After two weeks' intensive coaching he went up to Liverpool to sit the written papers and the oral test: young Joseph had to face Captains McNab and John, the fiercest examiners on the Board! However, to his relief and pleasure he was successful at his first attempt, and Wilfrid Hine kept his side of the bargain. To continue in Captain Millican's words:

Having secured my Master's Certificate, I had just a few days at home and then the final interview with the owner, who was, as I always found after many years' service under him, most kind and considerate. Among other things he said that I, being young, might come across some difficulties re chartering, etc., but that I would always find some elderly ship-masters who would be glad to give me a helping hand. I got to London in time to sign on the crew, and with the guidance of Captain Robinson, the overlooker, everything went well. Having some business still to finish, the Hazel Holme left dock with Captain Robinson in charge. I stood on the pier-head until she was out of sight. During that short period I was overcome with a wondrous love for the beautiful little barque that was now, as it were, "all my own." To me she was not a mere construction of wood and iron, but a something which had come into my life as a

living force that meant all the world to me. What I had always striven for – the command of my own ship – had come to pass in what, looking back, seemed a very few years and, as she faded away in the distance on the fine June morning, I turned away with a happy heart and some little moisture about my eyes.

So Hine Bros. recruited another skilled young mariner onto their team of captains, and J.W. Millican began a career which spanned 30 years and four ships, lasting into the twentieth century and the steamship era of the company.

Another long-lasting partnership was about to begin for the young mariner: on his first voyage in "Hazel Holme", Joseph fell in love! To quote his memoirs again:

This was my first visit to Australia, and as for Rockhampton I had never heard the name until I joined the Hazel Holme. Here we experienced to the full the wonderful hospitality of the people, and everyone was made so comfortable that it was a hard matter to leave as heart-whole as one entered it. To myself this port remains the first milestone on life's journey. Being a young man of 23, it was natural that I should fall to the charms of one of the many charming young girls of the place, and it makes me rather proud of my good judgment to be able to say, after nearly 50 years' close acquaintance, she is as charming as ever!

Joseph married his sweetheart Lily Jones in Australia in 1881. Mrs. Millican, a resourceful woman, later worked in the company's office in Maryport, and she is known to have made at least two trips home to Australia between 1883 and 1891 in the "Myrtle Holme" while Joseph was the captain. They had two daughters, christened Hazel and Myrtle after the clippers their father loved. His family story also entwines with that of the Hines: Myrtle Millican later married Joseph J. Hine's son Ernest!

Chapter Three
The Springboard to Business: 1878-1881

FOR WILFRID AND ALFRED HINE, 1878 was a fortunate year. The company they had formed just five years before had grown into a prosperous enterprise which was now beginning to reward them for their foresight and hard work. Whereas previously they had ploughed their profits back into the venture by commissioning new steamers, and buying out other shareholders in profitable ships such the "Florence Richards" and the "Aikshaw", they now decided to benefit themselves and their families.

The brothers were living modestly but comfortably in High Street, Maryport. Alfred was at No.98 and Wilfrid at No.104, which was a four-bedroomed house with drawing room, dining and breakfast rooms, attics, a kitchen and, as a description delicately puts it, "every convenience". However, in 1878 they purchased a large plot of land on the cliffs north of the town, adjoining the old Roman settlement at the top of Camp Road. The land was owned by the Lord of the Manor, Humphrey Pocklington Senhouse, and local legend has it that the site cost the brothers a huge sum; firstly because Senhouse was particularly pressed for cash at the time (he was to be married the following year), and secondly because houses on this site would be the only buildings visible from the Manor at Netherhall. Be that as it may, the houses were built to the design of Charles Eaglesfield, a local architect and friend of the brothers. They were named Camp Hill and Park Hill; Wilfrid lived in the former, Alfred in the latter. The two houses are in fact semi-detached and are large, roomy and substantially-built: they remain to this day as private residences and retain many of the elegant original features. Each house boasts a turret room with stunning views of the Solway and the port approaches, and it requires little imagination to visualise the brothers scanning the scene, watching with satisfaction the movements of their fleet.

1878 was also an election year for three of the seats on the Board of Trustees of the Town and Harbour, and Wilfrid was persuaded to stand as a candidate. (He had been approached in previous years but repeatedly declined to be nominated.) This year, however, he received what he referred to as an "influentially-signed requisition" – presumably from his business colleagues and maybe even H.P. Senhouse – which he felt he could not refuse. His sponsors had judged the situation shrewdly too, for Wilfrid was elected with the highest number of votes in the poll. In his letter to the electors appealing for support, Wilfrid had declared his enthusiasm for the future development of the trade of Maryport, which he saw as linked inseparably to further expansion of harbour facilities. Earlier that year the Trustees had determined to commission a plan for another new dock to allow larger ships – the modern iron steamers – access to the cargoes of coal, timber, grain and iron which kept harbour and town alive.

Increasingly, difficulties were arising in loading these ships. In July the "Maitland" had to leave the harbour without 200 tons of her cargo because her draught would otherwise be greater than 12 feet 6 inches – the depth of water in the dock on that tide. The remainder of the cargo was loaded from lighters once the ship was in deeper water, an inefficient and costly business. Ingenious solutions were sometimes found: in the same week the *Advertiser* described a "Novel and Interesting Operation at Maryport" in which Capt. Wilkinson (Hine's overlooker of ships) supervised the departure of the "Alne Holme". She had been loaded to a draught of 16 feet, so at the height of the tide the ship's hull was within six inches of the bottom of the dock. With no safety margin to manoeuvre in the harbour because of mud banks, there was just one chance of escape: had she been unable to leave port she would have been delayed nearly a fortnight, or forced to unload again. Early in the morning, as the tide reached its highest point, the "Alne Holme" was taken in tow by the tug "Maryport": stern first they inched out of the dock into the channel, round the South Jetty and safely to sea – amazingly, without once touching the bottom! If she had stranded, the heavy-laden steamer could have blocked the port entrance for days; and as the tide ebbed and she settled on the bottom she could have broken her back and become permanently wrecked. However after loading fully in the Roads the "Alne Holme" left for the Baltic the same evening. The press praised Captain Wilkinson, Captain Mounsey of the "Maryport" and Mr. Baylis the Deputy harbourmaster for their part in the undertaking, but the report concluded:

Surely, when things have come to such a pass as this, it is high time more dock accommodation with deeper water were provided, if Maryport is to maintain the good position it holds as a seaport on this coast.

This was precisely the platform upon which Wilfrid won his place as Trustee, and he took up the cause of the new dock with his customary vigour.

As the year progressed, and the evenings drew in, another matter engaged the attention of the Trustees: an application from the owners of Park Hill and Camp Hill for six street lights to be provided on the road to their newly-erected houses! It must have been with mixed feelings that Wilfrid, the newest Trustee, witnessed the rejection of his request (on the grounds that other parts of the town needed lighting more urgently) and set off home in the November gloom!

Nonetheless, both the brothers could look back with pleasure on the year. Mary Hine had presented Alfred with yet another daughter, Florence Elizabeth, on November 3rd; and in the following month his son Alfred, now 10 years old, was awarded his Honours Certificate from the Maryport British School.

As 1878 turned into 1879, the Company's fleet numbered 21 ships – 14 sailing vessels and seven steamships – engaged in trade and transport all over the world. One ship had been lost – the little "Earl of Carrick", wrecked at Oban – and one purchased. The **"Henry Scholefield"** was another J.L.

West Cumberland crew, with William Brown in the bowler hat, middle front row

Thompson-built steamship, launched in 1872. Like most steamships of the period, she was also rigged for sail; in this case, as a two-masted schooner. The company acquired her from Tully and Co. late in 1878, and in February 1879 they took delivery of another new steamship built by J.L. Thompson & Co. to Hine Bros.' commission.

This was the **"West Cumberland"** – at 1,387 tons gross, the largest steamer to have entered Maryport at the time. As with the "Alne Holme" and "Esk Holme", Captain Wilkinson had supervised her construction at the shipyard, and the new vessel had up-to-date features to fit the needs of the trade. She boasted four steam-powered winches for rapid cargo handling, a double-bottomed hull with compartments for water ballast (easily unloaded and adjusted), and a 150 horsepower engine, half as powerful again as the "Alne Holme". It was noted that although the "West Cumberland" was intended to ply the Mediterranean and Baltic routes, she would be *"suitable for the North American trade, should she be required for such service."* Captain George Brown, now almost 32 years old, was promoted to take command – another rung up the ladder in his career – and set off for the ports on the Spanish and Mediterranean coasts.

The intrepid Mrs. Isabella Brown often accompanied him, obviously undeterred by her earlier adventures in the days of the "Robert Hine"! Sadly, this proved her undoing: in 1879, returning from Genoa in the "West Cumberland", she contracted dysentery and rapidly became very ill. The ship put in at Gibraltar, where Mrs. Brown was taken ashore and placed under the best medical care. The "West Cumberland" resumed her journey home, but when Captain Brown arrived in Maryport a fortnight later it was to be greeted by the news that his wife had died of her illness a couple of days after his departure. Isabella's body was brought home to the town where she was widely known and liked, and her funeral took place early in September. Later that month there was further cause to mourn; Alfred and Mary's baby daughter Florence died, just ten months old.

In the business sphere, the brothers were concerned to discover that the Shaw Savill Company, who had chartered the "Abbey Holme",

had used her to ship a cargo of dynamite and gunpowder – and expected them to pay for the special magazines installed to store the explosives in transit! Thomas Devitt wrote from London offering to sort out the situation, and seems to have succeeded to everyone's satisfaction; but he advised Wilfrid and Alfred to tighten up their charter contracts to avoid future difficulties.

The life of the community went on, although not always smoothly. There was a minor scandal at the Baptist Church, and in July Wilfrid wrote to their Headquarters in London:

*My dear Sir, I feel greatly obliged by your note containing information about Mr. *****. I told you he borrowed £5 from us before he left and faithfully promised he would return it but since the day of his departure he has never written us a line. I am not at all surprised at his being a 'sly drinker'. He cannot be completely honest else he would not have left this place in debt to so many people. I was not aware until now what his trade was.*

The brothers' support for the campaign against the evils of alcohol continued: in June the newspaper noted that:

on Friday night last, (Fair Day) the usual entertainment was given by the members of the Trevelyan Lodge for the purpose of drawing people from the allurements to vice and drunkenness, which are scattered broadcast at Fair times, was held in the Athenaeum, Mr. Hine presiding.

This Lodge was a part of the Order of Good Templars, a Christian and social society to which the brothers belonged; but the press does not relate how successful they were in keeping the locals on the straight and narrow! With the same objective, Wilfrid addressed a meeting later in the year and proposed the establishment of a 'coffee tavern' in the town. The idea of a place where people could gather without having to drink alcohol caught the imagination of the citizens, and it was decided to go ahead with the scheme.

The other enterprise which occupied Wilfrid in his role as a Trustee was the planned new dock. Throughout the year he set about writing to friends, acquaintances, local dignitaries and those with influence in business and financial circles, urging them and their companies to invest in the project. There was more than usual importance attached to this fund-raising: the Trustees realised that the very survival of the port and the town depended on the success of this venture. As Commander Brian Ashmore points out in his book on Maryport harbour:

By 1879 the Trustees were again enmeshed in the relentless truth. In spite of everything, income had been inadequate to reduce the capital debt. Outstanding years in the period from 1866 to 1879 had permitted repayments totalling £6,800, but over the whole period the debt had crept up from £77,295 to £79,795. Over good years and bad, the undertaking simply could not earn enough to pay off its borrowing.

The cost of the new dock, including the railway, the harbour machinery and appliances and the land, was estimated at £91,000 – a staggeringly large sum, because the plan was to build out from the coastline into the Solway to provide a large deep-water basin accessible at all stages of the tide. The public response to the idea (and to the importuning and campaigning by Wilfrid and others) was astonishing: nearly £110,000 was invested, covenanted, pledged or subscribed! This represents over £5,000,000 at present-day rates: a phenomenal vote of confidence in the future by the Victorians of the north. Work began on the site in 1880, and was confidently expected to be completed in about two years. In the meantime the day-to-day work of the harbour went on, and the Hine Brothers' steamships continued to play a major role in the life of the port. There were some unusual cargoes too: in June 1879 the "Henry Scholefield" was loaded with 1,000 tons of granite setts (cobblestones) which were to be used for repairing the streets and squares of the city of St. Petersburg in Russia.

Although the sailing vessels were registered to Maryport it was very unusual indeed for the clipper barques actually to visit the port; but in the first quarter of 1880 no less than three of them arrived, exciting great interest and comment. The first was the "Castle Holme", at the time the largest sailing ship ever to have entered the port. For three weeks she remained in the Elizabeth Dock while 1,800 tons of steel rails destined for Adelaide, South Australia, were loaded into her holds. The *Maryport Advertiser* reported that when Captain Williamson took her out of harbour on February 12th to begin the voyage, "*...a great company of spectators thronged the pier to witness the grand sight.*"

In March both the "Brier Holme" and the "Myrtle Holme", under Captains Johnstone and Ritchie, arrived within days of each other, also to load cargoes of steel rails: Hine Bros. had secured a contract for the work from the Agent-General of South Australia, and had persuaded him to use Maryport rather than Workington. This caused some problems of space in the Elizabeth Dock, however, and the colliery owners wrote to the Trustees complaining that these large vessels were obstructing the coal-loading bays. Wilfrid replied accepting that this was so, but pointing out how much the Harbour Board was making in cargo dues and fees for the use of their cranes during this time. It was generally agreed that the sooner the new dock was ready the better – indeed, Wilfrid himself had complained a few weeks previously that ships ready to sail had been delayed by the congestion in the harbour – but that in the meantime it was 'first come, first served' at the quayside. (For some time there had been a slight slump in trade, so these difficulties were at least a sign of the return of business).

The two barques attracted great attention and approval from the local population, who were knowledgeable and sound judges of ships: the newspaper announced that the masters would be proud to show the townspeople over the vessels, and later noted that the "Brier Holme" had been visited by "vast numbers of admiring visitors" before she sailed in mid-April.

The "Myrtle Holme" weighed anchor the following month and made remarkable time on her

A late twentieth century photo showing the Elizabeth Dock and basin

outward voyage – only 86 days at sea! The ship was delayed for six weeks in Australia while the rails were laboriously unloaded and a large cargo found for the return journey, but she set off for London on October 14th Captain Ritchie had less luck with the weather this time, as his subsequent report makes clear:

Had very light winds and fine weather to Cape Horn, which was passed on November 25th. Very light winds and fine weather to Equator, which was crossed December 29th.

(Already 76 days at sea, and still a long way from home; but if the sailors had been 'whistling for a wind' they soon found their wish granted – with a vengeance!)

Had N and NE Trades, but a very heavy sea from the north; wind going from NE to NW daily, with heavy thunder and lightning, up to latitude 44ºN. The barometer for 9 days stood at 28:70 to 28:80 inches, with a heavy sea and bad weather.

Two thousand miles of beating into the wind, which must have seemed to change direction maliciously to defeat the crew's efforts and hamper progress: add to this the storms, the rain, the great waves always ahead, and the increasing cold as the ship approached the northern winter; this part of the voyage can be classed as an unpleasant month by any standard! To cap it all they met thick fog in the Channel, and the "Myrtle Holme" finally arrived in London after 102 days.

The "Brier Holme" had returned a month earlier, to Liverpool, while the "Castle Holme", which had departed first, was back in London on November 12th 1880. On that same day the "Hazel Holme", under Capt. Millican, set sail from London docks bound for Swan River, Western Australia, while the little "Glenfalloch", Captain Saul's command, left Boston, Mass. to return to Maryport. The "Eden Holme" was also homeward bound from Adelaide to Gravesend on her regular run under Capt. Randall, whereas the "Abbey Holme" (Captain Bryce), was outward bound to Adelaide from Workington.

The "Aikshaw", Capt. Tate's ship, was en route from Glasgow to Honolulu. The movements of the "Robert Hine' (Capt. Hall) are not recorded at all during this time, and only a cryptic report that the "John Norman" (Capt. Nicholson) left Samarang for Surabaya early in 1881 gives any indication of her whereabouts. (Java and Indonesia were not normal territories for Hine Brothers' vessels, so it is likely that both vessels were chartered to other users during this period.)

The movements of the "Aline", however, are all too well known. On June 21st, 1880, the wooden barque left Liverpool bound for Montevideo with a mixed cargo. Her master was John G. Turney, a Maryport man from a respected local seafaring family; and of the 14-man crew, four were Cumberland men, the rest taken on in Liverpool. The voyage was uneventful by all accounts, and after 84 days at sea the "Aline" was approaching her destination: she was about 75 miles away, in the mouth of the River Plate, by early morning on September 13th.

A heavy sea was running and there was slight fog but visibility was good enough for the watch to spot a light some distance away; this was identified as the light-vessel, and an appropriate course was set. The light was passed and all seemed well, but some little distance further on another light unexpectedly came into view! The navigator consulted his charts but could find no record of this second mark, so he concluded it must be the riding-light of another vessel and the ship maintained its course.

The consequences of this mistaken assumption soon became disastrously clear: at three o'clock in the morning, in the dark and the fog, the "Aline" ran aground on the coast of Uruguay approximately 30 miles from Maldonado. The sea was still rough, and waves repeatedly swept over the ship; the crew remained on board, clinging on grimly and hoping that conditions would improve.

Daylight brought no relief from the waves and pounding surf, but the shipwreck was spotted by some of the local inhabitants, who gathered on the shore to help the sailors. Captain Turney's men tied a rope to a lifebuoy and cast it overboard: the buoy drifted inshore and the locals seized the line, holding it tight while the crew began to abandon the "Aline". One by one they struggled ashore through the angry sea, hand over hand along the line, drenched to the skin and numb with cold. Tragically, one crewman did not survive: young Henry Golightly, a 16 year-old Maryport lad on his first voyage as an apprentice, lost his grip and was immediately washed away. Although his shipmates kept watch for the rest of the day, his body was never seen again.

The local people, who were farmers and stockmen of Spanish and Portuguese descent, showed great kindness to the Captain and crew. They took them to a nearby ranch, where they roasted a whole sheep for them – a gesture much appreciated by the stranded and despondent crew, whose only possessions were the clothes they stood up in. The company remained for three days, visiting the coast regularly in the hope of salvaging their personal property, but they were obliged to look on powerless while the unabated violence of the sea beat their ship to pieces.

At the end of this time the party was able to travel to Maldonado in the company of a train of wagons drawn by bullocks: the 30-mile journey took two days. From there they obtained passage to Montevideo in a small schooner, and the crew then returned home by steamer. Captain Turney was obliged to remain in Montevideo to face a Naval Court of Inquiry: he was acquitted of blame, but in a letter to his employer he confessed to being "severely shaken" by his experience. He returned to England with the mail steamer later in the year.

Earlier in 1880 the brothers had lost one of their steamships, the "Maitland", off Ushant Island at the western tip of the Brittany coast. She was in dense fog, moving at half-speed ahead and with her steam-whistle blowing continuously, when she was struck by the steamer "St. Andreas" and "cut open to the waterline". The "Maitland' rapidly began to settle by the head, and there was time only to lower the boats and abandon ship: Capt. Kirkpatrick and his crew could save nothing from the vessel. After two hours in the boats they were picked up by the other steamer, and all were safely returned to England. However, such was the pressure of commerce in that era that Wilfrid and Alfred immediately bought the **"Ardmore"**, a 928-tonner built by Bartram, Haswell & Co. eight years before, and set her to work: within six weeks Capt. Kirkpatrick was back at sea. They also acquired the **"Bavington"**, a tiny 79-ton screw steamer, for the local coastal traffic, probably to replace the "Earl of Carrick". (The "Aline" was not replaced, though Captain J.G. Turney remained with Hine Brothers for many years to come.)

After the depression of 1879 the town began to prosper again in 1880, and Wilfrid and Alfred continued to play a significant role in its development. The 'Solway Club' reported that 105 ships were now insured with them, and despite the losses and claims their premiums were still cheaper than others. (Wilfrid was President of the Committee of Management, and Alfred the Secretary.) Wilfrid remained a conscientious and active Trustee of the Town and Harbour Board; he continued to attend the Literary and Scientific Society; and with a General Election in the offing he found himself more and more in demand to promote the local Liberal candidate.

Both brothers stayed loyal to the cause of temperance, and were concerned in several schemes in support of the movement. One of these was a petition to the newly-elected Parliament to pass an Act closing public houses on Sundays: in May an announcement in the newspaper declared "the town will be canvassed for signatures, and all above 16 years-of-age are expected to sign". (Nothing more was heard of this particular initiative, however!).

Wilfrid's proposal to the Trustees to "consider the desirability of providing a place of recreation for the people" fell on deaf ears too, but one of his ideas did blossom. In January, the "Maryport Coffee Tavern Company" was formed, with Wilfrid and Alfred buying 50 £1 shares each – by far the largest holding. As members of the Board of the Company, they applied their characteristic energies to the project, and on August 6th 1880 the new "Cocoa and Coffee House" opened its doors in Irish Street. Mrs. Senhouse performed the opening ceremony, and Alfred presided at a concert, *"in a large room crowded to suffocation"* as the *Advertiser* reported. Less suffocating, but every bit as popular, was Alfred's next conducting engagement; the Sunday Schools' Centenary celebrations the following week.

No less than 1,400 children gathered in Fleming Square for hymn-singing; the whole throng then went in procession through the town to the grounds of Netherhall for an afternoon of games.

The brothers seem to have been indefatigable supporters of so many facets of the life of the town, and at this time their younger brother also began to join in the activity. Joseph Jackson Hine was by now 36 years old, married with three young daughters, and running his business successfully enough from his base in Kirkby Street. In December 1880, his name appeared on the programme for the first weekly saturday night entertainment at the coffee tavern; his contribution was a song called "Norah Darling"! The following week it was Wilfrid's turn: he does not seem to have been endowed with great musical talent, but he did his bit with a comic rendition entitled "How to doctor a cold". On the Saturday after that, both Alfred and Joseph were amongst those who entertained – mostly singing worthy Victorian ballads with titles such as "The Blind Girl" and "The Empty Chair".

The new year saw the dramatic conclusion to an affair which had been brewing for some months. In March, 1880, an article had appeared in the *West Cumberland Times*, a Cockermouth newspaper, purporting to be an account of a meeting of the owners of the "Castle Holme". According to the report, some of the shareholders accused Hine Brothers of overcharging them – both for the actual cost of the ship and also for their commission as brokers and agents of the vessel. They also maintained, the report went on, that the brothers' charges for managing the "Castle Holme" were excessive, being more than double what their competitors were asking!

The embarrassment which these statements must have caused, and the potential damage to their business in this highly competitive area of commerce, can readily be imagined. Stung by the imputations of dishonesty and sharp practice Wilfrid and Alfred went to law, instituting a libel action against the journalist concerned. The action was due to be heard at Carlisle Assizes in January, 1881, but at the last moment the reporter admitted that the account had been untrue and misleading, and apologised publicly.

The retraction and apology were accepted by the brothers, who withdrew the lawsuit: the *Maryport Advertiser*, however, seized the opportunity to score heavily off its local rival. Its contributor 'Pendragon' concludes:

the prostitution of the press to personal purposes, and making it the vehicle for attacks on private character, is as dangerous as it is discreditable.

The next week's editorial weighed in with fine style:

...one of the most scandalous acts of injustice ever committed by a journalist...

...a Cockermouth newspaper which entirely miscalculates its influence in the community, and is apparently never so overjoyed as when it makes itself pretentious and ridiculous....

Fine moral rectitude! It is almost unfair to mention that in the same issue there is a report that the brothers attended a presentation of an illuminated address and a Dock bond for £100, to which they had certainly subscribed, as a testimonial to Mr. Robert Adair. (As well as being a friend of Wilfrid and Alfred, Adair was the proprietor of the *Maryport Advertiser*!)

Interestingly though, the disputed report contains figures which cast light on the financial side of shipping at the time. For instance, the "Castle Holme" had cost £16,444 from the shipbuilders in 1875, representing 1,027 gross tons at £16 per ton. The broker, who sold the shares in the vessel to the owners, received 1% commission on the transaction at the outset, as did the manager. Thus each 1/64th share must have cost at least £160 in 1875 – an equivalent investment of over £10,000 today! Incidentally, the vessel made no profit at all on her second voyage so there would have been no return on their money for the owners that year, and this may have been the source of disgruntlement for some of the owners! While all this legal and editorial activity was going on, however, the "Castle Holme" herself left London for Melbourne with

every prospect of a successful trip. The "Eden Holme" departed for Adelaide again with general cargo on January 21st; and life in the company returned to normal for a while.

In the first half of 1881 it was the steamships which made the news. In February the "Esk Holme" damaged the North Pier on her way out of harbour, and it was a bad month for the "Alne Holme" too. Returning to Workington from Carthagena she met a severe gale, and had to put in at Milford with a damaged bridge and lifeboats swept away. Her next trip was a cargo of coal from Newport, in South Wales, destined for Gibraltar, so she set off back across the wild and wintry Bay of Biscay. Four days out, she was rocked by an explosion in one of the cargo holds which blew off the hatches, set fire to the sails, and killed a crewman. Despite this the "Alne Holme" was able to continue her journey, having suffered only slight damage overall. When the subsequent Court of Inquiry convened in Liverpool it was stated that the cargo was 'Risca Black Vein' coal, which was known to give off explosive gases, and the Board of Trade's counsel was able to convince the Court that the lack of proper ventilation of the hold was the cause of the accident. The owners of the vessel were ordered to pay £100 to the costs of the Inquiry – effectively a fine, indicating the Court's opinion of who was to blame. The *Maryport Advertiser* indignantly defended Wilfrid and his fellow owners, calling the verdict an injustice, and making valid points about the 'incomprehensible regulations and unhelpful attitude' of the Board of Trade. They also noted that the explosion had occurred in the hold of the "Alne Holme" which *was* ventilated, and not in the unventilated one next to it! Nonetheless, coal was known to be a hazardous cargo (such explosions were by no means rare), and the captain had received a B.o.T. notice that the vessel was not properly ventilated (but had not passed this on to Wilfrid). Furthermore, ventilation of the holds was by means of hatches which could be battened down in rough conditions – and probably had been, in the Bay of Biscay in February! All in all, Wilfrid must have considered that the owners had been dealt with fairly lightly: the ship and cargo were saved, and Capt. Markham's certificate was not even suspended. Whether the dependants of John Sponge, the unfortunate sailor, felt similarly was not recorded.

The company continued to acquire steamers; the **"Ovington"**, nearly 700 tons and eight years old, was the first in this year, and Capt. Winterhoff took command of her. Captain Joseph Wilkinson also had a busy winter, supervising the construction of two new ships being built to the brothers' requirements by J.L. Thompson & Co at Sunderland. The first of these was launched in March, and was named **"Thorn Holme"**. Like her predecessors, this new ship was purpose-built for the transport of large quantities of bulk cargo: she was a 1,700-tonner, designed to take more than 2,000 tons of cargo in six watertight holds, and yet to draw only 18 feet of water when loaded. She had four steam winches and a crane for swift cargo-handling, and her holds had vertical boards which prevented cargoes such as grain from shifting. The "Thorn Holme" had been fitted with very powerful engines and boilers: she also had accommodation for 'First Class Passengers', with cabins and saloon fitted out in maple and teak with crimson plush upholstery. As master for the newest showpiece of their fleet the brothers once again turned to Captain George Brown, as they had for "Esk Holme" and "West Cumberland". Once again Capt. William Brown moved to take his namesake's place, and Capt. J.G. Turney, now recovered from his "Aline" ordeal, moved into his first steamship command aboard the "Esk Holme".

Within days of her launch the "Thorn Holme" obtained her first assignment: to carry pig-iron from Maryport to New York. This cargo would be the first shipped direct from the port to the United States (previously they were sent via Liverpool), so after fitting-out and sea-trials Capt. Brown took on ballast and set out from Wearside to Maryport with the new ship. She carried not only ballast, however: Wilfrid and Alfred themselves were on board as passengers, with their friends Messrs. Eaglesfield and Douthwaite. The maiden voyage from Sunderland lasted three days, and was by all accounts a pleasant one: "Thorn Holme" arrived in the Roads on a Saturday afternoon, and when she entered the harbour on the evening tide a great number of the local people gathered to see the largest ship that had then ever dropped anchor in Maryport.

At the other end of the scale in many ways was the **"Ivy Holme"**, the second vessel off the Thompson slipway for Hine Brothers. Registered at only 174 tons, just 115 feet long and with a mere 8 feet draught, this little steamer was intended for the general coasting trade and lighterage work (carrying cargo to and from larger ships outside harbour). As an extra feature, "Ivy Holme" had a roomy deck, and lounge facilities for passengers; the enterprising owners intended her to prove *"a great acquisition to the ports in the district, particularly during the summer season... an attractive and desirable vessel for pleasure purposes."*

"Ivy Holme" was launched on April 2nd and left Sunderland four weeks later with a cargo of coal for Dublin. Capt. John Connell from the "Bavington" was her master, and as well as the crew she carried Mr. Robinson and Mr. Todd, from Hine Brothers' Maryport office, as passengers. This voyage was presumably meant as a treat for them, in the same way their employers had enjoyed their recent trip in "Thorn Holme".

For the first day or so the weather was fine and the ship made good progress round the northern coast of Scotland, but over the next two days the weather deteriorated and by the fourth day a howling gale was blowing. By this time the ship had turned southwards into the North Minch channel, between the Hebridean Isle of Lewis and the mainland. At eleven in the evening of that day witnesses recounted that the vessel was "struck by a tremendous sea on the port bow, which made her vibrate from end to end".

By the next morning it was obvious that something was very wrong with the little "Ivy Holme". She was lying low in the water, and beginning to settle by the head. At quarter to seven the crew and passengers were awakened and called up onto the deck while the captain went below to assess the situation. It did not take him long to confirm his worst suspicions: the hold was filling with water and nothing could save the ship. Though the gale had partly subsided the sea remained very rough and launching the lifeboat was itself a difficult and risky manoeuvre. It was accomplished in a very short time nonetheless, and in about five minutes the ship's company had taken to the boat.

By this time the sea was washing onto the deck and the engine-room door could not be opened, so the Second Engineer and a Fireman had to escape through a skylight. As the Fireman was clambering out the ship rolled and he lost his balance, toppling backwards, but amazingly his fall was broken by one of the moving piston arms of the engine, which propelled him upwards again and out of the skylight to safety! By now the ship was clearly sinking fast, so the men in the lifeboat bent to the oars to row clear. They had not gone far when the end came for the "Ivy Holme":

....the vessel's bow suddenly went under, and she quickly sank, assuming first a perpendicular position, which was only altered when she was about disappearing by turning completely over.

A local fishing-smack, attracted to the scene by the distress signals on the ship's whistle, took the seafarers on board and brought them to Stornoway. They transferred to the island steamer that evening to begin their journey home. (Unexpectedly they discovered a friendly face in Stornoway too: the Customs Inspector there, Mr. Ritchie, had been transferred from Maryport only a few weeks before and was not a little surprised to meet some old acquaintances again so soon!)

Not all the news was bad, though. The "Thorn Holme" had a successful first voyage across the Atlantic and back, having found a return cargo without difficulty, and arrived in Plymouth on May 29th. She was then due to return to Maryport to collect her next load of iron, but this time Captain George Brown came home ahead by train: he had an appointment he could not be late for. On June 1st, 1881, at the Maryport Baptist Church, he was married – to Barbara Robinson, née Hine, the younger sister of his employers and the widow of the captain of the "Mersey". Meanwhile six weeks before, on the other side of the world, Captain J.W. Millican and his sweetheart Lily Jones were married: she had travelled right across Australia from her home in Queensland to Fremantle, Western Australia, for the wedding. Both couples were destined for long and happy married lives. After their tragically short first marriages George and Barbara Brown had 41 years together, while Joseph and Lily Millican survived to celebrate their golden wedding anniversary in 1931!)

Back in 1881, however, the *Maryport Advertiser* had another important event to report: in its issue of 17th June, the editorial proclaimed:

Our readers will perceive a reference in our advertising columns that Messrs. Hine Brothers of this town have, with their usual expertise, determined to establish direct communication by sea between Maryport and America.

And there too, for the first time, was an advertisement which heralded the new development in the partnership which Wilfrid and Alfred Hine had started just eight years before. It began:

HOLME LINE
Direct Steam Communication
between
NEW YORK and WEST CUMBERLAND

With this, the HOLME LINE came into being. The paper's editorial concluded:

This new means of transit will be of great service to the public: it cannot fail, we think, to provide a commercial advantage: and we have no doubt but that the well-known readiness of Messrs. Hine to serve the trading community of the district will be appreciated as it deserves.

Chapter Four
Setbacks and Advances: 1881-1883

As WELL AS the Holme Line Steamers the firm continued to operate their other lines of business: the Hine Clipper Barques, the coastal and European trade of their tramp steamers and the brokerage and insurance of their own and other vessels. To consolidate their place in all these spheres of activity as the industry became even more competitive, the company needed the capacity to respond quickly to change and the skill to forecast the trends in the markets required. Trade at this time was in a state of continuing fluctuation, and the rates charged for shipping freight cargoes could – and did – alter hugely and sharply as hundreds of shippers, brokers and agents competed to attract the eye of the customer.

The secret of success lay in fixing a rate which reflected the costs of the voyage and the risk of not finding a cargo for the return trip, the company's overheads, the maintenance of the vessel, plus any special requirements of a particular cargo – perishable or inflammable goods for instance. The rate also had to produce a return on investment, yet remain competitive and attractive. In strategic terms, companies had to decide whether to increase their fleet in good times and to meet the increased demand by buying, commissioning or chartering ships; and conversely, whether to lay up ships and pay off men in quieter times. They also had to plan longer-term policies – expansion of the business, and diversification or specialisation of operation. For Hine Brothers, one example was the passenger trade. Since the 'Brier Holme' in 1876 most of the Hine ships had incorporated facilities for fare-paying passengers; sound commercial sense, as this produced income which was not offset by the high costs of extra cabin staff and the 'trimmings' which 'liners' had to provide.

Another factor to be considered was the replacement of ageing vessels in the fleet, and those which had become obsolete in an age of technical advance: this presented a formidable challenge. In almost the same month as the Holme Line was born in Maryport, a little steamer arrived in Melbourne on her maiden voyage. What made this event remarkable was that the "Aberdeen", built by Napier of Glasgow, had taken only 42 days for the journey from Plymouth! She was powered by the latest innovation, the Triple Expansion steam engine, which ran at higher pressures and produced vastly more power than the old compound engines. Moreover, it used less fuel (more room for cargo, fewer stokers to be employed), and could burn cheaper grades of coal (lower fuel and bunkering charges). The triple expansion engines were lighter, as they incorporated improved designs of boilers and pistons made possible by the use of steel instead of iron.

The use of steel to build the ships themselves, or at least for the hull plates, was also feasible by this time as steel production in Britain became more widespread and quality more reliable. As well as being lighter, steel also had the advantages of being both stronger and easier to maintain than iron. Although some steel sailing ships were built, it was mainly steamers which were to benefit from this advance; the financial savings were greater and the potential profit higher in this type of vessel.

For the time being, however, the iron clipper barques could fend off the challenge by a combination of realistic pricing, efficient seamanship, and on occasions a little entrepreneurial opportunism. In Fremantle, Captain Millican was offered a cargo of sandalwood for Shanghai, under unusual circumstances:

Two firms at Perth agreed, simply on a note of hand, to load the ship and despatch her as quickly as possible, each firm loading its own chosen end of the ship. There was no charter party; the contract being based on good faith, which prevailed throughout, and all went well, otherwise I would have been in the soup!

It took two stevedores five weeks to load the cargo: the Captain comments:

...the wood... was in pieces from 18 inches to 8 to 10 feet long and 4 to 10 inches thick, every piece as crooked as a dog's hind leg, carefully cut and each piece stamped at both ends with the private mark of the shipper.

The delay had a brighter side for Joseph Millican however: it allowed him time for a honeymoon! On arrival at Shanghai he was able to find a cargo for his homeward passage: the wood was rapidly replaced by tea, and less than a month later the "Hazel Holme" was following in the traditions of the windjammers on the China Clipper run. No speed records were broken this time though; light winds all the way home, and a severe gale in the Channel.

The 'Myrtle Holme", with Capt. Ritchie, continued to demonstrate the unpretentious efficiency which kept the company going, and maintained Britain's trading supremacy throughout the world. Keeping up her reputation as a clipper, she took only 88 days from her anchorage in the Downs to her arrival in Adelaide, and this included taking a little time for humanitarian duties. St. Paul's Island is a volcanic crater from a bygone age – a tiny, isolated spot on the map of the Southern Ocean, 2,000 miles from South Africa or Australia: any shipwrecked mariners marooned there stood no chance of escape and little of rescue. Finding himself in the vicinity, Captain Ritchie ordered the "Myrtle Holme" to stand in close while he inspected the coastline thoroughly, "...so as to make particularly certain no persons were alive on that desolate spot."

The value of this practice was dramatically demonstrated a year later. The "Abbey Holme" under her new master Captain John Rich decided to check another of the inaccessible islands in these wastes of ocean – and discovered no less than 60 castaways! The "Shakespeare", a splendid four-masted ship of 1,314 tons bound from Cardiff to Calcutta, had been wrecked in fog, and the passengers and crew had spent several weeks there, cut off from the world. One can imagine their relief

"Abbey Holme" at anchor, c. 1881

at being discovered and carried back to civilisation! The "Abbey Holme" was en route for Adelaide loaded with rails, but with so many extra mouths to feed the barque probably had insufficient fresh water and provisions to have gone on; so she retraced her course back to the southern tip of Africa and landed her unexpected guests at Simonstown in time for Christmas.

Meanwhile, in 1881 the "Brier Holme" met rough weather in the Southern Ocean during her passage to Australia: Captain Johnstone, in an interview with the "South Australian Register" described:

...some very heavy weather, a series of gales following from nor'west to south-west, setting up such a sea as washed on board an immense volume. One of the boats was smashed into fragments and a whole suit of sails was blown away. The havoc committed amongst the deck gear was something terrible, but being brought to the wind with a tarpaulin in the mizzen rigging the barque behaved extremely well though so deeply laden. The violence of the gale had hove the vessel so much over that the cargo had shifted; but when the weather moderated matters assumed a much more favourable aspect.

Despite this, the "Brier Holme" arrived in 91 days, and her master still found time to welcome aboard a party of pleasure-trippers who had come out in a steam launch from Adelaide to watch the barque arrive. The newspaper adds:

Captain Johnstone was eagerly interviewed by his visitors, who found in him the same genial shipmaster of old!

After such a voyage! The Captain obviously combined nautical skill with a shrewd eye for public relations!

Back in Maryport, the August of 1881 brought another election for the Board of Trustees; Wilfrid stood again, but this time the hustings were by no means uneventful, as earlier in the year the Board

had raised the harbour dues for smaller coasting vessels. This provoked an angry reaction from local mariners, and Wilfrid was accused of protecting his company's interests at their expense. There also seems to have been a personal vendetta against the other two Trustees seeking re-election. Wilfrid's robust defence of the Board's action at a public meeting just before polling day (reported in depth in the local press), together with his record of activity on behalf of the new dock project, just preserved his seat on the Board for another three years: his former colleagues, however, were ousted.

The Harbour Company's financial position was seen to be improving, to the encouragement of the investors in the new dock, and the port was thriving. At one stage there were so many ships waiting to discharge cargo in the Elizabeth Dock that the harbourmaster was ordered to moor the vessels end-on to the quayside and to unload them over the bows! The company's steamers prospered too, but not without incident. In September the "Alne Holme" had to put in to Copenhagen for repairs after colliding with a Dutch steamer and sinking her (fortunately with no loss of life). Captain Wilkinson, the overlooker of steamships, was sent to supervise the work, but he soon had to deal with another problem – the "West Cumberland", stranded on a reef near Trelleborg. With a salvage steamer and a lighter, 800 tons of pig iron were unloaded so the "West Cumberland" could be floated off and towed back to Copenhagen. Luckily the weather had been fine, the ship had not been pounded on the reef, and only minor hull damage was found. Over the next couple of months, however, the meteorological picture changed drastically, and the shipping reports tell a tale of damage, delay and disruption over the seas of northern Europe. The really catastrophic effects of the storms became evident at Maryport when, lashed by a wild south-westerly wind, the sea broke through the partly built sea wall and into the site of the new dock.

The nearly-completed construction was devastated. The sea wall was almost completely destroyed and seawater flooded into the basin of the new dock, scattering or washing away the builders' machinery, materials and timbers. Not since the storm which demolished the new South

Pier in 1853 had the port – and town – faced such a disaster. Wilfrid and the Trustees – not to mention the Dock Bond holders – must have viewed the havoc with dismay, and considered the likely cost of the damage. The first estimate, a week after the storm, was £25,000 (about a million pounds at today's rates); the final figure, following further damage before the weather finally abated, reached nearly three times that figure. The Trustees immediately set about raising capital, and once again the Senhouse family stood surety for the loans.

The diabolical weather continued through December 1881: as mentioned before, Captain Millican arrived in the Channel from Shanghai, and recalled:

We were thankful to get into the Downs before the weight of it broke, and with both anchors down rode out the heaviest gale I have ever experienced, when at anchor the barometer went down to 28.40.

On Christmas Eve 1881 the "Henry Scholefield" came to grief while returning home carrying water as ballast. Having rounded the Skerries rocks off the Anglesey coast the night before, she was on a north-easterly heading and making for Maryport. When the Master, Captain Clark, came on deck at six o'clock in the morning the ship was steaming full ahead, on course, but enveloped in a dense sea-fog. He ordered a reduction in speed, but at that moment a flare was seen; Captain Clark took this to be from a nearby ship, confirming his belief that he was still safe, in deep water, and well away from the coast. Almost immediately, however, the noise of waves breaking on a shore was heard; and before anything could be done the "Henry Scholefield" – still travelling at speed – ran aground at Nethertown, south of St. Bees Head. Stuck fast and holed below the waterline, she gradually filled up as the tide rose. There was a company of 19 aboard, plus three passengers including the wives of the Captain and Chief Engineer, but a heavy sea and a strong wind made it hazardous to abandon ship.

The Whitehaven Rocket Brigade arrived, and were able to rescue three crewmen by breeches buoy before the wind and storm tangled the lines. The steamer then launched its lifeboat and the Captain and Chief Engineer, with their wives and three more crewmen, came safely ashore. The Chief Engineer, Mr. Cummins, and another sailor then offered to return to rescue more of the crew, but could not persuade any other volunteers to man the lifeboat. By this time the sea level was up to the steamer's deck and waves were breaking over her, but fortunately the "Henry Scholefield" remained intact throughout the day and the crew was rescued at low tide. The company summoned a powerful steam tug from Liverpool in the hope of refloating the "Henry Scholefield", which had recently been overhauled and fitted with new boilers, but the continuing bad weather frustrated all the attempts and another particularly violent storm during the first week of the new year finally caused her disintegration.

The Court of Inquiry opened the next week, and heard that the flare which had reassured the Captain was indeed from another ship – the schooner "Laura Ethel", which had stranded in almost the same spot some time earlier, and was trying the warn the "Henry Scholefield" to keep clear!

Captain Clark stated in his defence that the light on St. Bees Head was not visible to ships approaching from a bearing south of south-west, and was thus useless for anyone in his predicament. It was also so high, he said, that it was frequently obscured by low cloud, and pointed out that in the previous six months no less than eleven ships had gone ashore along that short stretch south of the Head. The Committee consisted of a magistrate and two sea-captains, who were obviously not impressed by the standard of navigation; they were also singularly unhappy about Captain Clark leaving his ship while members of his crew were still aboard and in danger. The fact that the flare was misleading, and that taking to the boat had probably been a greater risk than remaining, probably saved his Master's Certificate, but his name never appears again in command of a Hine ship. The points Captain Clark had made about the St. Bees light were however taken up by Wilfrid Hine, who prompted the Trustees to petition the

Board of Trade. In March 1882 Wilfrid and the local M.P. went to London to meet Admiral Sir William Collinson, Deputy Master of Trinity House, and secured his agreement to investigate the matter.

In the meantime, tragedy struck another steamer of the fleet. The "Thomas Vaughan", commanded by Captain Branthwaite, left Whitehaven on January 2nd 1882 loaded with pig iron and heading for Rotterdam: four days later she put into Fishguard with her pumps out of order, and it was decided to go to Milford Haven, further round the coast, for repairs. The following morning she set out again, with a Fishguard pilot aboard to guide her round St. David's Head. At about three o'clock that afternoon the inhabitants of Skomer Island noticed a small steamer with a red funnel and two masts, sails set on the foremast, entering Jack Sound, the channel between the island and the mainland.

This whole stretch of the Pembrokeshire coast was – and still is – a navigational nightmare for the inshore sailor, and Jack Sound might almost have been designed to lure and ensnare the luckless mariner. It is narrow, with a current that can reach six or seven knots and which changes direction with the tides. At one point a dangerous eddy can appear, and the Admiralty Pilot Manual's description of the shallow inlets and rocky slabs to be negotiated makes bloodcurdling reading. It states:

Unless compelled by circumstances, Jack Sound should only be used by vessels with local knowledge and goes on ...a vessel must be careful of the helm, for the rate of the stream is such that a broad yaw might sheer the vessel onto the rocks on one side or the other to her certain loss.

It was presumably the Pilot's decision to take this route, though in retrospect the outcome was almost inevitable. A ship with engines of low power, lying deep in the water with a cargo of iron, and leaking, would respond sluggishly to her rudder. While using the current to help her through the channel, the "Thomas Vaughan" either lost control of her steering or caught the eddy, swinging out into the hungry

jaws of the waiting rocks. The hull plates would have been torn like paper, and the laden steamer would have no buoyancy whatsoever. Eye-witnesses confirmed that she was "making a fair speed when she foundered, and sank instantaneously."

Over the next few days debris from the wreck began to be washed ashore, and the worst fears of the Cumberland community were finally realised when a cigar-box containing a sailor's personal papers was found the beach. The vessel lying in 40 feet of water 300 yards from shore was indeed the "Thomas Vaughan". Two unidentifiable bodies were later found and buried locally; but of Captain Branthwaite, his crew, the cabin boy and the Pilot, no other trace was ever found.

The "West Cumberland" was more fortunate. Ten days out in the Atlantic from Londonderry to New York with a cargo of potatoes, she found herself in a bank of impenetrable fog. Real danger then arrived in the shape of a 20 foot high iceberg: before avoiding action could be taken the ice was upon them, gouging a huge hole in the port bow. The forward compartment filled with water within seconds, and the order was given to 'lighten ship'. Over 200 tons of potatoes were jettisoned, while Captain William Brown resourcefully devised a way to repair the leak.

First the crew managed to pass chains around the hull, and secured a sail across the hole in the bow; they then threw bags of potatoes into the flooded compartment to provide footholds for a team of crewmen to enter the hold. There was a large number of grain sacks on board ready for a return cargo and these were packed tightly into the hole, forming a makeshift plug which was kept in place by a huge heap of bags of potatoes. The "West Cumberland" then crept gingerly on her way, and despite a battering from headwinds she arrived in New York nine days later. Captain Brown reported that the makeshift repairs had just held out, and had undoubtedly prevented the sea from breaking through the bulkhead into the main hold. In dry dock the damage was found to be extensive, and it was more than a month before the ship could put to sea again.

Luckiest of all that year though were the crew of the "John Norman", which left Swansea in January bound for Valparaiso with a cargo of coal. One of those on board was a young apprentice, William Wilson; nearly 50 years later he wrote the following account in a letter to a magazine:

When a few days out, she was found to be leaking so badly that she had to put back to Swansea, where she had her topsides caulked and resumed her journey. A month later, however, the crew threatened to 'down tools' unless the Captain put into the nearest port; we therefore went to St. Vincent (Cape Verde Islands) where the cargo was sold.

Further repairs were carried out when the coal was unloaded and on April 29th, more than two months later, she left St. Vincent. William Wilson continues:

...we then took in ballast for Lota (Chile) and set sail. Three weeks later she sprang a leak, and the water gained on us to such an extent that it was decided to abandon her; this we did one afternoon, in two lifeboats, and had the good fortune to be picked up next day by the steamer "Mondego" and in due course landed in Southampton.

The 511 ton "John Norman" was the oldest of the Hine barques. Wooden hulled, she was built as a ship and had served 15 years on the China run before being sold, restored and reduced to a barque in 1870. She had been with the company from the start, and Wilfrid must have been sorry to hear of her going.

Nearer home there was excitement too. February saw a strike of 'pig-lifters' – dock workers who loaded pig iron into the holds. They were after a rise in pay – six shillings (30p) a day for loading, with one shilling (5p) per hour overtime. The strike failed: on the second day the managers of the Ironworks sent their own workers to load the ships, and two days later the dockers capitulated.

In April 1882 the Trustees again became concerned about public health. An outbreak of fever in the town had renewed doubts about the adequacy of sewerage and drainage, especially in the low-lying and populous areas of Maryport; the town's Medical Officer was asked to investigate and report. The problem persisted, until in July cases of Typhus were diagnosed among the townsfolk. The Trustees had few resources of finance or skill to tackle the problems, and could only look on helplessly: in August the situation was compounded by an epidemic of measles.

In November the 'Solway Club' and the 'Maryport Club' – the local Marine insurance co-operatives with which the brothers had been involved for nearly 20 years – were wound up. The number of ships insured had been falling for some years, and the rates were no so high for the remaining members that the loss of a vessel could constitute a ruinous expense to several of them.

There had been brighter moments though. The "Brier Holme" returned to Maryport in May and once again became the object of much public admiration – in fact a special train from Carlisle was arranged to bring folk to see her! Sixpence (about £1 today) bought a guided tour of the handsome barque, and the owners donated the proceeds to the Cumberland Infirmary. As the "Brier Holme", dressed overall, prepared to leave port to the cheers of a large crowd, the brothers and a party of their guests joined the ship. After lunch on board they returned with the tug, while in the roads the barque prepared for her journey.

The invited guests were not the only ones determined to see her on her way safely; two local ne'er-do-wells, Parkin Petrie and Thomas Todhunter, decided to join in. Under the influence of liquor they 'borrowed' an open boat and put to sea. Although "Brier Holme" remained at anchor within sight of Maryport all afternoon, Petrie and Todhunter managed to find themselves at Workington; there they sold their coats, filled up with drink and set off again. Two days and three nights later they landed once more – on the Scottish coast at Drummore, some 60 miles away! (It is not recorded how the intrepid mariners – or Robert Maize's boat – got home!)

Wilfrid and Alfred continued their campaigns against the social evils of alcohol: the Good Templars, the Band of Hope and the newly-formed Blue Ribbon Army received their enthusiastic support, as did the Literary and Scientific Society, the Baptist Church and the Liberal Party. The coffee tavern made a profit of over £100 and declared a 5% dividend on its shares! Alfred organised and conducted musical events, while Wilfrid continued his service to the town as a Trustee and a Magistrate. In May 1883 Wilfrid and Jane's seventh child, Robert Wilfrid, was born, and George and Barbara Brown also had a son a month before.

There was also an addition to the Holme Line steamer fleet. In the summer of 1882 the company acquired the "Margaret Banks", a twelve-year-old iron screw steamer; Captain Thomas Morwick, of the "Horatio", was put in command and for six months she plied the North European trading routes as the "Henry Scholefield" and "Thomas Vaughan" had done. On November 14th she arrived at Greenock, on the Clyde, now refurbished and re-named the **"Glen Holme"**. More additions followed in rapid succession.

In the first six months of 1883 the brothers took delivery of three steamships commissioned by them from the yards of J.L. Thompson – in the same way that eight years earlier the three clippers from Bartram Haswell had come into service. In February, Wilfrid's daughter Jane went to Sunderland to launch the **"Fern Holme"** of 2,610 gross tonnage; a cargo steamer 320 feet long and with specially-designed facilities for carrying up to 20 passengers in conditions of some style. One of the upper cargo decks could be adapted to transport livestock; and the Admiralty had also placed the vessel on its list of available troopships. The "Fern Holme" boasted two masts and could be rigged as a schooner with double topsails – a much larger spread of canvas than was usual. The ceremony went smoothly and the ship was christened in the traditional way, but it was a bottle of pure Keswick lake-water that was dashed across her bows!

Six weeks later, the **"Ivy Holme"** was launched: like her ill-fated namesake, a small steamer for the coastal trade and for lighterage, and also equipped with powerful towing gear. Miss Thompson, the shipbuilder's daughter, performed the ceremony, repeating the process a month later for the third ship of the trio, the **"Dent Holme"**. The "Dent Holme" was an iron and ore carrier; just over 230

feet long and with a draught of only 15 feet, yet capable of shipping over 1500 tons of cargo between Workington and the ports of the Baltic and Mediterranean.

The choice of commanders for these new ships is significant. The brothers gave the "Ivy Holme" to the man who had captained the first "Ivy Holme" on her disastrous maiden voyage: Captain Connell of the "Bavington". No such misfortune occurred this time however – no doubt to everyone's relief. Later in the year though he relinquished his command and appears to have retired from the sea.

The "Dent Holme" went to Captain James Ritchie of the "Myrtle Holme", an experienced mariner and long-time associate of Wilfrid (they had been co-owners of the "Cereal" at the beginning of the company's history). He now transferred his skills to steamships, while the "Myrtle Holme" was entrusted to the enterprising young Captain Millican.

Wilfrid and Alfred chose their brother-in-law George Brown for "Fern Holme". With a party of friends, they joined the new ship after her sea-trials and brought her to Maryport for her maiden voyage. The "Fern Holme" was too large to enter the harbour (completion of the new dock having been delayed) so the tug "Florence" ferried out another group of friends and interested townsfolk to the ship. A pleasure cruise, a picnic and an impromptu party ensued, with songs, dances and instrumentals from the crew! The "Florence" then returned all the passengers to shore and the "Fern Holme" began her working life.

The first journey was an eventful one: at anchor in Bombay she was struck and damaged by another ship leaving port, and on arrival at Le Havre on her way home she was detained on suspicion of carrying cholera! One of the engineers had been taken ill and died during the voyage and the French authorities insisted on quarantine at St. Nazaire, complete unloading of the holds and fumigation of ship and cargo alike! Needless to say, there was no cholera aboard, but the "Fern Holme" was a fortnight late in resuming her work and missed her next scheduled trip: the brothers complained bitterly about the cost to the company of all this, but to no avail.

Chapter Five
Brisk Business: 1883-1890

THE HINE FLEET was at its largest in 1883 with 23 ships in all registered to the Company with Lloyd's, but by the end of the year there were changes as two more of the wooden-hulled sailing vessels left the Brothers' service. The "Glenfalloch", one of Wilfrid's earliest acquisitions, was returning from Australia via the West Coast of the U.S.A., but did not complete the homeward run: arriving at Valparaiso in Chile she was examined by the Admiralty surveyor there and condemned. Re-named "Natalia" she was sold locally, and presumably ended her life as a coastal trader. The little brigantine "Clara" was also sold, to a Captain Shilton of Maryport.

In September 1883 one of the Hine steamers met a dramatic end under the horrified gaze of onlookers at her home port. A south-westerly gale had been blowing all day, and by noon had increased to a "perfect hurricane" as a contemporary account put it. At about three in the afternoon a small steamer was spotted running for the harbour through the wild seas, sails blown to tatters. It was the "Bavington", with a crew of five under Captain Tully, returning to Maryport with a full cargo of iron ore. Despite the conditions the ship reached literally to within a stone's throw of safety, and was at the harbour mouth when a wave caught her and drove her against the outside of the south pier. The next wave broke completely over her from stem to stern, extinguishing the boiler and leaving her helpless.

Hundreds of townspeople had gathered on the pier by this time, and the cry went up to launch the lifeboat. It is a tribute to the bravery of the local seamen that a crew was mustered promptly and the "Henry Nixson", the town's first lifeboat, set out without delay. The lifeboat's journey was a short one in distance, but the combination of breakers, wind and incoming tide made it almost impossible to make

headway out of the harbour. Meanwhile, the "Bavington" was in deeper trouble. She was now being blown northwards across the harbour entrance, her hull striking the rocks and the shallow sea-bed with every roller: the crew, terrified that she would break up beneath them, clung to the forecastle.

To shouts of encouragement from the townspeople the lifeboat eventually managed to clear the harbour entrance: several times they had been washed against the north pier, and only their dogged perseverance kept them to their task. No sooner were they in the open sea than a mighty wave caught them too, shooting them round the pierhead and right underneath the bows of the "Bavington". At once, two of the stricken ship's crew made a desperate leap for the lifeboat; by great good fortune they landed head-first among the rowers! The next wave drove the "Henry Nixson" away from the steamer, and the skill and strength of the lifeboatmen were again put to the test as they fought back to the doomed "Bavington" to receive the rest of the crew and Captain Tully. So bad were the conditions that the rescued sailors had to be lashed into the lifeboat to prevent them being washed overboard on the journey back!

Thanks to the courage and fortitude of the lifeboat crew, all landed safely at last. To add to the excitement a little girl called Dockray was blown off the pier into the sea, and narrowly escaped being drowned herself! The "Bavington", pounded by the storm, broke up and sank shortly afterwards, but within a couple of months the brothers had replaced her and Captain Tully was at sea again: he now commanded the **"Elizabeth and Ann"**, a similar steamer built on Tyneside in 1875.

The year ended on a sombre note for the company with the death in November 1883 of Captain Joseph Wilkinson: his friendship with Wilfrid and his association with the firm stretched back many years. He had been the captain of the "Robert Hine" in 1868; of the brothers' first steamship, the "Florence Richards", in 1874; and of their first new steamer, "Alne Holme" in 1876. Since then he had supervised the design and building of every one of the steamers the company commissioned, taking many of them on their sea-trials or maiden voyages. To succeed him as Marine Superintendent, Wilfrid and Alfred chose their brother-in-law, Capt. George Brown. By now Captain Brown was an experienced steamship commander, familiar with most of the company's ships, and had proved himself a skilful and conscientious mariner. (The promotion may also have helped to ease George and Barbara's grief at the death of their little son a month earlier).

As Captain Ritchie moved to command the "Fern Holme" his successor in "Myrtle Holme", Captain Millican, was showing the older masters what he could do, given a clipper barque and a fair wind! For the outward trip "Myrtle Holme" took only 73 days from the Lizard to Adelaide; and to prove this was no fluke, the return leg to the Lizard lasted only 91 days. Between Adelaide and Cape Horn, a distance of 2,880 miles, the journey had taken only twelve days, with the log recording the astonishing tally of 290 and 288 miles covered on the best days. The

"Castle Holme" also clocked up a good journey back from new Zealand in 97 days under her new master Captain Bryce – newly promoted from "Abbey Holme" – while the seasoned Captain Johnstone brought "Brier Holme" to home waters in 91.

In the affairs of the town, it was a time for tying up loose ends. Wilfrid's deputation to London had borne fruit; in June a new lightship and more buoys to mark the harbour entry had been provided. In October the Trustees received a memorandum from the shipowners and masters of Maryport, requesting extra protection of the harbour entrance against the elements. The Trustees agreed, H. P. Senhouse commenting "everyone could see on Wednesday that something was necessary" – an allusion to the "Bavington" shipwreck. Wilfrid reported that the Dock Committee engineers already had proposals to extend the north pier at an angle which would shield the harbour, and also to make the south pier about 50 yards longer.

Less satisfactory, however, was the record of the Trustees in the matter of the town's drains. In spite of criticism from Whitehall and instructions from the government no decision had been made about provision of proper sewers. Wilfrid objected to the proposed scheme because he believed it would not work in the lower-lying parts of Maryport, which were prone to flooding at high tide; he voted against it, earning himself castigation in the *Maryport Advertiser*, which called him a "jellyfish representative" and an "undecided carrier pigeon".

1884 was a remarkable year for Maryport. In February the young Oscar Wilde visited the town, and delivered a lecture on "The House Beautiful" at the Athenaeum. What impression the "Apostle of Aesthetism" made on his audience (or on the hard-working, church-going, teetotal Wilfrid, who presided at the meeting), is not recorded!

Crew of "Fern Holme", (Capt. Ritchie), New York, 1885

The Trustees were busy. They were being sued by the owners of the "Luigi", an Italian barque which had been damaged by grounding while being towed into the harbour, and £3,599 compensation was claimed. They were preparing another Bill to Parliament to allow them to raise a further £80,000 for harbour improvements, and in April the Dock Committee had to buy a new dredger to keep the port free of silt.

Their main preoccupation during the first months of the year, however, was the opening of the new dock. The great day was chosen, and for weeks ahead celebrations were being planned. It was Wilfrid who proposed to the Trustees that it be named the "Senhouse Dock" and this was adopted unanimously. He went on to suggest that Mrs. Elizabeth Pocklington Senhouse, the Chairman's mother, should be the one to open the dock formally: Humphrey accepted the offer on her behalf, and so it transpired.

Tuesday May 27th 1884 dawned bright and clear, and by early morning Maryport was filling with people from the surrounding country districts and spectators from further afield arriving by special trains. Mr. F. Kelly, writing in "Sea Breezes" in 1927, describes it:

The town was decorated as it had never been decorated before. There were bands of music and processions of Friendly Societies and school-children. The leading citizens boarded the S.S. "Alne Holme" from the North Quay and she, attended by a number of other steamers and sail ships in tow, steamed out to sea and re-entered the port. Her yards were manned by men of the Royal Naval Reserve; as the steamer passed through the dock gates and the only barrier (a blue ribbon) was broken, Mrs. Pocklington Senhouse, on board the "Alne Holme", declared the dock open for traffic amidst the plaudits of thousands of spectators lining the docksides and the piers; and a solitary gun from the pierhead joined in the glad acclaim.

A civic luncheon followed, and for the rest of the day the town gave itself over to festivities of all sorts.

"Alne Holme" enters the Senhouse Dock, May 27th 1884

A late-twentieth century photograph showing Senhouse Dock and Basin, and the subsequent silting-up of the entrance which was to be a constant problem

It was not long before larger ships, including the Holme Line steamers, were using the new facilities to take advantage of an upturn in trade after a relative slump. The Maryport Haematite Company had folded the previous year and general trade had decreased sharply; however, the "Elizabeth and Ann" unloaded the first grain cargo of the new Senhouse Dock only four days after the opening. The level of harbour dues once again became a problem: too high a level would drive shippers into the arms of competitors, while a low level might mean that the Trustees' huge capital debts would never be repaid.

As August approached election fever once more gripped the town, and the 'sewerage issue' surfaced again. Wilfrid's attitude – in favour of a sewerage system, but opposed to the proposals before the Trustees – was becoming understood by the populace; particularly as it was pointed out in July that there would be a risk not only to the lower-lying parts from flooding but also to the higher areas of the town from build-up of sewer gas! This vindication and his tireless work for the Senhouse

Dock ensured Wilfrid's re-election: again, his fellow members were unseated – this time by two nautical candidates, Captains Penrice and Williamson (the recently retired master of the "Castle Holme").

The "Castle Holme" herself, under Captain Bryce, again made good speed from Adelaide; 97 days to Falmouth, like the year before. Coincidentally, the "Brier Holme" also returned in the same time as she had taken in 1883. Hine Brothers took the opportunity during 1884 to sell two more of their wooden sailing ships, the "Robert Hine" and the coasting schooner "Tom Roberts". The flexibility and consistency of the company's business policies enabled Hine Bros. to prosper, but others were not so fortunate: in November 1884 the local firm of J. Melmore and Co., which mainly owned coastal sailing vessels, went bankrupt. Wilfrid and Alfred continued their personal commitment to Maryport's progress. As well as their church, temperance and temperance allegiances they had found time during 1883 to help the committee of the British School, which provided primary education. In 1884 they steered the coffee tavern to another profitable year, ran choirs and bazaars and supported the Literary and Scientific Society's initiative in forming a local branch of St. John's Ambulance Brigade.

The Company itself was undergoing considerable change. In 1886 Hine Brothers took over the City firm of Moses and Mitchell, and made the manager, Mr. E.P. Willis, a partner in the London end of the business dealing with the Insurance and Shipbroking aspects. 'Hine Brothers and Willis' continued to prosper, using their office at 6 Crosby Square, London, but they never severed the long-standing connection with Devitt and Moore, who continued to act as their agents for business associated with the sailing vessels.

These years marked a period of relative stability, and for the next five or six years the lives of the brothers and their families, the business affairs of the company, the development of Maryport and the voyages of the Hine fleet followed an even pattern. Naturally though, there were incidents worthy of note, and landmarks of various types, during the rest of the decade.

In 1885 the "Myrtle Holme" again made a fast passage to Australia, but on arrival the young Captain Millican had to face his first (and only) mutiny! In fact it was a very minor affair – a drunken spree by four of the sailors while the barque was being moved between berths in Port Adelaide – and it was speedily quelled by the Captain and the local Police.

More serious for the company was the loss of the "Dent Holme", the newest of the Holme Line steamers, which was run down in dense fog by the steamer "Lake Champlain" in the St. Lawrence River in July 1885. Captain Hurst and his crew all survived, and later in the year Hine Brothers successfully sued the other shipowners for the damages.

In 1886 the "Hazel Holme" was sold off to a South American company in Valparaiso. On arrival at that port she was surveyed on the orders of the British Consul, and it was found that expensive repairs would be needed: the brothers must have weighed the cost of these against the benefit and decided to sell, as they had done three years earlier with the "Glenfalloch".

In June of 1886 the gates of the Senhouse Dock were accidentally opened, causing a sudden drop in the water level inside. The "Fern Holme", docked and loading cargo, grounded sharply and sustained damage to her hull: Wilfrid found himself in the delicate situation of having to sue the Harbour Trustees (of which he was a member) on behalf of his company! It had been an unfortunate year for the Trustees in litigation; they had had to pay up for the damage to the "Luigi"; and Mr. Smith, a local builder, also seized some Harbour property to satisfy a court judgement for arrears arising from repairs to the dock in 1884!

Nor was the company itself immune from legal actions: in 1887 Hine Bros. defended a suit brought by a dockworker in London who had fallen through a deck hatch while unloading the "Alne Holme". The plaintiff won the first hearing and £45 damages, but this verdict was overturned on appeal in 1888. By then, another disgruntled shareholder in the "Castle Holme" was suing the them over their handling of the ship's finances back in 1880. Wilfrid and Alfred were once again vindicated, receiving judgement with costs in 1889.

In 1887 the "Aikshaw" lost her master, Capt. George Tate: he fell ill and died during the voyage to New Zealand, and the barque was brought home by a Captain Humphries, who only stayed with her another year.

1888 saw Hine ships in the limelight several times. In August the latest newcomer to the fleet, the **"Nether Holme"**, was launched from J.L. Thompson's yard in Sunderland. She retained the slim lines (length 277 feet; breadth 37 feet) and shallow draught (19ft 6") of her predecessors, which allowed her to use the Senhouse Dock, but the "Nether Holme" was designed and built to the most up-to-date specification. Most importantly, she was made of steel, and driven by a triple-expansion engine. Her manufacturers estimated that, with her high-pressure steel boilers, steel crankshafts and modern power unit, she would steam all day at ten knots on less than twelve tons of coal. Like her predecessors, she was also schooner-rigged and could carry sail; however, the "Nether Holme" had telescopic masts which could be shortened to allow her to pass under bridges such as those on the Manchester Ship Canal, then nearing completion. After sea-trials, the new steamer was placed under the command of Captain Ritchie, who moved from "Fern Holme" earlier in the year.

Captain Markham of the "Alne Holme", took over the "Fern Holme", but not for long. In July 1888, returning to London fully-laden from Montreal, she ran aground on a Newfoundland beach during a storm and was broken open in four places by the force of the waves pounding her against the land. The vessel was a total wreck, but there was no loss of life.

Unfortunately this was not the case later in the year, when the "Horatio" met her end. News of this shipwreck was slow to break: first reports merely stated that the ship had gone ashore on the Dutch coast, that the ship's lifeboat had been smashed to pieces by the sea, and that the crew had left the steamer in two boats – a small dinghy and the ship's pinnace. The following week's newspaper, however, carried the story of J. Gorley, the steward, who described how he had nearly been left behind on the stricken "Horatio". Having cut the rope to free the pinnace containing Captain Brough and nine of the crew he was only just in time to scramble aboard the dinghy, manned by the mate Mr. Grieves and a seaman called Bennett. The two craft pulled away from the ill-fated vessel, but soon afterwards the Captain ordered them to come alongside the pinnace and take another man, as they were overloaded. Despite the danger of this manoeuvre in the darkness and the heavy seas, the mate complied and a sailor named August Kieb was transferred to the dinghy. The boats pulled apart again, but within a short time the pinnace was struck by a huge wave and disappeared.

An hour or so later, as daylight appeared, the lucky quartet in the dinghy came ashore on dry land. They had no idea where they were, and in fact they feared their respite might only be temporary as the terrain looked like an island that could disappear at high tides. The sight of a rabbit, therefore, was a great reassurance! Shortly afterwards they came across signs of habitation and were soon enjoying the hospitality and kindness of the residents of Texel, the largest island in the Friesian Archipelago. Hearing the story of the shipwreck the local fishermen immediately launched a lifeboat and searched all day for the

pinnace, but in vain. One body was later washed ashore, but the Captain, his brother Daniel Brough and the rest of the crew were never found. Captain Brough, previously of the "Ivy Holme" and again only recently transferred, left a widow and five young daughters.

The same storm also grounded the "Esk Holme" 50 miles further up the same coast at Borkum, in fog. The ship was stuck on a sandbank, but local people rowed out and brought the whole company ashore. At the next high tide the Dutchmen returned them to the ship and put a tow-rope aboard: with the aid of a local tugboat they refloated the "Esk Holme" and brought her safely into Delfzyl for survey. The hull was found to be damaged, so she was later moved to Sunderland for repairs. A Board of Trade Inquiry was held the following month, and the Tribunal found the master, Captain J. G. Turney, at fault: its determination read:

The Court, having carefully inquired into the circumstances attending the above-mentioned shipping casualty, finds, for the reasons stated in the annex hereto, that the stranding was caused by the neglect of the master in not verifying the position of the ship by the use of the lead at any time during the voyage. The Court finds the master, John Graham Turney, in default for such stranding, but taking into consideration his long service and good character hereby suspends his certificate for three calendar months only from the date hereof. The Court blames the second mate, William Gill, for not stopping the engines and putting the lead over the ship's side when the man at the wheel reported that the ship had struck something. The Court recommend that the master be granted a chief mate's certificate in the meantime.

Dated this 22nd day of December 1888."

(John Graham Turney, a Maryport man, was 50 years old and had been a master mariner for 26 years. He had worked for Hine Brothers since 1872, commanding the "Aline" until her shipwreck, and the "Esk Holme" since 1881.)

By the end of 1889 the company had replaced its losses. With the launch of the **"Rydal Holme"** (1,931 gross tonnage, with a steel hull and a triple-expansion engine) from the yard of J. Blumer of Sunderland, the Holme Line maintained its thriving transatlantic cargo trade: Captain William Brown was moved from the "West Cumberland" to take command of this new steamer. In November 1889 the **"San Domingo"** was bought, destined for the Company's Mediterranean and Baltic concerns. She was an iron screw steamer of 1,079 tons gross, built in Stockton by M. Pearce, and launched in May 1874.

At the end of 1889 therefore, the list of Hine Brothers' vessels read as follows:

HINE CLIPPER BARQUES:

"Abbey Holme"	Captain Rich
"Aikshaw"	Captain Humphreys
"Brier Holme"	Captain Johnstone
"Castle Holme"	Captain Bryce
"Eden Holme"	Captain Randall
"Myrtle Holme"	Captain Millican

HOLME LINE STEAMERS:

S.S. "Alne Home"	Captain Dawson
S.S. "Esk Holme"	Captain J.G. Turney
S.S. "Glen Holme"	Captain Morwick
S.S. "Nether Holme"	Captain Markham
S.S. "Rydal Holme"	Captain W. Brown
S.S. "Thorn Holme"	Captain Holmes
S.S. "West Cumberland"	Captain Kirkpatrick

HINE BROS. COASTAL/EUROPEAN STEAMERS:

S.S. "Ardmore"	Captain Greggans
S.S. "Elizabeth and Ann"	Captain Tully
S.S. "Ivy Holme"	Captain Wilson
S.S. "San Domingo"	Captain Gorley

The S.S. "Ovington" does not appear on this list because early in the morning of December 29th 1889, she was struck by the S.S. "Queen Victoria" in the Firth of Clyde and sank within five minutes. She was bound from Greenock to Hamburg with a general cargo, and at the time of collision was stationary and in the process of lowering anchor because the weather conditions – snow and thick fog – made it dangerous to continue. Most of the crew of the "Ovington" were able to scramble aboard the other vessel; some had to be rescued from the water (one died from injuries and cold shortly after he was pulled from the sea), but four others – two stewards and two engine-room firemen – went down with the ship.

This loss compounded the unhappy end of the decade for Hine Brothers, following the death in June 1889 of the company's Superintendent of Sailing Vessels. Captain Wedgewood Robinson had been connected with the company since its inception – indeed, as a friend and associate of Wilfrid Hine his links went back even further, to the launch of the "Abbey Holme" 21 years earlier. Since 1875 he had ensured that the design, construction and fitting-out of all the company's beautiful clippers was to an uncompromisingly high standard. He also supervised the operational aspects of the business, as young Captain Millican witnessed in 1876, with the skill born of experience and understanding of ships and men. Locally his good humour, philanthropy and personal qualities earned him universal popularity. Flags in the harbour flew at half-mast in his memory; his funeral was widely attended, and a memorial erected in the cemetery by the captains and officers of the company testified to their esteem and respect. He was 55 years old.

Just as Hine Bros. seemed to evolve during this time, relatively stably but with occasional setbacks and tragedies, so too did Maryport itself. An upturn in the general climate of trade and the influence of the new dock resulted in an improvement in the financial position of both Harbour and town during this time. In January 1886 alone, 20,000 tons of imports – iron ore and grain – and 12,000 tons of exports, mainly pig-Iron, were dealt with, together with 3,200 tons of various coastal traffic cargoes – the largest tonnage ever recorded at Maryport. This brought in over £1,600 in harbour dues and tolls, more than double the previous January figure. In 1887 the Harbour revenue exceeded £24,000 – a healthy 164% rise in three years! The Trustees had been able to pay off the arrears and the interest they owed on the various loans, and had even redeemed some of the capital bonds: optimistically, Wilfrid claimed in February 1888 that they would "in a very short time extinguish the whole of their debt".

Ever keen to enhance the facilities of the harbour, Wilfrid tried to persuade the Trustees to raise another £20,000 for a graving dock for the repair of larger ships, pointing out that there was no such amenity between Barrow and the Clyde on the West Coast. The Trustees had other concerns, however – it had been discovered that some of the concrete in the new Senhouse Dock was already crumbling (apparently due to a high magnesium content) and it would be necessary to drain the basin for repair work. They also had to make plans for provision of water and gas to the town, and arrangements for celebrating the Queen's Golden Jubilee, so it was finally decided merely to enlarge the existing gridiron for ship repairs.

In 1888 Alfred was active in civic affairs too. Early in the year the town was rocked by a series of disasters, as the winter storms claimed the crews of three local ships, the "Glenavon", "Abercorn" and "Agnes" in rapid succession; while in April an explosion at St. Helen's Colliery, Workington, killed more than 30 miners. As president of the Maryport Choral Union and of the Orchestra, Alfred arranged a series of concerts to aid the Appeal Funds for these tragedies.

In June 1888 the managers of the British School decided to form a Higher Grade School, to extend the educational facilities to cater for older children. Alfred, the secretary of the management committee, called a public meeting for "interested gentlemen" to map out the scheme. It was proposed that 60 pupils would be enrolled, bringing £208 per annum in fees and grants – enough to keep the venture solvent. A draft curriculum including arts and science was prepared and by September the plan had general support: the schoolroom would be at the Assembly Rooms in High Street, and by the end of the year the first pupils were enrolled. Alfred had been obliged to give up some of his many commitments by this time, due to pressure of other duties: Humphrey

Senhouse and he now represented Maryport on the newly-formed Cumberland County Council in Carlisle.

Wilfrid's political life changed radically during this period. W.E. Gladstone, the Liberal Prime Minister between 1880 and 1885, had been plagued by the parliamentary tactics of Charles Stewart Parnell and his highly disciplined group of Irish MPs, and since 1882 had come to believe that Home Rule for Ireland was necessary. Ousted from office in June 1885 by Lord Salisbury's Conservatives, Gladstone nonetheless returned to power in February 1886 and pledged his government to Home Rule, a move which split his party, both in the Commons and in the constituencies. Wilfrid (the President of the Maryport Liberals) supported Gladstone's earlier proposals for more local self-government in Ireland and the amendment of earlier unjust Land Acts, but he felt that Gladstone had no mandate from his party to go further. In June 1886 he tendered his resignation from the local party, and for the rest of his life declared himself a Liberal Unionist. Alfred (the Hon. Secretary) remained with the Liberal Party and their local candidate Sir Wilfrid Lawson, who does not seem to have let the political difference interfere with his friendship with both the brothers. For his part, Wilfrid deplored the split; despite his convictions he never allowed his name to be put up against Alfred or Sir Wilfrid Lawson as a candidate for any office.

(Gladstone's Home Rule Bill was defeated in Parliament shortly afterwards, and he 'went to the country' in August 1886. Deserted by the Whigs and Radicals, he lost the general election, and Lord Salisbury returned to lead a Conservative and Liberal Unionist government.)

The brothers lost their mother in June of 1887, in her 80th year, after a long illness: she had been bedridden and living at Park Hill with Alfred's family for some time. Wilfrid retained his seat on the Board of Trustees in 1887, coming top of the polling figures. In 1889 he was appointed a Justice of the Peace, and sat regularly in the Police Court and Petty Sessions in Maryport thereafter.

Chapter Six
Flourishing and Growing: 1890-1895

AS A WINTER OF FOUL WEATHER ushered in a new decade none of the frivolity of the 'Naughty Nineties' was yet apparent in the world of ships and men, and 1890 was to be a year when 'life is real, life is earnest' for seafarers of all nationalities. On December 7th of the previous year the "Millie G. Browne", the largest four-master of the American merchant fleet, set sail from Boston with a huge cargo – 'a million feet of lumber' in the hold, together with a deck load that stacked three feet above the rail: 5,000 cases of kerosene, 500 barrels of resin and other goods – bound for Montevideo. At two in the morning of the fifth day the ship ran into a howling gale which lasted four days continuously, increasing in severity the whole time. On board the "Millie G. Browne" as a passenger was George Coleman, an American journalist, and his full account of the adventure appeared in the "Boston Sunday Herald" on January 5th 1890. He recorded his experiences in dramatic detail as the seas ran higher and the ship's hold began to fill fast:

We were all in the engine room where desperate efforts were being made to keep the pumps going when the spanker mast toppled over, breaking about 50 feet from the deck, and carrying with it the mizzen and main masts. The latter hung upon the foremast a few moments when that gave way, taking with it the jib-boom...

Lashed by the storm, dismasted and shipping more water with every wave, the ship was helpless and adrift; life for those aboard became decidedly uncomfortable:

Our mode of living during the storm was catch as catch can from canned goods, fingers taking the place of knives and forks,

while we slept – all 13 of us – in the engine room, crouching round the boilers trying to get warm or dry, lying on the floor by the coal-bin or elsewhere nestled among stiff old sailcloth or upon a battered-down door...

In a few days enough water had been pumped from the galley to get into the upper locker and the stores were carried forward to our abode.

Coleman then describes how they then started a makeshift oven on deck in the engineer's tin ash-barrel and could fry bread, ham and potatoes 'to their hearts' content'! The ship's company lived for a week in this way, maintaining a watch and at night raising a light upon the remains of the foremast. These were anxious hours:

Every moment, through long hours and weary nights, the horizon was scanned at every point in the hope of sighting some craft. We might be picked up in an hour; perhaps not in a month; and perhaps not at all...

Imagine their feelings then when just after dark on Sunday December 22nd the cry "Light Ho!" was heard from the mate on watch! Coleman again:

At once everyone was on his feet scrambling for the steps: but no-one but the mate could see the light, and sometimes he lost it. 'False alarm' was the thought of more than one, but no-one was willing to voice it...

After an agonizing wait, however, a faint glimmer became discernible in the distance and the crew set about drawing attention to their plight:

...torches were ordered and the heavens made lurid by the glare of hemp, manila and oakum soaked in kerosene.... Torches were carried fore and aft to show the friendly craft our length. It was a steamer, and as she drew near our stern there came across the water in stentorian tones the welcome cry 'Ship Ahoy – What assistance do you require?'.

This was Hine Brothers' "West Cumberland", loaded with steel rails and on her way to Norfolk, Va. to take on coal. She proceeded to put out her boats to bring the relieved group aboard the steamer, where they were *"given a hearty English welcome and shown every possible kindness, the officers and crew sharing with us their best in everything."* Captain Kirkpatrick later told Coleman that he had been on watch on the bridge when he noticed an unusual glow in the sky and had summoned the first officer for a 'second opinion'. They decided to investigate, *"so as to miss no chance to assist a distressed vessel."* (Incidentally, at the time the off-duty officers had been holding a service below decks, and had been singing "Rescue the Perishing"!)

Fortunately, the gales had abated sufficiently for the crew to be evacuated safely, but their ordeal was not yet over: two days later, on Christmas Eve, Coleman recalls:

...it stormed fearfully and heavy seas were shipped, some of which found their way into the cabin, down through tightly shut doors and windows, and we could make no headway.... Our coal was running out and it became a serious question whether we should not have put in at Bermuda.

In such conditions, and with the ship's complement increased from 18 to 31, a crowded, uncomfortable and possibly hungry festive season was in store: but by December 30th the situation had eased a little and the "West Cumberland" made as good speed as the fuel would allow. Until the following day, that is, when the engine broke down, leaving Coleman and his companions at the mercy of the wind and waves again! The ship's main boom came adrift, swinging across the foredeck and finally breaking in two over the rail. The engine was repaired after some hours, though, and as Mr. Coleman put it:

...our trials were at an end, and... January 2nd saw us in Norfolk, half dressed in rags and tatters but happy to have come through with our lives.

Among the many hazards of these voyages such as storms, uncharted reefs and shallows, disease and accidents, are 'derelicts' – the semi-submerged hulks of abandoned vessels littering the shipping lanes and posing a sinister threat to other craft. Collision with such an obstacle while under way could tear the bottom out of a hull or breach bow-plates in an instant, and must have been the cause of the unexplained loss of many otherwise sound and well-managed ships. Coleman recounts that to prevent this the crew set fire to the stricken hull and *"...left the 'Millie G.', or what was left of her, to the destruction of the flames."* The following year Captain Kilpatrick was presented with a fine gold chronometer watch by a grateful U.S. Government in recognition of his rescue.

Nearer to home another shipwreck must have caused much distress to many involved with Hine Brothers' activities, though again no lives were lost. In April 1890 the "Abbey Holme", one of the original barques with which Wilfrid had started his business career and in which several of the Company's Captains had been employed, was proceeding from Leith to Middlesborough to collect a cargo and begin her voyage. She was in ballast and riding light, and was being towed by a tug from Leith; and as the wind was north- to north-easterly the "Abbey Holme" had set some of her sails to reduce the load on the tug. As the little convoy moved south the wind became a gale and the "Abbey Holme" repeatedly overran the towing vessel, so the sails were furled, the yards braced fore-and-aft and it was decided to make for shelter. They reached the mouth of the Tyne with some difficulty, but just as the ships were about to enter South Shields harbour the towing hawser snapped. The "Abbey Holme", without the capacity to make way or manoeuvre,

The Wreck of the "Abbey Holme", April 1890

was suddenly helpless: adrift in a gale and a rough sea, close to the shore and being blown inexorably towards the harbour walls and the pier.

Her predicament was spotted from the land and the maroon was fired. As well as mobilising the rescue services the alarm alerted many hundreds of local folk, who thronged the seafront to watch the spectacle. The doomed barque struck the eastern end of the south pier, then gradually ground her way towards the shore until she stuck fast against the rock beneath the ironwork of the pier. By this time the sea's fury had increased even further, and waves were breaking right over the pier and the ship.

Although lifeboats from both North and South Shields had been launched, the rescue of those aboard the vessel was carried out by the men of the local rocket brigade and the coastguards: the "Abbey Holme", though irrevocably stranded, had 'parked' on an almost even keel against the pier, and the main danger was not of sinking but of men

being swept away by the breakers. Thirty-four local Brigadesmen turned out to help, rocket lines were fired from the pier to the vessel and two officers of the Brigade boarded the "Abbey Holme" to assist in rescuing the crew. A 'breeches buoy' was rigged, and the Captain's wife, Mrs. Rich, who had been accompanying her husband, was then evacuated to safety. As the local newspaper put it,

> She was in a very prostrate condition and was assisted to the Watch House and there carefully attended to. Dr. Crease, the honorary surgeon to the Brigade was already at the place and under his direction the poor woman gradually recovered from the shock which she had sustained".

Her husband and the crew were also brought safely to shore and were taken to the Brigade headquarters, where it is reported they were given *"dry clothing, hot tea and other refreshments."*

Poor Mrs. Rich's discomfiture can only have been increased when the *Maryport Advertiser* reprinted the story word for word the next week. In the local press, the account read: *"The first person to be landed by the breeches buoy was the Captain's wife, **a stout, elderly woman.**"*

The "Abbey Holme" was surveyed shortly afterwards and certified as a total wreck: she subsequently broke up fairly rapidly under the pounding of the waves and the rocky shore, but her 'bones' remained for many years as a reminder of her fate. The following month the regular annual meeting of the vessel's owners was due to take place, and this gave Wilfrid and Alfred the opportunity to present the 'total loss account' to their fellow shareholders. The "Abbey Holme" had in fact had a very profitable year, and the brothers were formally complimented on their management of the vessel. Their management of the "Castle Holme", which had been the subject of litigation by two disgruntled shareholders in the vessel over the last two years, was also finally vindicated at this time with the Lords of Appeal in London dismissing all allegations against the Company.

In the following month Hine Brothers acquired another sailing barque to replace "Abbey Holme" and put Capt. Rich in command of her. She was the "Star of Denmark", 998 tons, built in 1863 by Harland & Wolff of Belfast to the order of the Corry Line and destined to join their 'Star Line' of jute clippers plying between London and Calcutta. Launched just a week after the Prince of Wales (later King Edward VII) married Princess Alexandra of Denmark, not only did she bear this appropriately loyal name but also a figurehead carved to resemble the Princess! Hine Brothers changed the name immediately on purchasing the vessel, however, renaming her **"Denton Holme"**, and within a month she had loaded a general cargo and set sail for Fremantle, Western Australia.

The summer of 1890 was to turn out to be a dramatic season for the Company. All started well enough in June, with the successful launch of the latest steamer built for them by J.L. Thompson & Sons of Sunderland. A Miss Laura Dickinson performed the ceremony, christening her the **"Forest Holme"**. (As the boilers and engines of this and most of the other steamers of the Holme Line had been built by the firm of John Dickinson of Palmers Hill Engine Works in Sunderland, it is probably safe to assume that Miss Laura was the boss' daughter). Unusually for a steamer of this time, the "Forest Holme" had a 'clipper' stem like a sailing vessel, with a short bowsprit and a

"Forest Holme"

figurehead carved to resemble a lady: not royalty this time, but Wilfrid's wife Jane Hine! As usual, Capt. George Brown had supervised the construction of the 2,400-ton ship, which incorporated several innovative design features which would fit her for the Line's particular needs. The holds of the "Forest Holme" were wider and easier to load or discharge because the vessel had no beams between the decks or the holds (the hull itself was specially strengthened to compensate for this) and the officers' and crew' quarters were above the deck level and so did not impinge upon the cargo space. The Company continued its policy of fitting retractable masts (the ship was rigged as a two-masted schooner as well as using steam power) with the Manchester Ship Canal transit in view – a far-sighted decision, as at this time the Canal was still five years away from its opening. Although the new steamer's draught was only 20 feet and 5 inches (a vital requirement for any ship planning to enter Maryport's shallow harbour) she could carry 3,400 tons of cargo of all sorts. Her modern steam winches, capstan, windlasses and steering gear, together with cutting-edge engineering features and even 'state of the art' lifeboats, added up to make the "Forest Holme" as modern, complete and efficient as possible. After fitting out, she would be brought to Maryport on her first sea trial before being loaded with a cargo of steel rails for Canada.

Accommodation for a few passengers had also been included in the design, and the *Maryport Advertiser's* preliminary announcement of the launch ended:

Many of those who enjoyed an afternoon's cruise on the "Fern Holme" a few years ago would be delighted if Messrs. Hine Brothers could see their way to entertain them in a similar manner when the "Forest Holme" comes home get her baptism in the waters of the Solway!

This subtle angling for an invitation seems to have been successful, as a few weeks later the paper contained a description of the trip from Sunderland, on which,

by the courtesy of the owners... a small party of friends were invited to accompany the steamer.

The reporter was particularly impressed when

...running from the Mull of Galloway to the Harbour of Maryport the steaming capacity of the vessel was tested and she attained the high speed of 14 knots....

Command of the new vessel was given to Captain J. Johnstone, making his debut in steamers after nearly 20 years with the Company as master of the "Glenfalloch" and "Brier Holme". Only a fortnight after the "Forest Holme" was launched, however, the first of a series of blows rained on the firm.

The "West Cumberland" – the rescuer of the Americans six months before – was the first. Steaming from Cartagena for Mostyn fully laden the ship was in collision with the "Minero", a barque sailing out of Cardiff. The "West Cumberland" went down, but there was enough time for four of her crew to be taken on board the "Minero", which returned to Cardiff; the Captain and the rest of the crew were rescued by the "Montana Bay", a passing steamship which delivered them safely to London some days later. All except the second engineer, a Whitehaven man called Thornber, who drowned: he had been due to be married when the ship returned to Maryport.

The next blow fell in July. The "Thorn Holme", the large steamer whose maiden voyage Wilfrid and Alfred had joined just over eight years before and which had been purpose-built for the transatlantic trade, ran ashore while passing up the St. Lawrence River in Canada. Having stranded at low water on a rocky shore with her holds full of steel rails she did not float off as the tide rose: as the tide rose the hull filled, and by high water the ship was reported to be completely covered. Despite attempts to save her by unloading part of the cargo the "Thorn Holme" remained stuck fast, and was declared a total loss. (A major salvage job was undertaken later that year by the Canadians: the ship was purchased from the underwriters by a local shipbuilder, refloated and towed to a shipyard where about a workforce of 150 men spent a winter repairing her! The ship was then re-sold, her name changed to the "Louisburg", and she spent another 27 years in the service of the Black Diamond Steamship Co., Ltd.! She was eventually wrecked in 1918.)

The third disaster struck the following month, with another stranding; this time it was the "Denton Holme", purchased only months before and on her first voyage for the Holme Line. Captain Rich – apparently not accompanied by his wife this time – had brought his craft to within ten miles of his destination half way round the world, only to strand the "Denton Holme" on the reefs of Rottnest Island in the Swan River approaches. No lives were lost, and at first it was hoped that the cargo (1,500 tons of water pipes, and general goods for Perth and the Swan River colony) could be saved; but by the 27th September, two days after the disaster, Lloyd's List contained the following message from their local agent:

Denton Holme is full of water. All of the cargo is damaged. Every exertion is being made to save what is possible.... Saving of the cargo will depend on the weather.... Arrangements have been made to salve the cargo at 50 per cent value when recovered.

Worse news was to follow:

October 4th: Fremantle: Denton Holme broken in two...

then:

October 6th Fremantle: The ship is gradually breaking up. She has been formally condemned. According to best advice obtainable, an immediate sale is best for all concerned. Recommend that matters be allowed to take their course...
and finally:

October 8th: Fremantle: Salvage recoverable will be very small...

There had been lighthouses and beacons on Rottnest Island since about 1850, and a pilot boat service: the charts and pilot manuals also warn of the reefs to the north and east of the island, and detail the deep channels – and the shoals and shallows around them – giving soundings to guide the navigators into the harbour. The area is prone to strong north-westerly gales at this time of year, but no explanation has been offered for the captain's mistake, albeit an error made by many a hapless mariner in the area before and since.

The formal Court of Enquiry in Fremantle found Captain Rich to have been culpable in the loss of his vessel, in that he had strayed in too close to the land and neglected to 'heave the lead', i.e. have sufficient soundings made of the depth of water under her keel. For this error of judgement the Court ordered that his Master's Certificate be suspended for three months. It seems that the double disaster and the Australian Court's ruling did not diminish the brothers' regard for Capt. Rich's ability, however, because by the beginning of the next year he appears in Lloyd's Register as the master of the "Brier Holme", where he remained for a further 13 years.

Back in Maryport, three new building projects involved Wilfrid and Alfred particularly. The first was the new Baptist Church which was due to replace the existing chapel in High Street. A generation before, Alfred Hine senior had been involved in the initial establishment of the High Street Chapel, whose congregation actually built the place themselves – members donating materials, labour and services as well as cash – and it was ready by 1834. The church grew in numbers so much that it had to be enlarged to seat 400, and a Sunday School building was added in 1840. The brothers were at the forefront of the new fundraising exercise and had pledged significant amounts themselves, and doubtless shared in the excitement when the foundation stone was laid at the new site in Station Street. (Indeed, it was reported that Alfred had already hunted out and bought an organ for the new church!) The second project was the coffee tavern, which moved to new premises in Senhouse Street and was still providing alcohol-free entertainment for the local people – and making a profit! In August of that year the Tavern opened a Billiard Room, and Wilfrid and Joseph Williams, the Secretary of the organisation, played the inaugural match (Wilfrid lost). Lastly, in November, the Maryport Seaman's Institute opened its doors, set up to provide a welcome, help and support to sailors from visiting vessels as well as from the local area.

With all these commitments it is not surprising that Wilfrid only managed to attend eleven out of the 85 meetings of the Harbour Board during his term of office (he wasn't the worst – one member had only attended four times in three years): nevertheless, he 'topped the poll' again at the election of Trustees in August 1890 – and promptly missed the September and October meetings! This was unfortunate, because one item on the Harbour Committee's agenda was the matter of the damage done to the sea wall of the dock by the "Forest Holme" on her arrival in September. Wilfrid wrote challenging the Trustees' estimate for the cost of repairs, maintaining he could get the work done for half the price, but was voted down in his absence. This was only the second visit to the port by this steamer since her launch, and it is noticeable that with the advent of larger ships – not only from the Holme Line – the incidence of this type of accident increases: an indication of the narrow margin for error while negotiating the restricted harbour entrance.

Over the next couple of years the fortunes of the town of Maryport were racked with uncertainty as it was affected by the fluctuations in world trade and local resources. A slump in demand for iron dealt the final blow to the Maryport Haematite Iron and Steel Company – which itself had taken over the business of the Harrington Company which had 'gone bust' in 1883. The new administration tried their best, but within a year had had to close the factory down for several months; things later improved, but eventually despite short-time working and pay cuts the Company could not go on. The workers struck for a fair wage, management suspended operations and the company went into receivership in March 1891. This had the 'knock-on effect' of finishing operations at two of the local pits, Ewanrigg and Ellenborough, which had been

Wilfrid and Jane, an informal photograph c.1890

leased to the Company: Ewanrigg closed in 1891 and Ellenborough in 1892, though this latter reopened some years later. The Lonsdale Colliery at Dearham closed down in 1894, and in that year also the Solway Ironworks' furnaces were finally blown out after a decade of decline in business. The prosperity of the port naturally suffered with the reduction of iron, steel and coal passing through the harbour, inbound and out. The 1891 accounts for the Harbour, published in the press in February 1982, made dispiriting reading: receipts (from harbour dues etc.) were only £22,607, while expenses amounted to £20,193. The loans remaining outstanding – on the upgrading works done years before – still came to over £312,000, so it would be most unlikely that those who had invested in the new harbour would see a dividend for that year. By October 1893 the *West Cumberland News* reported that after the "Forest Holme" left the port bound for Canada the Senhouse Dock was empty of shipping; and that the "Ivy Holme" was available for charter, presumably because the company had not found a cargo. In April 1893 the press also carried an item which was in a way related to the situation: a complaint about youths bathing off the port pier on Sundays. It was not clear whether the correspondent took exception to the place, or the day – or merely the fact that the lads had not equipped themselves with bathing suits!

There were more serious problems in the docks during this time, however. Throughout 1891 and 1892 trouble had been brewing among the labour force over pay scales and the use of non-union labour: this came to a head over Christmas 1892 when the dockers refused to work with two others, non-union members, who had been employed to unload a vessel. Mr. Robinson, Hine Bros.' agent at the dock, suggested to the Captain that his crew could unload their ship, and this was done: and when the "Alne Holme" subsequently docked the dockers were told (by somebody) that their services were not required here either, as non-union labour was being employed! This resulted in, as the newspaper put it, *"a good deal of feeling... among the men"*, but *"no disturbance has occurred"*. It later transpired that the "Alne Holme" had also used its own crew and discharged the cargo themselves, and the local Dock Labourers' Union secretary wrote to the paper the following week to clarify the matter and calm the situation down. (He also explicitly accused the dock stevedores of 'creaming' the wages of the workers, claiming that the labourers made less than £1:10 per week, whereas the stevedores took home £4 – 6 per day!). Another indication of troubled times was an increase in damage and vandalism in the dock area, and Wilfrid had proposed in Autumn 1891 that the Trustees should approach the Chief Constable for an increase in the police force for the town, for this reason and also because of the increase in Maryport's population. This had increased the work of the magistracy too, and in that same period Alfred was appointed to join Wilfrid on the local bench. Alfred also retained his seat on the new county council early in 1892.

For his part Wilfrid remained a Trustee, and when an Act of Parliament in 1894 separated the running of the Town and the Harbour he found himself a member of the newly-formed district council as well. For many years prior to this he had been a conscientious – and at times controversial – member of the Harbour Trustees' General Purposes Committee, which tended to concentrate on urban issues such as the town's water and gas supply and the sewage system with all their shortcomings, and when elections came around in August 1893 he was again re-elected unopposed, even though he was not in Maryport at the time! A month earlier he had embarked on the "Forest Holme" (Captain Johnstone) and crossed the Atlantic for the first time, travelling to Montreal with his wife and one of their daughters together with their friends Dr. Little and Mr. McGowan. (The *Maryport News* reported that no less than five stowaways were discovered on board and put ashore before the ship sailed!) Wilfrid's objective was to explore the potential of increased contact and business with the Canadians; the rest of the party may have had their sights fixed on the Chicago Exhibition which was taking place at the same time! The "Derwent Holme" left port the same evening, carrying another (legitimate!) group to the same destination; relations and friends of the family taking advantage of the Holme Line's passenger capacity. One of these was Captain Johnstone's daughter, and another was Wilfrid's niece Jane Leighton, who may have been taking the trip to take her mind off the death of her mother three months before.

Mary Leighton was 58, the eldest of the five surviving Hine children, and had been aware for nearly a year that she had a malignant growth in the liver. Despite this she remained closely associated with all aspects of the benevolent and charitable life of the town and of the Baptist Church up to the last few weeks of her life. The *Maryport Advertiser*, the *Maryport News*, the *West Cumberland Times* and the *Carlisle Journal* printed glowing and affectionate obituaries, and more than 500 people attended her funeral service. Mary had been married for many years to William Leighton, a well-respected and old-established draper who like herself was a stalwart of the Baptist Church: he was ten years her senior, and sadly only survived her by less than two years.

The new Trinity Baptist Church building had opened, amid great celebrations, 18 months before, and soon became known as "The Baptist Cathedral": the old chapel in High Street was sold, which helped to offset the considerable cost, but even after a second transfusion of funds by Wilfrid and Alfred there remained a shortfall of over £2,000 which the congregation hoped to clear with a grand bazaar in October 1893.

During these years the core business of the Holme Line continued to flourish. The "Thorn Holme" and "West Cumberland", lost from the Transatlantic routes in 1890, had to be replaced, so in January 1891 Hine Bros. acquired the "Crest", a large steamer built by J.L. Thompson two years earlier for a Newcastle company, and re-named her the **"Derwent Holme"**. At 2,107 tonnes gross, and drawing only 19 feet, this nearly-new ship was pressed into service immediately: Captain Holmes from "Thorn Holme" took her over, first delivering coal to Hamburg and thence to Maryport and on to Montreal with steel rails.

In June of the same year The Thompson yards produced another steamship, this time custom-built: the **"Loughrigg Holme"** had almost the same dimensions as her new 'half-sister' at 2,069 tonnes gross, 300 feet long overall and a draught of 20 feet. Like almost all the vessels the yard constructed for Hine Bros., the "Loughrigg Holme" had masts and sails, and a 'clipper stem' like a sailing ship, rather than the orthodox straight stem: she also had a figurehead, this time *"carved from a photograph of Miss Barlow of Accrington"*, according to the reports of her launch. After fitting-out and sea trials the ship made her maiden voyage to Maryport, with several members of the staff of Hine Bros. on board (as usual the ship had been fitted with passenger accommodation) and on arrival took further local guests aboard for a trip to the Isle of Man – a gesture much appreciated by the Company's land-based workers on their return the next day! Thereafter, though, it was 'back to business' and the ship was loaded, also with rails for Canada – a trade for which she had been specifically designed and built.

At this time there were four Holme Line steamers plying the route, as the "Nether Holme" (Capt. Markham) and the "Forest Holme" (Capt. Johnstone) found themselves bound for Quebec and leaving within an hour of each other. Both captains denied there was a race; indeed, thanks to days of fog and gales neither ship had any sight of the other for ten days after they had passed north of Ireland into the Atlantic. Then one afternoon, almost at their destination, the fog lifted and an astonished Capt. Markham spotted the "Forest Holme", a mere two miles behind him! Captain Johnstone had obviously seen him first and had ordered full steam ahead to overtake the "Nether Holme": the latter, however, was able to beat off the challenge and reached the Pilot boat first, eventually arriving in port 45 minutes ahead.

1892 was a year of drama for the Turney family. The Company had employed two Captain Turneys; both were the sons of Capt. R.A. Turney senior, master of the local coaler "Esther and Jane", who had been lost at sea in 1849. Richard Ansley Turney, born in 1828, had been the master of the "Alne Holme", the "West Cumberland" and the "Horatio" over the years before leaving the Company in 1884. His younger brother, John Graham Turney, born 1838, began his career as a Captain with Hine Bros. back in 1873 with the "Aline". After his shipwreck in 1880 he was transferred to the "Esk Holme" and had converted successfully to the role of a steamship captain, with the reputation of being a careful and cautious mariner. So on January 31st 1892, when the "Esk Holme" left Newport harbour in South Wales and encountered increasing westerly winds and stormy weather, Capt. Turney decided discretion was the better part of valour and the ship rode the storm out at anchor in the Newport Roads. She was loaded with iron and heavy machinery and bound for Valencia, and the next morning set out again, making reasonable progress down the Severn Estuary towards the Bristol Channel and the open sea: but by the afternoon a fog bank drifted in, and became so thick that it was decided to reverse their course and return to safe anchorage once again – in Penarth Roads – rather than remain in the main shipping lane. The "Esk Holme" turned east, then north-east, and gingerly attempted to retrace her steps.

There are several interesting hazards in this part of the estuary: all are marked with buoys, lighthouses or beacons and are marked on the Admiralty charts, well known to seamen. Into this category fall 'The Wolves' – three protruding rocks in the middle of the channel, marked with a red and white buoy on either side, east and west – and they have a long and savage history. In 1736, 60 soldiers were drowned when their ship struck the Wolves and sank. In 1817 a sloop, the "William and Mary", foundered on the rocks and went down within 15 minutes (the first mate and another sailor made off in the only lifeboat, leaving the passengers and the rest of the crew at the mercy of the waves: 15 passengers survived by clinging to the ship's rigging until they were rescued, but 50 lives were lost).

In the swirling fog, with the tide running hard and the compasses possibly affected by the iron cargo , it was not easy to be sure of the "Esk Holme"'s position; so when a buoy loomed out of the mist the Captain's calculations convinced him it was the East Wolves buoy and the vessel held her course. Unfortunately, he had miscalculated: the ship struck the rocks almost immediately and stuck fast. The Captain went ashore in one of the ship's boats and summoned a tug, but the ship was firmly impacted and the ebbing tide steadily made matters even worse. There was nothing for the ship's company to do but abandon the "Esk Holme" and return to dry land with the tugboat. No lives were lost this time, but the ship broke up and the 'Wolves' claimed another victim.

The subsequent Court of Enquiry took exhaustive evidence from the first officer, the engineer, several of the crewmen and Captain Turney himself. As well as two magistrates (one was Mr. John Ritson) the Panel was made up of two experienced captains as independent nautical assessors, while lawyers representing the Board of Trade and Hine Bros. spoke and questioned the witnesses. The official report of the proceedings shows that the matter was comprehensively reviewed, and that the Company's advocate went to some length to impress Capt. Turney's reliability, length of service and his record of careful practice upon the Panel. There was a reason for this: three years previously he had also been in charge of the "Esk Holme" when she had run aground in fog on Borkum, one of the Friesian Islands off the Dutch coast. On that occasion his certificate had been suspended for three months but, in consideration of his long service and good character, he had been allowed a first mate's 'ticket' during the suspension period. There was no way that this previous mishap could be ignored or glossed over: one of the nautical assessors in those earlier proceedings had been a Capt. Kenneth Hore – who was sitting on the present Panel too! Despite the many similarities between both cases, there was obvious general concern that Captain Turney should not 'lose his ticket' for this error. After a two-day hearing, the verdict appeared:

The Court, having carefully inquired into the circumstances attending the above-mentioned shipping casualty, finds, for the reasons stated in the annex hereto, that the "Esk Holme" was stranded and lost on the Wolves Rocks in a fog, through the master, John Graham Turney, having mistaken the east buoy of the Wolves Rocks for the west one, and altering his course to the north-east accordingly, under the impression that he was between the West Wolves and the Ranie Spit Buoy.

The Court, taking into consideration the circumstances of the sudden fog, consider he made an error in judgment in so doing, and therefore does not deal with his certificate.

The *Maryport News* reports that when this was announced there was a spontaneous burst of applause from the assembled audience: Captain Turney, no doubt greatly relieved, went back to sea shortly afterwards as master of the "Alne Holme".

Daniel Stalker Turney, Captain Turney's son, had followed the family's seagoing tradition and was advancing his career with the Company. At the age of 22 he was already the second mate of the "Aikshaw" under Captain Cobb, and in December 1891 the barque was bound for Antofagasta in Chile carrying coals from Newcastle (New South Wales). From there they sailed north with part of the load, making for Tocopilla, further up the coast. While passing round a headland the vessel 'missed stays' –

that is, did not answer her helm when the sails slewed round as the ship went about – and found herself driven onto the rocky coast. With a heavy swell crushing her against the rocks the "Aikshaw" lay almost on her side: the ship's boat was lowered into the stormy seas – or rather, dropped, according to one report – and Daniel Turney jumped down with a rope to draw it closer to the ship's side. As he did this about seven of the crew leapt into it – against the instructions of the Captain, though one survivor subsequently stated he had been "ordered into the boat". Turney was able to jump back on board the "Aikshaw", but the boat immediately capsized and five of the men were drowned.

At this point Captain Cobb relates that:

the next I saw of Mr. Turney he was running ashore along the mizzen mast, and was the first to land. Immediately... he went to the assistance of the first mate, who was clinging to the seaweed and unable to help himself until the second mate, at the risk of being washed off the rocks, climbed down and succeeded in pulling him out.

The first mate, James Allen, stated that he had been:

washed off the rigging when the ship capsized and could not get up the rocks to dry land, and was in great danger of being washed away by the sea, which was sweeping over me.

Mr. Turney went to his assistance:

lying flat on his stomach and leaning over the rocks, seized me by the beard on the second attempt and lifted me up to the higher ledge where he was.

Both he and the captain stressed the risk that Daniel Turney had taken: Captain Cobb's statement continued:

I saw him rescue the first mate, and for a few moments it was very doubtful whether either

of them would escape being washed off the rocks... I may also state here that the second mate was unable to swim, and if he had once got into the water I don't think he would ever have got out.

Turney next went on to pull another member of the crew – Samuel Nomo, variously reported as the steward, the cook and the sail maker, who had been in the ship's boat when it turned over – from the waves in the same way (though possibly not by the beard!). He then became aware of the plight of the youngest apprentice on the "Aikshaw", Julian Bulmer. He had been in the ship's boat too, and described the scene:

...before we could haul her clear the ship gave a sudden lurch onto her beam ends and crushed the boat to pieces.

Remembering the events nearly 40 years later, Julian – by now Captain – Bulmer goes on:

After struggling in the water for some time I found myself clinging to the main top where I was seen by Mr. Turney, who threw me the end of the royal brace... (a rope he had cut from the royal yardarm) ...I was just able to secure this round my body and he, with another apprentice, Harry Smith, hauled me over the wreckage, rocks and sea to safety... I certainly owe my life to Mr. Daniel Turney.

All in all seven of the ship's company lived to tell the tale, and at the Enquiry in Valparaiso Daniel Turney was commended formally for his bravery. Captain Cobb was admonished for not having tacked sooner and taken the ship away from the danger, but his certificate was not cancelled.

A few days later they set off to return to England on board the "John Elder", a liner of the Pacific Steamship Navigation Company – and almost unbelievably, were shipwrecked again!

The ship was carrying 139 passengers and a valuable cargo of silver when, just 24 hours out of Valparaiso on the January 17th 1892, she stranded on Cape Carranza rocks. No lives were lost, and it is

The S.S. "John Elder"

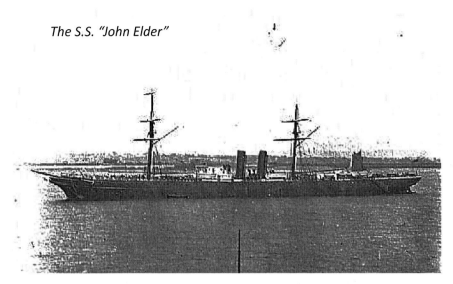

reported that Capt. Cobb, Daniel Turney and the rest of the "Aikshaw" party gave valuable assistance to their colleagues in rescuing the other passengers.

In May Daniel was the guest of honor in Maryport when Wilfrid and Alfred, together with many of the town's dignitaries, assembled to see him receive the Board of Trade's Silver Medal in recognition of his courageous conduct. Wilfrid made a speech introducing the new Superintendent of Customs Mr. Erupt, who was to make the actual presentation, and revealed that the Royal Humane Society had also voted to award Daniel Turney and Harry Smith citations for gallantry in rescuing Julian Bulmer.

There was an interesting footnote to this story: in 1930, 38 years after the disaster, two local Chilean fishermen lost their gear in a storm in the bay. When the weather improved, they went back to try and retrieve their nets and tackle by dragging the sea bottom; and they also brought up a brass bell engraved "Aikshaw – 1875 – Maryport"! There was a move at the time to try and retrieve the bell for Maryport, but this was unsuccessful and the whereabouts of the relic remain a mystery.

Captain Cobb remained the master of a Hine clipper barque by being appointed to command the "Myrtle Holme" later in 1892. This fine vessel had continued to ply between London and the Australian ports, regularly turning in fast times – 85 days for the return voyage in that year – under Captain Millican (and usually with Mrs. Millican

aboard too!). Hine Brothers had decided on some 'career development' at this stage for the skilful and productive young Captain Millican and promoted him from sail to steamships, giving him the 'plum' post of master of the new "Loughrigg Holme". Daniel Turney continued his career and gained his Master's certificate in 1897: he too was given the command of the "Loughrigg Holme", when it was relinquished by Capt. Millican in 1898. He later went on to captain the "Forest Holme" and then went to the Australian Mercantile Marine.

The same sort of prompt action and concern for ones shipmates was displayed the following year, when the "Glen Holme" was in collision with a Danish steamer, the "C.P.A. Koch" in the Sound of Islay. The "Glen Holme" had set out to deliver a cargo of railway sleepers to Ardrossan, but had a problem with her engine: she had had put in to Stornoway, and early on a Sunday morning was actually being towed to Ardrossan for repair. The "C.P.A. Koch" was on her maiden voyage, and was travelling at some speed: she struck the "Glen Holme" amidships and 'cut her down to the keel'. (Such was the force of the impact that it took five hours to disentangle the vessels.). What happened at the time cannot be better described than by the account of John Robinson, the carpenter of the "Glen Holme", in a letter to the *Maryport News* of June 10th 1893:

Sir,

On the morning of the 28th of May at 2am I was awakened in my berth by the chief officer calling my name and immediately I fell foremost out of my berth. When I came to my senses I found that I was buried among splinters of bunk boards and bedding, and the whole room was jammed up to the deck with sleepers, leaving only two foot of space and no way of escape. I then heard the poor cook moaning beneath me, with his foot jammed in the sleepers. I then heard Mr. Tully (the first officer) say that the steamer was fast sinking, but our captain jumped on board the colliding steamer and found that she was going full speed astern. He however, with great presence of mind, banded the telegraph 'Full Speed Ahead'. This kept our steamer from sinking, and the captain stood by the telegraph for three-quarters-of-an-hour and dared anyone to touch it, saying he would charge them with manslaughter, until his two men were extracted from their perilous position. Our chief officer and crew were busily engaged in cutting us out and it took them three quarters of an hour to do it. I got one of my ribs broken and also splinters of collarbone fractured.

I beg on behalf of myself and the cook to thank Captain Wilson for his prompt action in the matter, as we would undoubtedly have been drowned if the steamer had got clear of us. I also beg to thank Mr. Tully and those men who nobly cut us out of our prison.

I remain, Yours truly, Jno. Robinson.

Mr. Robinson was right: as soon as the two vessels disengaged the "Glen Holme" sank. The ship's company of the "Glen Holme" were taken by the tug to Glasgow: the Danish ship had to go there too, for repairs to her damaged bow, but on her arrival the "C.P.A. Koch" was placed under arrest by the port authorities on the testimony of Captain Wilson of the "Glen Holme". Hine Bros. immediately sued the Danish company for the loss, quoting £8,830 as the value of the lost steamer: their opponents had the audacity to enter a counterclaim for £3,000 damage to their vessel, denying liability for the collision and maintaining that it was entirely caused by the fault of those aboard the "Glen Holme"!

Fortunately for the Company's Canadian trade, Thompsons were about to complete another Hine

steamer built to order under George Brown's supervision, and at the end of 1893 Alfred's daughter Molly Hine went to Sunderland to launch the **"Greta Holme"**. Larger and wider than the other ships of the line, the "Greta Holme" was 320 feet long, 41 feet wide (towards the maximum for squeezing in through the Maryport dock entrance) and displaced 2,700 tonnes gross. As usual, she had all the modern appliances and equipment, and the telescopic masts, and was particularly designed to carry the heavy cargoes that Hine Bros. were dealing with at the time. As an extra, "Greta Holme" had the capacity to load and transport cattle, and a pipe system for providing the stock with water during the voyage. She followed the Hine tradition, however, in having a figurehead *(from a photograph of Mrs. Burgis of Manchester)*; she had accommodation for more passengers, so this time a trio of the next generation of the Hine family – Alfred E., Alfred junior and Wilfrid junior – and friends joined the "Greta Holme" for her maiden journey to her new home port in April 1894. Capt. George Brown retained command of the ship for her first trip across the Atlantic, too: he wanted to be in position for the melting of the winter ice and the opening of the St. Lawrence seaway. After this trip, however, he handed her over to Capt. Ritchie.

There had been contact of a more light-hearted nature in 'home waters' between these two senior colleagues, old friends and master-sailors in the old tradition during 1893 which had attracted the interest of a growing audience in Maryport. Hine Bros. had acquired a sailing yacht, the "Clymene", while the Maryport Pilot (Captain Thomas Brown) was in charge of the pilot cutter, a trim vessel called the "Nickey". Throughout the first half of 1893 there had been a series of races between the two craft: George Brown and his crew in the "Clymene" and James Ritchie and his team in the "Nickey". On one occasion another yacht, Mr. Kirkbride's "Olympia", also raced, but came in a disastrous third (beaten by at least 20 minutes!). By mid-June the series was 'neck and neck', so the two rivals met to settle the matter: two laps of a course round the Solway light-vessel and a boat moored outside the harbour pier, amounting to about 20 miles in all. The "Nickey" had a crew of six and Capt. Ritchie; the "Clymene" was manned by Capt. George Brown, Alfred E. Hine and four others. (A third yacht, Mr. William Walker's "Irene", was also racing; but again, was never in contention in this company.)

A goodly number of the townsfolk took advantage of the fine weather to stroll along the pier to watch the contest, and the next *Maryport News* contained a blow-by-blow account of the race, including – no doubt for the benefit of the many knowledgeable readers in this nautical community – details of the crafts' various tactics and manoeuvres. All sorts of excitements and mishaps occurred to the contesting boats, but when they rounded the lightship for the second time and headed for home the "Clymene" led the "Nickey" by four minutes and the "Irene" by ten, and despite a drop in the wind maintained her lead to the finishing line. The newspaper commented, prophetically:

The race seems to have given an impetus to yacht sailing in this district.... It is hoped that Maryport will develop considerable yachting talent, so that ere long a flourishing club may be established among us.

Throughout this whole period the Company's business between England and the Australian ports, carrying general cargoes of everything from linoleum to livestock outbound and wool on the return, went on as before. The four 'Hine Clipper Barques', as they became known – the "Brier Holme", "Castle Holme", "Eden Holme" and "Myrtle Holme" – consistently produced fast times for their voyages: Basil Lubbock, in his book "The Colonial Clippers", comments that they were *"rarely much over 80 days going out, and generally under 90 coming home."*

Chapter Seven
Winds of Change and
Troubled Waters: 1890-1900

THE SECOND HALF OF THE DECADE opened with the sale of the "Ivy Holme". In mid-January 1895 a Spanish master and crew arrived in Maryport to take over the little steamer, which by this time had been re-christened the "Chindor" and registered at the port of Bilbao, and she headed off for Newport to take on a cargo of coal. The local press comment was unusually frank:

> She departed, I have no doubt, unregretted by her owners, to whom she has not been an remunerative investment. The Spanish, however, have got her cheap, £2,400 was, I hear, the price, and she will... have a chance of doing more than pay her way.

There is probably more than a grain of truth in this assessment: the "Ivy Holme" was too small to be useful to the Company's transatlantic business, and in a rather depressed market the rates she could charge as a coaster would probably not recoup her running costs and the initial capital outlay (she was only ten years old).

For several years, Hine Brothers' larger new steamships had all been built with telescopic or retractable masts with a view to passing under the bridges along the Manchester Ship Canal. Construction had started back in 1885 but it was not opened formally until May 1894, and at the end of January 1895 the "Loughrigg Holme" became the first ship to come up the Canal to Manchester direct from Virginia. It was a murky afternoon, but the Canal Company's headquarters had been informed of the steamer's impending arrival and a distinguished welcoming committee gathered. Sir William Bailey, one of the Directors of the Canal Company; Mr. J. Addison, the local MP; Judge Jordan; Mr. Marshall Stevens, the general manager of the Canal, and Wilfrid Hine, among others (including a *Manchester Guardian* reporter) boarded a launch to greet the arriving vessel. The press report continues:

> About 3:30 the "Loughrigg Holme", which had just passed through the locks, was seen with her red and black funnel and white deckhouse looming through the grey mist that hung over the water. As she passed the launch one was able to form some idea of her great size.

The ship docked, and unloading of her cargo began immediately – when daylight faded the work continued under electric lights, a notable innovation – and the party from Manchester were shown round the ship by Wilfrid.

The *Guardian* reporter interviewed the master, Captain Millican, whom he described as "quite a young man", about the voyage (slightly prolonged because of bad weather) and the cargo (over 1,000 bales of cotton; 1,700 tons of wheat; a consignment of lard and tinned meat, and "a considerable quantity of persimmon wood"). Capt. Millican said he had not found it particularly difficult to navigate the Canal, but *"if he were making any recommendation to the authorities, it would be that they should effect some improvement in the efficiency of their tug service!"* (The "Loughrigg Holme" had in fact entered the canal a day earlier but had to to lie up at Saltport overnight waiting for a tug and a pilot.)

The "Loughrigg Holme" next returned to Maryport, where as well as a cargo bound for the Mediterranean en route for Alexandria she collected a group of passengers which included four of the younger members of the Hine family and three of their friends. Later shipping reports disclose that in March the ship was 'struck heavily' by a mail steamer in the Greek port of Lavrion – no serious damage was done to the "Loughrigg Holme", but with the owners' family aboard Capt. Millican's reaction can only be imagined!

Another embarrassing collision occurred in the same month. On March 6th the Line's new acquisition the "Greta Holme" had just left Liverpool in ballast for Cardiff and was steaming down the Mersey when she encountered "Dredger No.7" steaming in the other direction. The dredger turned to port, but the "Greta Holme" ran into her, and the dredger sank. At a subsequent hearing in the Admiralty Division of the High Court before Mr. Justice Bruce and the Masters of Trinity House, the Mersey Docks and Harbour Board sued Hine Bros. for damages. The Company put up two lines of defence; firstly that the dredger had caused the collision by turning across the path of the steamer, and secondly that as the "Greta Holme" was being piloted down the river at the time the responsibility lay at the door of the pilot. The Judge rejected both these arguments, declaring that the steamer had not kept a good lookout, that she had turned to starboard as the dredger turned to port, and that the crew had not given the pilot *"that assistance which he required and had a right to expect from them."* (If this were in fact the case, it represents an uncharacteristic lapse on the part of a master who was as skilled and experienced as the utterly seamanlike Capt. Ritchie!) The Court awarded damages with costs, which must have been considerable as the plaintiffs had briefed two Queen's Counsel – both knights – to plead their case!

To make up the trio of March mishaps, the "Myrtle Holme" (Capt. Cobb) managed to foul a steamship in the Thames, but sustained no damage – or damages.

Litigation had been occupying a considerable part of the attention – and finances – of the Company during this period. In 1893 Hine Bros. had been in dispute over the "Glen Holme" sinking, and during 1894 they were arguing not only with the Canadian shipowner to whom the "Thorn Holme" had been sold but also with the owners of the Liverpool steamship "Priam". This ship had come to

the assistance of the "Forest Holme" (Capt. Johnstone), which had struck a submerged wreck in mid-Atlantic and lost her propeller. The **"Pram"** had towed her for four days before reaching harbour, and had entered a huge salvage claim against the Company. The Judge, hearing that the value of the "Forest Holme" and her cargo was £63,000, awarded the owners of the "Pram" £2,100, her master £350, and £700 to be divided between the crew. The bad luck of the "Forest Holme" seems to have continued, as in June 1895 she was run into by another steamer in thick fog at the mouth of the St. Lawrence River. Though there was significant damage it was all above the waterline and she was able to complete her journey, discharge her load and obtain temporary repairs. Other Holme Line ships were involved in close encounters at this time, too: the "Nether Holme" (Capt. Markham) collided with an American schooner in the same area, badly damaging her, while the "Daren't Holme" (Capt. Holmes) hit a local coaster while leaving Maryport harbour and had to return to port for repairs.

Saddest of all, though, was the fate of the "Alne Holme" (Capt. J.G.Turney), the steamer which had led the procession into the Senhouse Dock eleven years earlier. On May 5th 1894 she was at anchor off the port of Burriana, on the Mediterranean coast of Spain, and in the process of loading a consignment of oranges: nearby was the Liverpool steamer "Ambrose", doing the same. A strong northerly wind suddenly blew up, causing the "Alne Holme" to drag her anchors and blowing her side against the bow of the other vessel with such a force that the hull of the "Alne Holme" was breached from top to bottom. Unfortunately she was carrying 500 tons of pig lead and 100 tons of copper ore as well as the fruit, and this was sufficient to cause the vessel to sink in 30 feet of water. The Captain and all the crew were taken off by a Cunard Line ship who later delivered them to Liverpool safe and sound, but despite attempts to salvage her the "Alne Holme" was never refloated. As a replacement it was decided to press The "Ardmore" into service once more: she had being lying up in the harbour at Maryport for several months following an accidental grounding which had strained her hull plates. An estimated £1,000 of repairs were needed, and Hine Bros. commissioned Ritson's, the local shipbuilders, and others to do it. They certainly set about their labours with a will, for on the 31st August the "Ardmore" was listed at Lloyd's as "*for Renneberg, cargo steel rails*".

The "Castle Holme" (Capt. Bryce) appears in the shipping reports at this time too, having stranded in Sturt Bay, South Australia, while trying to get close enough to the shore to land a sick member of the crew. After jettisoning 600 bags of wheat, and unloading more onto a lighter which arrived to help, the "Castle Holme" was towed off the shallows by a tug and taken back to Adelaide for inspection. Fortunately there was no damage to the clipper's hull, and she was able to head for home.

Back in Maryport prosperity had not returned to the town, and when Captain Johnstone and the officers and crew of the "Forest Holme" gave a free tea in the School Hall for the poor children of the town in February 1895, 300 children attended. The room was draped with bright flags (bunting from the "Forest Holme", set up by the Captain and his officers, Hine Bros. house flags, the union flag and the red ensign) and the children were seated at three long tables in the schoolroom. They had tea, currant loaf and cake, and were waited on by a bevy of the local ladies led by the wives of many of the Captains. At the end of the meal all gave 'three cheers' for the Captain and his crew, and an impromptu concert followed. Wilfrid, in his speech of thanks, commented that he...

had often heard of landsmen subscribing to the relief of widows and children of seamen lost through wrecks, etc., but this was the first occasion on which seamen had subscribed to the relief of landsmen.

It was not the last: a month later the ship's company of the "Rydal Holme" (Capt. William Brown) repeated the generous gesture and this time benefited no less than 350 children!

The *Maryport News* carried another happy item in the same issue. Mr. James Thompson, the Second Engineer of the "Rydal Holme", married Miss Sarah Ann (Sally) Johnstone, second daughter of Captain Johnstone of the "Forest Holme", at the

Presbyterian Church. Says the report:

the Rydal Holme and most of the other ships in the harbour were decked with bunting in honour of the happy event... and... there was a large company of friends and acquaintances... to witness the ceremony.

One who wasn't present, however, was the father of the bride: the "Forest Holme" arrived in New Orleans the next day!

Other snippets of news surface during 1895, and there are two worthy of mention: the first is a 'follow-up' to the saga of Thomas Todhunter and Parkin Petrie, the inebriated duo who in 1882 had set off in a 'borrowed' boat to celebrate the departure of the "Brier Holme" and sobered up to find themselves in Scotland. Both renewed their acquaintance with the Hine brothers in 1895, as reported in the press: in February Alfred J.P. fined Todhunter 15 shillings or 14 days' custody for being drunk and disorderly: it was his 42nd appearance in court on these charges! Then in April, Wilfrid J.P. found himself trying the case of Petrie, accused of assaulting one of the dock stevedores. Petrie was defended by Mr. G.W. Turney, a well-respected local solicitor, but the outcome of the case is not recorded.

The second is a report of the cutting of the first sod of a new coalpit at Dearham. Wilfrid Hine made a speech praising the

self-reliance, energy and sterling commonsense of the men of Dearham in their efforts to resuscitate the industry on which the existence of their community depends.

His influence did not stop there, apparently, as within months his nephew and employee William Leighton was also acting as the Secretary of the Coal Company.

In 1896 the economic tide began to turn again, and Maryport's fortunes revived a little as the Solway Iron Company was taken over by Messrs. Cammells, who also owned iron and steel plants at Workington. Iron ore imports recommenced – nearly 200,000 tons in 1896 – and exports of coal rose to 350,000 tons. Nonetheless, difficulties remained: even the Trinity Baptist Church where the Hine families worshipped had not had the resources to pay their Pastor his agreed salary in full, and in May 1896 he resigned. (The press report also hints at *"differences of opinion having manifested themselves among the congregation"*, so the financial problem is probably not the whole story!)

The Holme Line widened its sphere of activity in transatlantic business by entering into an agreement with the Canadian Government to run a line of steamers between Boulogne and Antwerp and the ports of the eastern seaboard: when the St. Lawrence seaway was closed by ice for the winter the ships would dock in Halifax, Nova Scotia, or St. John, New Brunswick. The deal involved a subsidy from the Canadians, who were looking to expand their trade with Francophone Europe, and was a welcome diversification for the Holme Line: the "Greta Holme" and the "Loughrigg Holme" were initially assigned to this duty, and it was anticipated that as the trade developed more ships would be built. The speed, seaworthiness and levels of equipment of Hine ships had made a favourable impression over the years they had been operating the routes – and no doubt Wilfrid's visit to Montreal in 1893 had not been entirely fruitless! The "Greta Holme" sailed from Boulogne to Montreal on September 10th, and even before she sailed a full cargo for her homeward run had been secured. The "Loughrigg Holme" followed early in October from Antwerp.

Trade with the Canadian ports continued to occupy a large part of the Holme Line steamers' work throughout the year. On May 21st 1896, the "Nether Holme" was five days out of Quebec, bound for Greenock with a cargo of timber. Her previous master, Capt. Markham, had been taken ill a month previously while at sea and had died before the ship could reach port. Captain Markham, a Swede by birth, had been with the Hine fleet for nearly half his life: he was appointed second mate in the "Abbey Holme" back in 1870, had gone on to captain the "Alne Holme", "Fern Holme" and "West Cumberland" before taking over the "Nether Holme" in 1893. He was about 58 years old, and had been known to suffer from heart trouble for some time.

Captain Wilson was now in command of the ship, and was on the bridge taking one of the night watches when he noticed a faint light and a drift of smoke in the distance, some miles away on the ship's starboard quarter. He ordered the "Nether Holme" back to investigate and as they approached they saw two boats, containing in all 15 sailors in an exhausted condition. These were the Captain and crew of the Norwegian barque "Valborg", en route from Liverpool to Pugwash, NS, which had struck an iceberg in thick fog three days before. The "Alborg" filled with water and Captain Olsten and his crew had had to take to the boats before she foundered, leaving them in bitterly cold weather and in dangerous waters. Their ordeal was made all the more demoralizing when, after a day, a schooner passed close by their boats without spotting them, and on the following day a barque hove into sight but also sailed on without seeing them! The shipwrecked mariners then lighted a blanket soaked in paraffin oil and hung it up on an oar as a signal; but imagine their anguish, therefore, when the "Nether Holme" steamed past them into the distance, apparently oblivious to their distress! And their relief when they realized that after all they would be saved!

For many years, Hine Brothers had used the well-known and established firm of Davit and Moore to act as shipbrokers for the clipper barque, and even when they opened their London office for the Holme Line business they continued to entrust the sailing ships to them. Many other shipowners did the same, including Mr. T.B. Walker, a prominent London businessman (for many years he was Chairman of Lloyd's Register), who had a particular commercial interest in Tasmania. The pride of the small but efficient Walker fleet at this time was the "Berean", a compact and speedy wooden barque built in Sunderland in 1869 and skippered from her first day off the stocks by one of the most respected – even legendary – masters of the age, Captain John Wyrill. Unfortunately T.B. Walker died in 1894, and after two years his son decided to close the shipping business: Captain Wyrill looked on sadly as his pride and joy was sold to a Norwegian company to transport ice, and he realised his services would no longer be required.

Hope reappeared, however, when he learned that there was a job opportunity in the wind: Captain Randall, who had been with Hine Brothers for 23 years – including nearly 20 years in command of the "Eden Holme" – was about to retire. Moreover, as luck would have it, The "Eden Holme" was on her berth at that very moment loading cargo – and for Launceston, Tasmania!

Captain Wyrill and Mr. Devitt went straightaway to see Wilfrid Hine at the London office: the Captain's memoirs describe what followed:

Mr. Hine immediately offered me the command of the "Eden Holme", an iron Barque of 1200 tons; but when I mentioned the salary I expected he demurred, as it was higher that that paid to any of their captains. When I told him that it was definitely what I had been accustomed to in the "Berean" he replied "But you are not so young as you used to be, Captain". "No," said I, "but I am younger than many men 20 years my junior, for I have been a teetotaller all my life." He laughed and said "And so have I. I am about your age, Captain, and feel as fit as ever I did; so we will say no more about age!"

It was finally agreed that Capt. Wyrill would draw the same salary as the other skippers but would be paid a bonus to make up the difference, and he accepted the post.

In John Wyrill, the Company not only acquired the services of a fine sea-captain – he hailed from a Scarborough nautical family, and within three years of going to sea as an apprentice he was acting as second mate – but a master who for nearly 30 years had been engaged in trade in the Tasmanian ports. Capt. Wyrill was thus able to brief Wilfrid on the opportunities in this market (especially as the competition from the T.B. Walker ships had disappeared), and as a result of this it was decided to divert the Hine Clipper Barques to Launceston rather than Adelaide. His memoir continues:

to my delight therefore I resumed my associations with my many friends on the banks of the Tamar.... The only difference in our passages was that the "Eden Holme" being such a much larger vessel than the "Berean" our outward cargo had to embrace a consignment for Hobart, whither I would call first, proceeding to complete discharge at Launceston; which still remained, however, our port of departure with all Launceston wool.

Many of the captain's crew from his previous command followed him to the "Eden Holme", and it did not take long for his expertise to show itself in regular, rapid voyages. Captain Wyrill comments that he found his new vessel

one of the smartest ships of her class in the trade, well found in every respect, as tight as a bottle, and possessing the fine lines requisite for speed. Our passages were always made in good time; and with the confident knowledge of having a thoroughly seaworthy craft beneath my feet I had no timidity in pressing her for all she was worth in heavy weather.

And 'heavy weather' was indeed what he experienced on his first outing: the "Eden Holme" arrived in Hobart on November 8th having lost her longboat and foretopsails while rounding Cape Leeuwin!

In 1897 the Greek and Turkish nations went to war, and in April the "Nether Holme", returning from Alexandria, came across a small Greek coaster which had been attempting to run the gauntlet of the Turkish blockade of Crete with a cargo of flour and other provisions for the starving islanders. Despite several approaches the captain had been unable to elude the searchlights of the blockading Turkish cruisers: the ship had then run out of fuel and was adrift, at the mercy of the wind and waves, about 30 miles west of Malta. Once again it was Captain Wilson to the rescue! The ship was towed to Malta, and the "Nether Holme" was able to put in a claim for salvage.

England in 1897 was all agog with preparations for Queen Victoria's Diamond Jubilee, and one of the highlights of the celebrations was to be a Naval

Review of the Fleet at Spithead. Because of her age and frail health Her Majesty was not planning to attend in person, but would be represented by the Prince of Wales, the future King Edward VII. The great day, June 26th, arrived, and the might of the Royal Navy – which at this time comprised a huge and formidable armada, from 'ironclads' of implacable power to squadrons of smaller warships of all types – was held at anchor in the Solent: to quote the London *Times* correspondent, *"in lines so straight they could be ruled".* A rainstorm threatened to spoil the day – and apparently did wreak some havoc upon the finery of the privileged spectators – but all was clear by the time the royal party sailed between the ranks of the fleet, followed by other vessels bearing foreign royalty and dignitaries.

(There was also one unauthorised participant: the tiny "Turbinia", powered by a steam turbine, gatecrashed the procession and proceeded to demonstrate to the distinguished guests the astonishing turn of speed its revolutionary new engine could develop. The "Turbinia", driven by the inventor, Charles Algernon Parsons, comprehensively saw off the official security patrol boat, at one stage recording 34 knots. Though there was much disapproval expressed in the press in the aftermath of this sensational display, Parsons had made his point to an Admiralty who had up to that point been distinctly lukewarm about turbines: within a couple of years the Navy was fitting them in two of its new warships.)

Following in the official wake of the royal procession, a column of merchant ships then made its way between the rows: at the head of this column, proudly flying the Company's flag at her mainmast, was the "Rydal Holme" (Capt. William Brown), at a much more sedate speed! Five knots was the maximum allowed: a rigidly-applied set of rules for the course, speed and conduct of the ships had been laid down by the Navy's C-in-C, Portsmouth.

Something similar would have been useful in the Solway too: a fortnight previously no less than eight steamers, including the "Nether Holme", were either lying off Maryport or approaching the harbour to load or discharge their cargoes. As there were not enough berths for this number in the Senhouse Dock there was naturally considerable jockeying among the various captains to be at the head of the queue. First in the race to the harbour mouth on the morning tide was the "Jersey Moor", loaded with over 2,000 tons of iron ore. On reaching the entrance to the dock basin she discovered the hard way that she did not have enough water. She stuck fast and ground to a halt, leaving a bare 50 feet of space between the ship and the dock wall. The harbour authorities hoisted a signal to indicate that the entrance was blocked, but by this time no less than five ships had started to move in on the evening tide. Four saw the signal and held back, but a Spanish ship called the "Nina" had the Pilot on board and was able to squeeze through the gap and into the dock.

Seeing this, the other four masters all headed for the entrance as darkness fell, but then a further complication arose: the "San Domingo" appeared in the narrow channel from inside the dock, leaving

The "Turbinia" interrupting the 1897 review

harbour with a load of rails! Much sounding of hooters and horns ensued as the inbound procession had to come to a hasty halt and manoeuvre aside to let the "San Domingo" out into the basin. To add to the chaos, at this precise moment the tide reached its height, the "Jersey Moor" became unstuck from her mudbank and began to move!

The *Maryport Advertiser* described the situation, which now began to resemble a game of nautical Dodgem Cars. First, the "Jersey Moor" was hauled against the dock basin wall with winches, but the "Ardenbahn" banged into her while passing through into the dock, damaging her rail and boats. Then the "Twilight", the second in line, tried to enter, only to be struck several times by the "San Domingo" which was attempting to pull out of the basin to make room for the incoming ships. Next the "Nether Holme" arrived towed by the tug, but her bow rope parted: she drifted into the harbour dredger, crushing her against the dock wall, to the consternation of those on board. As the *Advertiser* reported

the dredger got a good squeezing, the crew meanwhile shouting out at the top of their voices "What are you doing?" (One suspects this may not have been an entirely verbatim record!)

Seeing this, the "Blakemoor", the fourth ship in the line, wisely decided to return to her anchorage, and came in without incident the following morning. The *Advertiser* notes that at the end of that day there were no less than twelve steamers of large tonnage in the Senhouse Dock. Other ports seem to have taken their toll of the Holme Line ships too: while in Constantinople in September the "Forest Holme" collided with the Austrian steamer "Ivan Brailli", which later sank. Intriguingly, the shipping report of the collision merely states *"both ships at anchor"*!

Both the Hine brothers continued their busy lives, intimately involved in many aspects of Maryport life as 1898 went by. Both Alfred and Wilfrid sat regularly on the local bench, several committees and societies in the town, as well as

widening business interests and the ongoing Coffee Tavern Company, which seemed to remain profitable on a regular basis. Trinity Baptist Church had appointed another minister the previous autumn, but serious disagreements between the new man and the deacons began to surface and in July he resigned.

For the wider family, life continued: Joseph J. Hine's daughter Mary Elizabeth had moved south, and was working in a business in London: in November she was married at St. Pancras Church to Mr. George Balderstone Rich (no apparent relation of the captain of the "Brier Holme") of Marlborough, Wiltshire. The *Maryport News* report even carried a description of the wedding dress *("a becoming costume of grey silk trimmed with pink silk, with white velvet hat trimmed with white plumes")* and the going-away outfit *("a green travelling costume with hat to match")*. A month later her cousin Jane Leighton also featured in the *Maryport News'* social page as her brother led her up the aisle to marry a sea-captain! He was Alexander Beaton, master of the steamship "Phyllis" of West Hartlepool. The marriage was by special licence, because the ship had just returned and was unloading in London: Capt. Beaton had not been able to obtain an ordinary licence in the time. This meant that the ceremony had to take place in a parish church, so Trinity Baptist Church was ruled out. All went happily, and the happy couple left by train for London that afternoon in a cloud of good wishes and confetti.

There were unhappy events too: in June of 1898 Eileen, the wife of Wilfrid's eldest son Alfred Ernest Hine, died aged only 26, while in November Alfred and Mary had rushed to London to the bedside of their youngest son, Wilfrid junior, who had required emergency surgery – probably an appendicectomy, which at that time constituted *"an operation which the medical profession say few people who are subjected to it get through"* as the *Maryport News* later put it. While there, Alfred himself was taken ill and found himself occupying a bed at the same hospital for over a month! Wilfrid junior and his cousin Robert (youngest son of Wilfrid and Jane, and a year younger) were both pupils at Mill Hill School in London at this time.

Wilfrid's involvement with the district council continued, and his comments and outbursts seem regularly to have made local news: he railed against their decision not to support the British School in Maryport – with which he had been involved for most of his life – out of the rates, leaving the managers no alternative but to close. *"Whilst in other parts of the country"* he complained, *"they were boiling over with benevolence in celebrating the Diamond Jubilee, it had been reserved for Maryport to act the penurious, shortsighted and shabby part of declining to assist in carrying on this school."* Not all his contributions were critical, however: he had made a gracious speech of appreciation when H.P. Senhouse left the Council at the end of 1897, and produced several constructive suggestions in the following months, including a proposal to beautify the town by planting trees in Curzon Street and Senhouse Street. (He had suggested this some years before but the Trustees had turned the scheme down because of the economic state of the town; by this time, however, things were looking better, and the Council decided to look at the matter again.)

Wilfrid's main interest at this time – indeed, the cause to which he devoted all his resources of persistence, enthusiasm and powers of persuasion – was the scheme to extend the Maryport dock. This would provide a deep-water anchorage with increased loading and unloading facilities and would permit the entry of larger ships which could not use the Senhouse Dock because of the limited depth of water and the narrow entrance (less than 50 feet across). The project would include enhanced rail

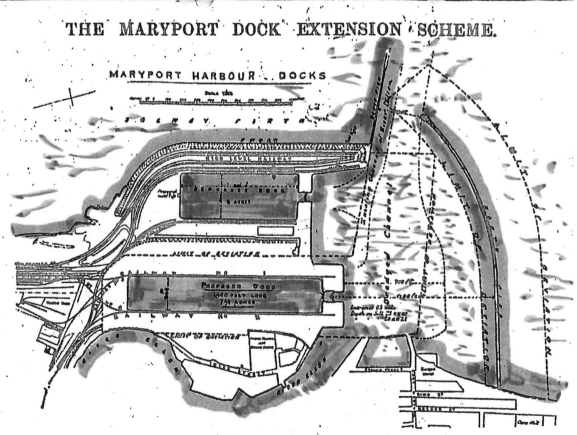

THE NEWS. SATURDAY, NOVEMBER 26, 1898.

THE MARYPORT DOCK EXTENSION SCHEME.

PLAN OF THE PROPOSED EXTENSION OF DOCK AND HARBOUR.
(From a Photograph by Mr. H. W. Rowland, Station-street, Maryport.)

access, and a channel that would be dredged to maintain a navigable passage to the sea. It would be constructed to replace the old Elizabeth Basin, dating from 1837, and the Elizabeth Dock, opened 20 years later: it would be 1,400 feet long, and with a depth of up to 29 feet and an entrance 65 feet wide. It would double the available quay length while also providing a further four extra acres of mooring and manoeuvring space needed by the modern steamers. Wilfrid himself was the prime mover in the development and presentation of the proposal, and despite the appalling record of the Senhouse Dock over 15 years (in terms of monetary returns on investment) he managed to attract enough outside 'venture capital' to place his vision before the Harbour Commissioners in November 1898.

The London *Times* described it as:

An important project affecting the iron and coal trades of West Cumberland" and a *"scheme which is regarded with enthusiasm at Maryport as a step towards the industrial works of the district"*, and noted that *"The Harbour Commissioners yesterday recorded their great approval of the scheme, and appointed a committee to consider the details.*

The *Maryport News* naturally gave great prominence to this in their next issue, devoting a full page to a plan of the scheme. In a long article about Wilfrid which described his background, the paper declared

...no other man in Maryport could have succeeded in working up and launching a scheme of such magnitude and enormous importance as that which astonished and delighted the Maryport people at the beginning of last week. No other man, it is safe to say, has that wide acquaintance with men of business and men of capital outside the county that made it possible to take up the scheme with the slightest probability of success, and... to tackle the difficult, and not a few would have said impossible, task of

seeking to enlist the support of financiers for such an uninviting project as the enlargement of a harbour in a small port on the Cumberland coast; a harbour moreover which, after a chequered career, had finally to be taken under the protection of the Court of Chancery. Whether the scheme falls through or whether it goes forward (and there seems to be a fair promise that it will go forward) rests in other hands now. Mr. Hine has done his best, and deserves immense credit for his pertinacious labours.

Wilfrid's 'pertinacious labours' involved gathering a group of interested local businessmen – shipowners, and the local iron and steel company Cammell & Co. – to form a public company to buy the harbour land and structures from the Commissioners and build the extended dock. The Commissioners and Trustees were not in a position to take on the task directly themselves as the affairs of the harbour had been transferred to administration by the Chancery Court in London some time before because of mounting debts and fluctuating harbour income. Despite this, the new company had secured pledges of nearly £300,000 of outside capital against the estimated £200,000 cost of new works, and proceeded – as a formality – to present a Bill before Parliament to authorise the enterprise.

What happened next almost beggars belief. In a six-month period which effectively sealed the doom of Maryport as a viable commercial entity and condemned the town to social obscurity, the local people put up one objection, reservation and procrastination after another. Public meeting followed public meeting: hours of debate in the local press argued round and about every aspect of the plan; and though Sir Wilfrid Lawson, Sir Alexander Wilson and Mr. Senhouse voted for the scheme the Maryport and Carlisle Railway Company's directors decided not to support it, for reasons which even at the time seemed completely incomprehensible. The local holders of harbour bonds, issued against previous investment in the various dock improvement schemes of the past, were also showing signs of not being prepared to back the scheme by selling their stake to the new company or accepting shares in the new project.

In February 1899 the intrepid *Maryport News* reporter bearded Wilfrid in his office for an interview, which was printed almost verbatim. Wilfrid had just arrived back in his office from London, had a pile of paperwork to go through and two meetings to attend that evening, so his responses were blunt and direct. He made it clear from the outset that the promoters of the Bill intended to continue with their plan:

...we have to get the dissenters to see that they have made... a very serious mistake, and throw in their lot with the scheme.

And what do you think of the response of the bondholders?

The support given from outside was, I have reason to believe, greater than was anticipated, but I regret to say that the same cannot be said of our own town, which has everything to gain and nothing to lose by the scheme being carried out. Indeed, the support accorded from Maryport has been less than anyone could have expected.

Some of the objectors have said that there is no need for enlarged dock accommodation?

I am inclined to think that those people fail to read the signs aright.... Trade is increasing on all sides, and there is no question but that there will be an ample revenue as far as I can see. These objectors should go and have a look at the dock. At present there are only two berths for loading rails, and there are three ships expected next week. How can trade be carried on under these circumstances?

Wilfrid went on to explain that the Commissioners had been consulted but were unable to float a concern in Chancery that would attract the investment needed: he recognised that alternative schemes were being mooted, but

pointed out that (unlike the others) this one was a practical project, already worked out by practical men, funded adequately and ready to go. Delay would mean waiting for another parliamentary session to present a revised Bill. One frank and telling comment came out of the interview:

Of course I know very well that some of these people will say that it is all very well for me to advocate a new dock for it is in my interest; but I may tell them that it does not much matter to our firm where a dock is built on this coast. We can easily move our ships, and if dock accommodation is not to be provided at Maryport then we shall have to lend our support towards getting a dock elsewhere.

In a similar interview a little later, this same point was echoed by Alfred:

In order to keep up with the times the firm has given orders for four new steamers, two of 5,000 tons and two of 6,000 tons; all of which, it may be mentioned incidentally – to illustrate how much we need improved harbour accommodation at Maryport – have had to be built of less breadth than otherwise would be the case, to permit them to enter the Senhouse Dock. Other owners, as Mr. Hine pertinently observes, will not show the same consideration, but will say let the Maryport people widen their gates and deepen their harbour if they wish our vessels to come.

The first of the steamers Alfred had mentioned was the **"Abbey Holme"**, launched in May 1899. The ceremony was performed on this occasion by Mrs. J. Thompson, wife of the managing director of the construction company (and whose likeness was used to carve the ship's figurehead). The *Maryport News* drew some interesting comparisons between the two "Abbey Holme" vessels that Hine Bros. had owned, to:

give a clear indication of the great progress of the British mercantile marine in the space of 30 years. The one was built of iron, propelled by sails, carried 750 tons and was manned by a crew of 15 hands: the other is built of steel, propelled by steam power, carries 5,100 tons, or nearly seven times the cargo, and will be manned by a crew of 24.

The new steamer underwent her sea trials under the eagle eye of Capt. George Brown, and the following month set sail for Maryport with both brothers on board, together with family members, and several representatives of Thompsons the shipbuilders. A large crowd of townspeople turned out to watch the ship's arrival, and with a breadth of 45 feet 3 inches she would present them with a very close-up view as she negotiated the dock entrance! All was well, and the "Abbey Holme" proceeded to load 4,500 tons of steel rails and 500 tons of bunker coal before setting off for Montreal the following week on her maiden voyage. Again, Captain William Brown moved to take over from his namesake.

The **"Isel Holme"** was the next new vessel from the Thompson shipyard for the Holme Line, the 18th they had built for the company, and again it was Mrs. Thompson who launched her in August 1899. Though packed with up-to-date equipment and technology, the "Isel Holme" retained the 'clipper stem' which was one of the Line's trademarks, and once again, a figurehead – this time, a likeness of Lady Lawson, wife of Sir Wilfrid Lawson, the brothers' old friend (the name "Isel Holme" referred to the Isel estate, the Lawsons' home). The steamer would hold 6,100 tons of cargo, and with a draught of 28 feet 4 inches and a breadth of 45 feet 10 inches was likely to require very skilled navigation in or out of her home port!

The firm's policy, mentioned by Alfred, of keeping up with the times had dictated several changes to the fleet, mainly involving the sale of their smaller, older steamers. The "Ardmore", only 597 tons and built in 1872, was sold in 1898, but after less than a year with her new owners she stranded in the Pentland Firth and was declared a total loss. The "San Domingo", 1,087 tons and dating from 1874, was also sold in 1898 to a Swedish company, and became the "Blanda". Of the four

coastal steamers on the Company's list in 1883 none now remained, the "Ivy Holme" having been sold in 1895 and the little "Elizabeth and Ann" in 1889.

The Dock Extension Scheme continued to exercise the minds of the businessmen, Harbour Commissioners and the townsfolk of Maryport. Despite the passionate arguments put forward by Wilfrid, the support of the Harbour Commissioners and the assured financial backing from outside, the Bondholders returned only a lukewarm response in support of proceeding with the project (365 voting papers were issued: only 256 were returned, and of these 168 voted for the scheme and 88 against). The Railway Company maintained their negative stance, apparently fearing loss of revenue while the project was under construction, and in an astonishing display of short-sightedness the townspeople themselves also voted against it. In June 1899 the Bill was put to Parliament, but was lost. Undeterred, Wilfrid continued his campaign and by September 1899 he was back, using almost every opportunity to publicise a second dock scheme, pointing out the urgent necessity for Maryport to accommodate the merchant shipping companies who were using larger ships and thereby making economies of scale in this cut-throat commercial arena.

Pushed into the relative background by these local events were several other topics, perhaps the most significant of which in the context of the company was the health of Alfred Hine. Since his enforced stay in London the year before the press had reported Alfred as being unwell on two or three occasions during 1899, and he had taken a couple of recuperative breaks in the Lake District and to Minehead (which was just emerging as a seaside holiday destination in those days). He was able to return to his business commitments, however, and still managed to fulfil the formidable list of outside interests – the bench, the county council, the church and Sunday School and the musical life of the town.

Alfred Hine junior, his eldest son, was now 30 years old, single, a keen sportsman, and commissioned as a Lieutenant in the Cumberland Volunteer Artillery Company. In a lighthearted comment in June 1899 the *Maryport News* "Things in General" columnist commented:

Lieut. Hine is an energetic and capable young officer who takes a keen interest on artillery work, but he will perhaps forgive me if I suggest that he has hardly as yet caught the true military style of giving commands. The first characteristic of the command given by a British officer is its loudness; the second, its unintelligibility to all but military hearers. Lieut. Hine is loud enough, but too clear and distinct!

In more serious vein however, echoes of the 'distant drums' of the second Boer War, which in 1899 had just begun, began to be heard even in the quiet of Cumberland, and the volunteers' exercises and training began to increase in frequency and urgency.

In August of 1899 the dock workers – there were about 300 employed in the harbour at this time – went on strike for higher wages. The "Greta Holme" had to be diverted to Ardrossan Port and thence crossed the Atlantic 'light', carrying only bunker coal instead of her usual cargo of thousands of tons of steel rails. Faced with the prospect of more empty ships the Company readily assented to a compromise settlement, and work resumed: during September and October 1899 the "Abbey Holme", the "Forest Holme", the "Greta Holme" and the "Rydal Holme" entered harbour, were loaded with steel rails and departed across the Atlantic. Finally the "Isel Holme", the Line's new acquisition, arrived at her home port on October 24th from Sunderland. As usual, Capt. George Brown had brought her round and on this occasion Wilfrid, together with a party of family and friends, had gone along for the ride: in pleasant weather the trip had taken a leisurely five days, including a stop at Tobermoray.

The "Isel Holme" was to undertake her maiden voyage with a cargo – not surprisingly, steel rails – to Valparaiso, and Captain Ritchie was detached from the "Greta Holme" to assume command of her. Loading began straightaway, as the timing of the ship's departure was critical: with more than 5,000 tons of rails aboard her draught was such that if she did not catch the high tides in mid-November the "Isel Holme" would have been stuck in the dock until the next spring tides. And so on November 5th, despite a rough sea and a strong south-westerly wind – and with a large audience of interested

spectators on the quays – Captain Ritchie, with the assistance of Capt. Nelson the harbourmaster, inched her skilfully out into the Solway.

Throughout this turbulent period the other arm of the Hine enterprise, the Clipper Barques, continued to ply their regular trade, with some notable passages: in 1898 Capt. Cobb brought the "Myrtle Holme" back to England in 86 days, and in May 1899 the "Eden Holme", under Capt. Wyrill, arrived in the London Dock after a passage of only 88 days from Launceston, Tasmania. (Captain Wyrill stated that the passage would have been even quicker had they not encountered 17 days of light winds just north of the equator!) The *Maryport News* recorded that, *"this was the fourth voyage out of six to and from Tasmania which this vessel has accomplished in under 90 days, which may be considered almost a record."*

But times were also changing in this type of trading. Sail had already yielded regular coastal trade to steam, along with the parcel-carriage and fast freight trade and, most importantly, the

Capt. Wyrill (left) and his officers; Boston, 1900

passenger trade. However, the sailing ship seemed to have found a niche which would last for many more years: they had been able to compete with steamships as long-haul carriers of bulk cargoes to and from destinations such as Australia, South America or New Caledonia. They could use ports that did not possess the large dock basins and expensive fast cargo-loading facilities necessary for steamers, and they could transport cargoes which were non-perishable and not 'urgent' at economic rates: the regular wool trade from Tasmania was a typical example. But by the time the nineteenth century gave way to the twentieth the ocean-going 'tramp' or cargo steamer was beginning to make significant inroads into these markets too. Even in the years since he had taken over the "Eden Holme" Captain Wyrill had been finding it increasingly difficult to find cargoes of wool to fill her hold for the return passage because of the competition from steam, until finally in 1900 he wrote:

after I had discharged my outward cargo, I learned bitterly that wool for the first time in all the long years would afford me no payable freight. There was nothing else for it but to

leave Launceston light, and I ran across to Melbourne and placed the ship upon the berth for Boston and London.

Fortunately a charter was available, and he returned home via Boston and St. John, New Brunswick.

There they loaded a cargo of wood, stacked up eight feet high on the deck, for London: Capt. Wyrill noted with disgust, *"This made the ship so crank that all her fine sailing lines were negatived, and we crossed the Atlantic like a haystack!"*

By chance, as they approached the Scillies they were offered a tow at a bargain rate by a steam tug returning to London after a job in the Bristol Channel. They thus arrived at the timber dock:

amid the Scandinavian drogers, the "Eden Holme" looking like a white-winged albatross among a lot of barnyard fowls. I felt it very much.

The ship was more fortunate in the wool trade the following year; but Captain Wyrill realised that the writing was on the wall.

At the turn of the century, "Brier Holme" as a troopship in 1900. The banner reads 'Success to the Tasmanian Troops'

Maryport Harbour showing Senhouse Dock (1884), Elizabeth Dock (1857) and Basin (1837)

Chapter Eight
Difficult Years: 1900-1905

THE 1900S DID NOT START WELL FOR THE TOWN. The Harbour Commissioners announced that the Senhouse Dock would have to be drained for repairs; they hoped this could be done as part of the works on the New Dock – if the Bill passed through Parliament this time! The outlook for this was not promising; at the February meeting of the district council Wilfrid was asked "how the dock was getting on", and retorted that *"he could tell them a great deal about how the dock was not getting on!"* He told them he had attended the annual meeting of the Chamber of Shipping in London the week before, where special stress was being put upon increasing the port accommodation all over the country to cater for the increasing size of ships. He went on to say that a new dock somewhere on that coast

had become a necessity if trade was not to be strangled in the district. Most of the people who traded with Maryport did not belong to it and did not care a rap whether it was made at Maryport, Workington or anywhere else.

The Council declared that it hoped that the project would go through, and soon; the insuperable obstacle seemed to be the Maryport and Carlisle Railway Company, who continued obdurately to oppose the scheme. Despite Wilfrid's repeated efforts in every forum to which he had access, local support also remained lukewarm. In March 1900 the second Bill was withdrawn, and an interesting glimpse into local politics at the time was given in a report in the *Maryport News* of March 24th, in which District Councillor Barnes remarked that *"what killed the Bill is spite, not business"*. The Senhouse Dock duly closed for repairs in June, 1900.

Ominously, another Dock Bill – closely resembling the Maryport plan – was laid before Parliament that same month. It was for Workington.

The year also began badly for the Holme Line. In January 1900 there was a dreadful accident while the "Nether Holme" was mooring at Genoa: the second officer Mr. McClorry, a Maryport man, became entangled in a hawser and was dragged against the barrel of the winch mechanism, crushing his head and killing him instantly. The funeral, at Carthagena, was a "decent and respectable" one, according to Captain Wilson who attended with the ship's company. Captain Johnstone and the crew of the "Loughrigg Holme", which had also been docked there, attended, and many other seamen from British merchant ships in the port at the time joined the procession to the cemetery and afterwards subscribed to pay for a tombstone for the grave. The unfortunate victim had been due to be married to a local girl on his return to his home port

At the beginning of March the "Derwent Holme" struck a large submerged rock while entering the Italian port of Civitavecchia, severely damaging to her keel, rudder, propeller and hull plates. Divers were sent down to assess the situation, but the underwriters' verdict was reported back as *"Possible to float and repair, but at enormous expense"* and the Company decided to cut their losses. The "Derwent Holme" was sold to a Belgian company who pumped her out, towed her to Genoa, repaired her, renamed her the "Flandres", and returned her to service. She was finally lost in 1911.

In May 1900 the third of the new ships ordered for the Holme Line from J.L. Thompson's yard came off the stocks. Captain George Brown, the owners' Superintendent, had overseen the construction of the vessel, and like her predecessors she had been fitted with all the most up-to-date equipment and accommodation, including electric light! As usual there was a figurehead – a likeness of Lady Bailey, the wife of a director of the Manchester Ship Canal Company – and on this occasion the launch was carried out by Mrs. Marr, wife of the manager of the firm, who named her the S.S. **"Hazel Holme"**.

This was the second time the Company had named a steamer after one of the original clipper barques of the line, but unlike the S.S. "Abbey Holme" this newcomer did not carry on its namesake's tradition of service. In fact the S.S. "Hazel Holme" never sailed under the Holme Line colours at all: while still being fitted out she was sold! Moreover, the Company chose not to take up its option on the last of the four vessels referred to by Alfred Hine as being "specially constructed to use the Maryport harbour" and already being built by Thompsons; nor did they replace the "Derwent Holme"; and early the following year the Company also sold the "Rydal Holme".

One can only guess at the brothers' motives for this change of strategy. Presumably Wilfrid and Alfred had come to the conclusion, after the further setback to the plans to enlarge the harbour facilities at Maryport, that commissioning more ships small enough to use the Senhouse Dock would restrict their prospects of remaining competitive and profitable in a market increasingly dominated by bigger ships and rates that reflected 'economies of scale'.

(The "Hazel Holme" was bought by Messrs. Charlton & Thompson, a local Sunderland company, and renamed the "Hughenden". She was subsequently lost in 1911 on a voyage from Smyrna to Dublin, when she foundered during a gale and sank with the loss of all but two of her crew. The fourth vessel was sold to another company by the shipbuilders and named the "Pretoria". The "Rydal Holme" went to a Newcastle businessman setting up a new company, but was sold again a year later and renamed the "Ronda". She traded until 1914, when she was purchased by the Admiralty at the outbreak of war and ended her days being sunk as a blockship.)

There is no doubt that Wilfrid was extremely concerned about the effect the withdrawal of the Bill would have on the town he loved. The *Maryport News* columnist 'Ewanrigg', for many years a mordant commentator on local affairs, gives an account of the Oddfellows Banquet at the Maryport Atheneum in September 1900. After listing the menu for the evening, a modest collation of

Hare and tomato soup; an entrée of Veal and Ham pie, followed by joints of Roast Beef and Lamb, boiled leg of mutton, boiled corned beef with caper sauce, potatoes, turnip, cabbage and carrots; then for sweets, Plum, fig and rice puddings, apple and plum tarts and desserts cheese and celery

…'Ewanrigg' goes on to refer to Wilfrid's after-dinner speech – a *"gloomy oration"* giving his

prophetic vision of a blight on the town, its prosperity having travelled to Workington with the new dock and the shipping.

In the family life of the brothers, however, there were happier moments. In August Alfred Ernest Hine, Wilfrid's elder son, remarried: his new wife was a Miss Marian Hopcraft of Anerley, South London. Because of a recent bereavement in the bride's family the wedding was confined to family guests, but after a wedding breakfast – there is no report of a speech by the bridegroom's father on this occasion! – the happy couple left for a honeymoon in Switzerland.

In June 1900 Alfred and Mary had celebrated their Silver Wedding by hosting a day's outing to the Lake District for over a score of family members. Setting out in two four-horse charabancs the party visited the sights – Borrowdale, the Bowder Stone and Derwentwater, lunching at Keswick and returning home to Maryport after tea, well pleased with their trip. They did not forget their staff either: the maids, the coachman and the gardener were treated to an excursion for the day, to various spots in the area. Alfred also had the chancel of the Trinity Baptist Church redecorated to mark his anniversary.

January 22nd, 1901 marked the end of an era, with the death of Queen Victoria at the age of 81 and the accession to the throne of the Prince of Wales, now His Majesty King Edward the Seventh. The whole of Britain and her Empire was plunged into deep mourning, and for a time the life of the country came to a halt. The ceremonial lasted several days as the Queen's body was transported from the Isle of Wight to lie in state before the royal funeral – a state occasion attended by the world's highest dignitaries, and mirrored in cities and towns throughout the realm. In Maryport it was decided to build a hospital in the Queen's memory, and Wilfrid was, needless to say, at the forefront of the Subscription Committee. The response, however, was very similar to that of the Dock scheme – a disappointing local outcome, with only £500 pledged by the end of the year (but matters did improve later). This may have reflected a 'dip' in the fortunes of the town, as the shipping news at the time mentions the "Nether Holme" among several vessels leaving the port 'light'.

The "Nether Holme" was bound for Brunswick, Georgia, and returned with a mixed cargo of cotton, resin, pig iron and timber to unload at Manchester early in March. Then it was over to Sunderland for repairs; at this point Captain Wilson, her master, left her for the last time. Suffering from severe lung symptoms he returned to his home in Maryport where he died a few days later of tuberculosis. He was only 48 years old, and had been with the Holme Line for many years commanding the "Ivy Holme" and briefly, the "Ardmore". As master of the "Glen Holme" in 1893 he had saved the lives of his crew members after a collision in the Sound of Islay; while in the "Nether Holme" had rescued a Norwegian crew adrift in the Atlantic in 1896, and a Greek Coaster in the Mediterranean in 1897. Described as *"...a man of quiet unostentation of character, who won the respect of all with whom he came into contact..."*, he left a widow and seven children, the youngest only eight years old. Captain Gorley took over the "Nether Holme", which departed for Miramichi Bay on the eastern seaboard of Canada in May.

The "Forest Holme", having delivered the usual load of rails, was returning across the Atlantic with a large cargo of timber and 70,000 lengths of deal, all for the Cork Timber and Iron Company of Ireland. The *Cork Examiner*, in a long article, marvelled at the amount of wood that could be shipped in one load *"...by steamers, it may be mentioned that they carry as much on deck as the old sailing ships used to carry on deck and under it..."* and noted that the

ship had made a record run of only nine days and five hours from Sydney, Cape Breton, *"...and arrived in Cork ahead of her papers from Canada..."*. The ship's master was now the young Alexander Ross Beaton, who had married the brothers' niece Jane Leighton three years before. He had been appointed to the command when Captain Daniel S. Turney took command of the "Loughrigg Holme". According to the *Shipping Gazette* in February 1901 the "Loughrigg Holme" had been in trouble; prosecuted for causing smoke pollution in London! The Company's solicitor blamed the poor quality of the coal available, but in vain: the Port of London Authority's counsel declared that, *"the ship's furnace was not constructed to consume its own smoke, nor was there a competent man in charge of them at the time."* The Southwark Magistrates fined the Company a hefty £5, with a guinea (£1:05) costs.

Alfred Hine Junior, Alfred's eldest son, had for some time been involved in the activities of the Cumberland Voluntary Artillery, with the rank of Lieutenant. As well as being a good rider and a fine shot he had successfully trained in Artillery at the Army School of Gunnery at Leith. In March 1901 he volunteered for Army Service and was commissioned into the Imperial Yeomanry with a view to service in South Africa, where the Boer War was at its height. After a rousing send-off from his fellows in the C.V.A., reported at length in the local press, he embarked on a troopship the following month.

On arrival he found himself posted to Edenburg, just south of Bloemfontein in what is now the Orange Free State, attached to the 1st Royal Sussex Regiment and in charge of *"a body of well-disciplined troops"* as he described his section. By June Alfred was firmly involved in the action, trekking about 200 miles between Springfontein and the veldt and hills north of Bloemfontein. They were in pursuit of a militia army of about 1,000 Boers whose guerrilla tactics often frustrated the more formal manoeuvres of the British. In a full and exciting letter home (which only took a month to arrive) he relates his adventures and escapades in a unit which was performing well and obviously high in morale. After recovering from a bout of dysentery he remained well and felt fit, and he admitted that he had not been subjected to much hardship during the exercise. The British troops ate well (both sides 'liberated' livestock from the local farms as they went, though the British at least paid for what they requisitioned) and the Sussex officers invited him to share their mess facilities. Alfred described his Captain as *"a rattling good sort"* and got on well with his brother officers, declaring that he would be *"very sorry to leave them when the time comes"*. In fact he remained with the Regiment, and received promotion to Captain early the next year. His first taste of action, when his company came under fire from the enemy, was on June 6th 1901.

On the very same day, back in England, his brother John McLennan Hine married Lydia Booth, the oldest daughter of Benjamin Booth J.P. The family home was Plashwood Park, a historic house near Stowmarket in Suffolk surrounded by nearly 800 acres of park and estate. The wedding appears to have been quite an event: no expense or effort seems to have been spared to make it an occasion to remember, in the traditions and style of the Edwardian age. Under the direction of the churchwardens the road outside the lovely old parish church of Wetherden was ablaze with triumphal arches, bunting and garlands, while the path to the church door was carpeted and the head gardener of the Park had decorated the nave with hothouse plants and palms. The bride, exquisitely attired in a dress of ivory satin and wearing a diamond and sapphire spray brooch given to her by the bridegroom, was attended by no less than six bridesmaids: her three younger sisters, together with Mary and Ethel Hine – the groom's sisters – and Elfrida Hine, Wilfrid's daughter. John McL. must have faced a heavy bill from his jeweller, as all six received presents of shamrock brooches in pearl and diamonds! His youngest brother Wilfrid, now aged 20, was his best man.

The service over, the happy pair left the church to the cheers of the villagers, who had all turned out to see the spectacle, and returned by carriage to Plashwood for a reception in the grounds, where a band played and photographs were taken.

Later in the afternoon the newly-weds, the bride now wearing a pale blue outfit with a pink hat, left for the station to travel to London and then to a honeymoon in North Devon, while that evening the Booth family hosted a dance for a large house party

Wedding Group at John McL Hine's wedding

of guests and friends. In the following week they laid on a dinner for all the tenants and workers on their estate, and also a tea party at Plashwood for the schoolchildren of the parish. With three more daughters to provide for, Benjamin Booth may perhaps have wondered whether he had set too high a precedent as father of the bride!

Back in Maryport, life went on. In January, Wilfrid had warned the Council that the town's water supply was becoming insufficient for its needs; and while he was in Suffolk at his nephew's wedding the Council decided to act. The *Maryport News'* columnist Ewanrigg commented gleefully:

> *One would like to see Mr. Hine's face when he reads in the News that the Council has decided to cut off the supply to the Baptist organ engine"* (the church apparently had a water-powered pump to power the organ).

Wilfrid does not seem to have risen to the bait, but William Leghton and Alfred, the elders of the church, wrote to the Council and complained bitterly. The families of the brothers were entering fully into the life of the church and the town at this

John McL and his new bride on honeymoon

Alfred, Mary, Jane and Wilfrid Hine at John McL Hine's wedding

time, and are mentioned frequently among those singing at concerts and taking part in events of various sorts: John McLennan Hine was active in the Cricket Club, and Ernest Hine, Joseph J's son, turned out regularly at full-back for the Maryport Hockey team!

With the dawn of 1902, Britain prepared itself for the launch into a new era: the twentieth century was still young, and the coronation of the new King would mark the official beginning of the Edwardian age. A year before, *The Times* had declared that:

> *To write the life of Queen Victoria is to relate the history of Great Britain during a period of great events, manifold changes and unexampled national prosperity.*

Yet there was evidence that the old philosophies, assumptions and attitudes that had characterised and stabilised the 'Victorian' society for the previous 50 years could not survive unchallenged and unchanged. Within a short time another leading article in *The Times* sounded a warning: the last 30 years, it asserted:

> *were the times of our 'unrivalled prosperity', advancing by 'leaps and bounds'; of our common assumption that the opinion of England was the most potent in the affairs of Europe, of our invincible belief... that we were the salt of the earth.*

But it also reported the words of Lord Roseberry, who urged the business community to *"get its house in order, and do it with brains"*; similarly the Prime Minister called for *"higher intelligence, for knowledge better organised and assimilated, in the conduct of our commercial affairs."*

Mr. Chamberlain continued, in a passage of prophetic accuracy:

> *It depends very much upon what we are doing now, at the beginning of the twentieth century, whether at its end we shall continue to maintain our supremacy or even equality with our great commercial and manuf- acturing rivals.*

The 'rivals' at this time were the United States and particularly the newly-emergent federation of Germany, whose rising influence in Europe and potential involvement in the South African war were of growing political concern in Britain. *The Times* leader goes on to quote the late Bishop of London, who had written,

> *our assumption of moral and intellectual superiority in the past has done more than anything else to make us unpopular* and to ask: *Is it too late? We still lead the world's commerce, but our lead has appreciably diminished of late.... We have been so self- satisfied that we have never taken the trouble to apply scientific methods the whole business of life as our neighbours less favoured by fortune have had to do.*

Certainly the merchant shipping industry was suffering a decline in trade at about this time, as evidenced by an item in the *Maryport News* in March, 1902. The article points out that when Hine Bros. had sold the "Rydal Holme" twelve months previously the new owner paid about £20,000, whereas she had been re-sold recently for only £13,700 – an illustration of the sharp fall in shipping values. The Holme Line steamships were still managing to find cargoes during this period, but the Canadian contract seems to have terminated and the steamers were having to deploy over a much wider range of routes than previously: examination of the Lloyd's Index for the year shows their activities:

The "Abbey Holme" (Capt. W. Brown) was engaged in transport between the ports of the River Plate and South Africa all year. Similarly, the "Greta Holme" (Capt. Millican) did not leave the South Atlantic, trading mainly between Table Bay and Buenos Aires, transporting general goods and livestock and without returning to home waters. It was the practice at Table Bay for the ships to unload their cargo of sheep as soon as possible after arrival and then, because the docks were so busy, to move out into the roadstead to clean out the holds. They would return some days later to discharge the dry cargo: by then, no doubt, both steamer and her crew had a more acceptable odour!

The "Isel Holme" (Capt. Johnstone) had been employed during 1901 in trade between Australia and Java, but in February 1902 she left Melbourne for Natal, South Africa. From here she sailed to Delagoa Bay, Mozambique, and thence back to home territory, arriving at Tyneside in May and on to Barry in June. Then it was off again, to Montevideo and the Plate River; then Buenos Aires; and to round off the year a couple of further trips to the Cape of Good Hope and back!

The "Forest Holme" (Capt. Beaton) plied the North Atlantic route, mainly to Montreal, alternating with shorter journeys to Sorrento or Genoa in Italy; returning to Cardiff or occasionally to Maryport. (On August 2nd, the "Forest Holme" departed with a cargo for Alexandria, Egypt, calling at Tripoli, Benghazi and Leith on the return journey: the chief Engineering Officer was obliged to cut short his honeymoon to sail with his ship, and according to the Lloyd's records was away from his new bride until November 1st!)

The "Loughrigg Holme" (Capt. Chadwick) was seen more often in her home port, continuing what remained of the transportation of steel rails to the ports of the St. Lawrence River from Maryport, plus moving bunkering coal and other general commodities. In the autumn of 1902 she too was routed to the Eastern Mediterranean, calling at Alexandria and Thessaloniki.

The "Nether Holme" (Capt. Gorley) saw in the new year in Charleston, Carolina, and for the major part of 1902 steamed between Maryport, London or Liverpool and various ports on the eastern seaboard of the USA and Canada. In October, however, she joined her sister ships in carrying cargoes to the ports of Greece and Egypt.

The four clipper barques were still managing to maintain their routine. The "Brier Holme" (Capt. Rich) continued her annual journeys between Tasmania and London. Captain John Rich was now in his eleventh year as master of the barque, and had become a well-known and respected figure in Launceston; reliably appearing and bringing the cargoes of goods the Tasmanians needed from 'home', and still finding a consignment of wool to fill the hold for the return journey.

The "Castle Holme" (Capt. Hurst) sailed from Kingston, South Australia, on January 11th 1902, arriving in London on May 16th after 128 days at sea. She did not leave London until the end of August – possibly a reflection on the difficulties of finding enough goods to transport at an economically viable rate – and arrived in Adelaide on Boxing Day: an outward trip of 118 days.

The "Eden Holme" (Capt. Wyrill) and the "Myrtle Holme" (Capt. Cobb) also fulfilled their commitments, with uneventful voyages. These were two sound ships, with highly experienced masters, both in the nautical and business aspects of their profession; but increasingly their sphere of influence was diminishing. To quote the President of the Society for Nautical Research, in the report of a symposium in 1972

...the life had long been an anachronism. Younger and farsighted men had gone to steam. At the turn of the century there had been successful auxiliary steamers for 75 years, and successful steamers for at least 60.

"Nether Holme" unloading steel rails, Bridgwater, Nova Scotia: 15 Sept., 1904

The remarkable thing was that the large sailing ship survived so long.

Matters such as these, however, were far from the minds of the people of Maryport as the year went on: more immediate was the sensation of the King's illness and the last-minute postponement of his coronation in June. Two days before the due date the grumbling appendicitis which had plagued him for some weeks flared up into an acute episode of pain and abdominal symptoms. In the opinion of all His Majesty's medical advisors, the King needed an immediate surgical operation. Given the condition of the patient – a portly man, in his sixties and certainly not a disciple of the healthy life – and the state of surgical and anaesthetic knowledge at that time, this represented a situation of significant risk both to the patient himself and to the monarchy. The Country and the Empire held its breath as Dr. Frederick Hewitt administered anaesthesia and Sir Frederick Treves wielded the scalpel. The diagnosis – 'peritiflitis' as it was then known – was confirmed, an abscess was drained and the royal patient made an uneventful recovery. The nation breathed a sigh of relief – the King had already, in the short period of his reign, endeared himself to his subjects – and the coronation took place six weeks later, on August 9th.

Further cause for celebration, again tinged with relief, was the signing of the 'Treaty of Vereeniging' on May 31st 1902, ending the Boer War. The 31st Yeomanry had been involved in fighting throughout the hostilities, taking casualties right up to the final days of conflict, and Captain Alfred Hine was treated to a hero's welcome on his homecoming. Upon his arrival at Maryport station on September 1st he was driven through the town in an open carriage drawn by his colleagues from the local Volunteer Regiment,

to the applause of the population who turned out in force to cheer while the Volunteers' band played "See the Conquering Hero Comes"! Outside Park Hill, Alfred's home, a triumphal arch had been erected; the Volunteers lined up, and speeches followed: Captain Alfred modestly admitted that he had been moved by the warmth of his reception, but would rather have gone through the war again! Notwithstanding, he heartily appreciated their kindness. He declared that he *"had had a ripping good time in South Africa, and did not regret going out as he had thoroughly enjoyed himself!"* (The *Maryport News* of September 6th 1902 carried a long interview with the returning Captain, and a photograph showing him resplendent in uniform and sporting a waxed military moustache.) Alfred, as the host, thanked everyone for turning out, gave thanks for his son's safe return and invited all the Volunteers to partake of refreshments before they left. Amid cheers and laughter he said he

Captain Alfred Hine, 1902

knew they were all teetotallers there, and had nothing to do with alcohol, so they would have to be satisfied with ginger pop!

The celebration was to be short-lived, alas. In the following week's edition, there was news of a different kind:

Illness of Mr. Alfred Hine, Maryport
We regret to state that Mr. A. Hine J.P., C.C., of Park Hill, is seriously ill. Mr. Hine was suddenly taken ill at noon last Saturday when in his office and has suffered acute pain since. He was attended by Dr. Little, but on Thursday morning dangerous symptoms manifested themselves and it was deemed well to obtain specialist advice. Yesterday

afternoon Professor Newman and Dr. Jowell of Glasgow attended and performed a minor operation, bleeding the patient in order to relieve the congestion at the kidneys, the seat of the disease. Last night the patient was in a critical condition and very weak.

On Sunday September 14th 1902 Alfred Hine died of acute nephritis, aged 61 years.

The funeral, five days later, was an astonishing event, even considering the enormous influence Alfred had had upon Maryport life. Preceding the cortege as it left Park Hill was a throng of over 400 children in all, shepherded by their teachers; the girls dressed in mourning black and carrying bouquets of white flowers. These were his pupils at the Sunday Schools, the various other church classes and the British School, of which Alfred had been Secretary of the Board. In their wake came a pair of carriages bearing past and present ministers of the Trinity Baptist Church together with Alfred's doctor, solicitor and the firm's manager. Following them was a wagonette laden with wreaths, and then the hearse, with an escort of the 'pioneer captains of the firm' – Captains Johnstone, Kirkpatrick, Holmes and Bryce – and senior members of the staff, marching at either side. Eight coaches containing the family mourners were next, and they led a long line of others; Sir Wilfrid Lawson MP, Alfred's friend and Liberal political companion of many years; Mr. Senhouse of Netherhall, and many more. Although Friday was a market day in Maryport the shops had closed all along the funeral route and blinds were drawn as a mark of respect, the population standing quiet and bareheaded as the solemn procession passed on its way to the cemetery. Even the Police Court adjourned its sitting for the afternoon as the magistrates wished to attend the funeral of, as the Chairman Mr. Cockton said, *"...one who always attended to his duties in a pleasing and efficient manner."*

The *Maryport News* filled several columns with its description of the event, listing those who had attended, sent wreaths or otherwise had been involved; and such was the demand that its edition of the 20th September completely sold out! The next week's paper contained the following:

As many people were unable to obtain copies of the News on Saturday owing to the heavy demand, a slip containing the portrait, obituary and the report of the funeral of Mr. Alfred Hine, suitable for forwarding to friends at a distance, may be obtained at the office in Senhouse Street. The funeral was one of the largest ever held in West Cumberland. The newspapers did their best but were not able to report the attendance of all who attended.

Wilfrid threw himself into a whirl of activity, taking on most of his Alfred's duties as well as his own, to the point where the *News* commented:

...Mr. Hine is distinguished by immense capacity for work and an energy that knows no curbing, but this honourable desire to take his brother's burdens upon shoulders already sufficiently loaded may result in the willing carrier being overtaxed.

Nonetheless, in November Wilfrid decided he would stand for election to Alfred's seat on the county council, and in the same month he was in the public eye again – with another set of proposals for a new dock!.

Wilfrid had never given up hope since the failure of the earlier two attempts to implement the first dock scheme. The new project would, in his view, put Maryport in the first rank of British ports by allowing the production from the industrial north to be exported direct to China and India from Maryport instead of going via Wales or the Clyde. His latest plan envisaged a huge new dock to the north of the existing structures, opening into the basin between the Elizabeth and Senhouse Docks but with an opening 70-75 feet wide and 30 feet of depth of water: *"...large enough for the Oceanic, Campania and Deutschland"*, he is quoted as claiming. He included comprehensive arrangements for railway connections to the docks, and even allowed room for a possible graving dock to provide ship repair facilities. Pointing out that the scheme would take two years, Wilfrid calculated that the new jobs the construction work would bring would generate over

£200,000 in wages alone; new industries would be attracted to Maryport thereafter and the benefits to the town's economy would be ongoing.

On that optimistic note Wilfrid and Jane left for their annual visit to Eastbourne, this time taking Alfred's widow Mary with them. Unfortunately all three caught influenza, and Mary was obliged to delay her return because of her illness! The turn of the year did have some brighter notes, however: in December in London Marian, Alfred Ernest's new wife, produced a grand-daughter for Wilfrid and Jane, while in January 1903 Lydia, John McLennan Hine's new wife, had a baby boy in Maryport – a grandson for Mary.

As so often in the past, the winter winds provided drama and danger for seafarers entering the waters to the west of Britain. In late February 1903 the people of Maryport were surprised and excited by the appearance in the Solway Firth of a large four-masted barque with all sails set, running before the fierce southerly gale. No such ship was expected and speculation was rife as to her identity; but as she came to anchor in Maryport's roads the refugee was seen to be the "Hougomont", 2,240 tons, one of the merchant sailing fleet of Messrs. John Hardie & Co. The "Hougomont", built in 1897, had left San Francisco the previous October with a huge cargo: 2,000 tons of wheat and barley in sacks, and another 2,000 tons of tinned fruits and salmon, packed in cases. She was due to discharge at Liverpool; but on rounding the north coast of Anglesey she had not been able to engage a pilot or a tug, and was forced to square away to avoid drifting to leeward into potential difficulties. The owners immediately commissioned a steam tug, the "Brilliant Star", to tow her to her destination and the following afternoon they set off from Maryport to return to Liverpool, unaware of what the elements were about to throw at them.

That night, the weather really broke: a gale described as 'of hurricane violence' swept the entire British Isles, causing widespread damage over land and sea. Out in the Solway the tow-rope parted, and while the battered "Brilliant Star" was able to stagger back to Maryport Harbour the "Hougomont" was driven up the Firth by the south-

The "Hougomont"

wester, at the mercy of screaming wind, mountainous seas and an inexorable tide. Their signal flares and distress rockets could not be seen, but in any case little help could have been given because of the awful weather.

Just before daybreak the next morning the vessel stranded in Allonby Bay, north of the town. The wind continued unabated in its fury, coming round to north-westerly almost as if to increase the attack on the ship: great waves broke over her, bringing down more of the upper sections of the masts in a tangle of spars and rigging. The crew – and the captain's wife, who was also aboard – retreated to the poop deck area, but this gave them only temporary respite. The "Hougomont" lay broadside-on to the surf, which soon washed all the fixtures from the deck: after a time the hatches were also breached, spilling the cargo of sacks and cans into the raging sea to be washed ashore. All the ship's company could do was to cling to the after-rigging and wait for rescue: they could be seen clearly by the crowd of villagers who had gathered on the shore but who were powerless to help. Because of the appalling conditions – and a communications problem at the Maryport lifeboat station – it took five hours for the lifeboat to arrive to take the survivors off the stricken vessel, and although there were no fatalities many were near the limits of their endurance due to the cold and exhaustion. The local people did all they could to succour the victims, and by that evening the Shipwrecked Fishermen and Mariners Society had come to their aid too. Hine Bros. were the local representatives of the Society, and provided a wagonette (from Joseph J's fleet, no doubt!) to bring the rescued company to the coffee tavern premises in Maryport: there they received warm food and dry clothing before being found accommodation, either at the Tavern itself or in local homes. The following morning the crew were paid off and were able to return to their various families: the weather by this time was noted to be 'gloriously fine'!

With the storm ended, attention could be given to the "Hougomont", lying damaged on Allonby beach. A relatively new ship, she carried a potentially salvageable cargo (all, that is, that had not been washed away by the tempest, ruined by seawater or already 'salvaged' by the local populace!). People had travelled from far and near to view the sight of the wounded giant, and despite the activity of the local police and the attention of the Receiver of Wrecks few left without a sample of the delicacies she had been carrying! Every effort was to be made to refloat the "Hougomont", and Captain Frederick Young of the Liverpool Salvage Association appeared on the scene to take charge of operations. The attempt was made two weeks later, taking advantage of the next high tide, with three large pumps draining the holds and with

The "Hougomont" stranded on Allonby beach

The "Hougomont" being towed into Maryport

powerful tugs standing at the ready offshore. As the Whitehaven paper the *West Cumberland Times* reported on March 18th 1903:

> *On Sunday the wind changed from east to west, and this certainly favoured the flowing tide. Long before mid-day the steam tugs and salvage boats were again alongside and made fast – the "Ranger" and the "Cruiser" towing astern and the "Wrestler" on the starboard quarter, close by the ship, pulled for all they were worth. Several hundred people stood again on the shore at 12 o'clock and gazed seawards. At last, when few expected it, the ships were seen to move a little, and continued to creep on and on till they gained deeper water. The speed increased and the ensign was hoisted on the Hougomont as a sign of victory. On board a cheer was raised for the chief engineer; and on shore expressions of joy, thankfulness, and regret were heard that at last she was away. Having towed her clear of the ground, the tugs got hold of her bows and soon sped away to the Maryport roads, where anchor was cast, and divers were sent down to the damaged sides. On Monday morning an attempt was made to reach Liverpool, but nearing St. Bees the weather and sea became so rough that the ships were forced to put back into Maryport as the three steam pumps, big as they were, could not keep down the water. She was safely berthed in the Senhouse Dock Basin.*

This was no mean feat in itself: the size of the vessel, lying low in the water because of the water still in her holds, required all the skill and experience of the Harbourmaster Captain Nelson to judge the exact time at which the tide would be high enough to allow the "Hougomont" to enter the basin without further damage. The operation was accomplished successfully, however, and after discharging part of her cargo and undergoing temporary repairs at Maryport she was towed to Liverpool by the "Ranger" on March 31st.

Damage was not confined to the ship, however: the *West Cumberland Times* again:

> *The big hole left by the Hougomont on Allonby sands constitutes A SERIOUS DANGER to fishermen and bathers, and ought to be staked in order to keep people from walking into the dam which is eight to ten feet deep and 30 feet wide and 100 yards long, and is exactly opposite the vicarage. Of course this is many hundreds of yards from the shore, but it must be attended to in the near future. When the ship came over the Scaurs she buried many a big boulder by sheer weight: one stone bigger that the rest has been smashed on the top and most probably made a hole in the ship. A deep gutter was*

Scavengers of "Hougomont" cargo on Allonby beach

ploughed up through the scaurs and sands on Sunday as the tugs hauled her away; and this mark will remain for weeks to come to show the way to the great lair in which this fine vessel was so firmly gripped for 14 days.

There is a happy ending to the "Hougomont" story. After being unloaded she was taken to her home yard in Greenock for repair and re-fit, rejoining the Hardie fleet in October of the same year. In fact despite several further brushes with the elements the career of the "Hougomont" with the company was to be a long and honourable one: one of the last of the real 'windjammers', she was eventually sold to a Finnish owner in 1924, and was finally condemned in Australia in 1932, having been dismasted on her outward voyage.

The first half of 1903 proved to be a busy time for Wilfrid Hine. In April he found himself appointed to the committee of the Victoria Hospital (as did Mary, Alfred's widow), and as a district councillor he became the chairman of the General Purposes Committee. In February he had made his maiden speech as a county councillor, on the subject – unsurprisingly – of the latest plans for Maryport's Docks. He had his opportunity to expand his views in London in May, when the Maryport Harbour Bill came once again before the House of Lords.

In a statement to their Lordships as a witness, Wilfrid pointed out the inadequacies of the now obsolete Elizabeth Dock, which at neap tides could only give ten to twelve feet depth of water – only enough for small coastal shipping, which made up only a small part of the industry. The Senhouse Dock, though deeper, was now too small, he declared: ships sometimes had to wait 10-14 days for a berth to load or discharge their cargo, and larger cargoes could not be shipped. This latter factor alone added approximately nine pence (4p) per ton to the shipping rate, such was the 'economy of scale', and the extra premium which shipowners had to charge to allow for possible delays at Maryport amounted to a further 1s. 9d.(9p) per ton approximately. The situation had become so disadvantageous that some owners were declining to charter vessels to Maryport at all:

Unless they had further accommodation and that very speedily", said Wilfrid, *"the iron trade, the steel trade and also the colliery trade in the whole of the district would be most seriously affected.*

He went on to show that trade in general in the town had quadrupled in the ten years following the opening of the Senhouse Dock; that the local traders agreed that the improved railway link envisaged would also benefit Maryport, and assured the Lords that the district council was unanimously in favour of the new scheme. How much influence Wilfrid's argument had in London is not known; but it is interesting to note that the Maryport and Carlisle Railway Co. withdrew its opposition to the Bill the following month. At this juncture Wilfrid and Jane decided to take a summer holiday in Switzerland – and while he was away he was re-elected to the chairmanship of the Board of the British School!

Indeed, such was his involvement in such local affairs that the columnist Ewanrigg likened him to:

an educational Poo-Bah: Mr. Hine represents the District Council on the Board of Managers of the British Schools to check on Mr. Hine the Chairman of the Managers and Mr. Hine the Secretary of the Schools

Perhaps not entirely fair on Wilfrid: he had taken on some of his late brother's duties, but Alfred Jnr. and John McL Hine – and their wives – were increasingly taking over Alfred's charitable and social role after their father's death. Nonetheless Wilfrid remained a busy man for the rest of 1903, missing several Council meetings and church events due to business in London. He was away from Maryport in December when his friend and fellow Commissioner H.P. Senhouse died: at the time Wilfrid was in Paris, one of seven British delegates to an International Conference of Sailing Ship Owners. The object of the conference was to fix an internationally acceptable minimum rate for freight carried in sailing ships, and the delegates – French, German and British – were successful in agreeing a scheme they felt would meet widespread approval throughout Europe.

Back in England, 1904 brought Wilfrid Hine – now in his 66th year – a period of indifferent health. He had forsaken his usual summer holiday haunt of Bournemouth for Tunbridge Wells, but had been laid low with a sharp attack of influenza and had not been well enough to travel home until mid-October, so (among other things) he missed the visit to Maryport of Buffalo Bill's Wild West Show! A three-day Bazaar was held in late September in aid of the Cottage Hospital project, and Wilfrid had hoped to attend; he wrote expressing his regrets at his absence, and his sadness that neither his brother Alfred nor Mr. Senhouse were alive to see it. The event raised £1,100 for the fund, a magnificent sum in the uncertain economic state of the time.

Wilfrid had left behind him an unsettled and unhappy situation in the Docks – strikes, and a riot of disaffected workers throwing stones at the police sent to restore order. He returned home to keep in touch with the business, but by mid-November he was still weak: on his doctor's advice he decided to take a trip abroad to recuperate. Wilfrid and Jane travelled to the Mediterranean by liner, and the local press commented:

It is expected that the warm, dry bracing winter air of Egypt will brace him up. It is to be hoped however that he will have good weather on the voyage... as a rough passage in his present delicate state of health would try him severely, for Mr. Hine, though a shipowner, is no sailor.

However, 'the best-laid plans of mice and men'... Ewanrigg's column in January 1905:

Mr. Hine's quest of the sun has not been quite so successful as we stay-at-home people who associate Egypt with a perfect winter climate and burning sun would have imagined. During the cold snap which struck the Mediterranean and caused the lightly-clad Arabs of Algiers to shiver as they walked the snow-covered streets, Mr. Hine found it necessary to wear his overcoat when out of doors.

The couple returned home in March, with Wilfrid reported as feeling much better: in an interview he said he had enjoyed the clear desert air, and that, *"although the Solway has the best sunsets in England those of the desert surpass both Solway and Switzerland!"*

This happy recovery was not to last. The *News*, April 8th 1905:

Mr. Hine has been ill again. He felt so well after returning from Egypt that, with more heroism perhaps than prudence, he reverted to his former daily custom and indulged in a cold bath. The result has been disastrous, as he has suffered great pain from an attack of a neuralgic character.... It is to be hoped that he will soon recover from this setback. Cold baths no doubt brace up and harden the strong and hardy, but it may be questioned if those people who are some time in recovering their normal heat on leaving the water had not better avoid the matutinal cold tub except in the summer months.

The invalid, suitably rebuked, was back in circulation in a few days, but in May took himself off again for the benefit of his health – to Bournemouth once more. He was nonetheless able to travel to London to attend a Dinner with the Elder Brethren of Trinity House, presided over by the Prince of Wales: and on June 3rd the local press noted that:

...Mr. Hine is improving in health and gaining in weight in Bournemouth. He has been occupying his leisure time in characteristic fashion by writing to the Shipping Gazette, *pointing out that a correspondent who stated that Maryport would suffer from the completion of the new port of Heysham "did not know what he was writing about". A little controversy is an excellent tonic, and will do more to brace up Mr. Hine than all the drugs in the British Pharmacopoeia.*

The prescription seems to have been successful, as Wilfrid was back 'in harness' by the end of the month. In August General William Booth – the founder of the Salvation Army – visited Maryport and was entertained to lunch at Camp Hill: according to the press report the General, a vegetarian, did not require a gourmet meal, requesting only dry toast and rice pudding!

The Holme Line steamers did not fare well in 1905: in May the "Abbey Holme" managed to run aground in Moreton Bay Harbour while en route from Saigon to Brisbane, and was stuck for nine hours before being towed off. A survey revealed no damage so she was allowed to go on her way, but only a few months later Captain Brown broke down at sea and had to be towed into Brisbane. The ship's crankshaft had broken, and the cost of repair together with the salvage claim made this an expensive setback for the Company. In the same month the "Loughrigg Holme" also found herself in difficulties, with a ten-day delay and a sizeable bill anticipated: again, the crankshaft was the culprit and she had to put in to Lisbon on her route from the River Plate to Hull. So it was just as well that later in the year Hine Bros. won their court action against another shipping firm in a dispute about a charter contract involving the "Loughrigg Holme" and the "Forest Holme". Their claim for loss of freight earnings was upheld by the King's Bench Division of the High Court, and with costs.

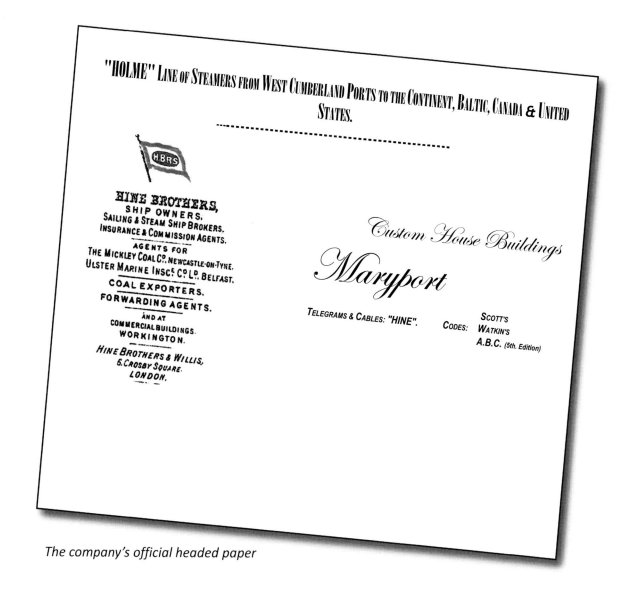

The company's official headed paper

Chapter Nine
Farewell to Three Masters: 1903-1905

Capt. J. Wyrill

FOR THE COMPANY'S CLIPPERS, it was 'business as usual', and the life remained arduous and dangerous. On August 8th 1903 the "Eden Holme" set out from London with a cargo of general merchandise, bound for Tasmania as usual. The voyage was to take 107 days, and would involve facing all the perils, tragedies, frustrations and hardships such an adventure entailed. At the outset the weather was against them, with south-westerly gales in the Channel and the Bay of Biscay, in Capt. Wyrill's words, was *"in one of its angry moods".* The "Eden Holme" sustained damage to sails and gear and made only slow progress against the wind as far as Madeira, where she picked up the Trade Winds, but these north-easters were not of their usual force and soon failed. This left the barque 'in the doldrums' for a while, whistling for a wind: from one extreme to the other!

Nearing the Equator the "Eden Holme" narrowly avoided being in collision with another ship – an almost unimaginable occurrence, given the thousands of square miles of empty ocean! It was a bright moonlit night, and when the light of another vessel was seen it was assumed that the other vessel should give way according to the 'rule of the road', the "Eden Holme" being on the starboard tack. However, Capt. Wyrill records:

she came on, until it was too late to bear up. The foreigners must have been asleep, for they only roused up to their danger at the last moment, when they broke out into wild shouting with much rushing about. To avoid a smash we tacked, but at the last moment the Italian did the same and we barely escaped hitting stern to stern.

(The Tasmanian newspaper which carried a report of the voyage on the "Eden Holme"s arrival mentions that, *"by her perforated sails, and other signs, she was judged to be an Italian ship".*)

Only a few days later, the Captain was on watch on a stormy night when the cry "Man Overboard" rang out. Running to the poop, he threw a lifebuoy in the direction he judged the man would be and

Capt. J. Wyrill

ordered the the ship be stopped and the lifeboat launched with all speed.

> *It was one of the apprentices who had gone over, and when he was picked up he reported he had seen the lifebuoy fall into the sea and had swum to it... from this point of vantage he had cheerfully set to whistle with his fingers and guide the boat to his rescue. He was little the worse for his immersion, but regretted having to lose his trousers to assist his buoyancy. "Shake hands, sir," he said to me as I met him at the gangway, "I knew you would do everything possible to save me." He, of course, was quite a hero with the other lads for a long time...*

The "Eden Holme" crossed the Equator on September 13th after 36 days at sea, and thereafter made good progress, taking a further 25 days to reach the latitude of the Cape of Good Hope.

In this area of the southern ocean devious currents and abnormal seas are often encountered: this voyage proved no exception, and nearly proved the undoing of the "Eden Holme" and her crew. On October 8th she was making reasonable progress, running before a strong westerly gale and with reduced sail, about 400 miles south of the Cape. Capt. Wyrill had experienced these treacherous conditions before, and feared that the ship could be 'pooped' – caught by a wave coming over the stern – and had actually gone aft to tie a rope round the helmsman for his protection at the wheel, when completely without warning the ship was struck by an enormous tidal wave which washed completely over the ship. Water rolled inboard from both sides, rushed aft and completely submerged the after half of the "Eden Holme", carrying away the bridge rail and causing major damage to the deck structures. Three of the ship's lifeboats were lost and their iron davits were twisted and bent over like wire: the hatches gave way and tons of seawater poured down into the cabins, saloon and galley. The Captain had been clinging to a rope attached to the mizzen mast; dragged aft underwater he released his hold, and was only saved from going over the stern to certain death by becoming wedged, half-drowned

and semiconscious, against a stanchion. Only the hub of the ship's wheel remained: the steersman, an Exeter man called John Wilson, was swept away and never seen again.

As the water cleared off the poop deck Capt. Wyrill heard a cry for help, and discovered that there was a man pinned down by the wreckage and hanging half over the stern of the ship. It turned out to be the apprentice who had fallen overboard earlier in the voyage – a youth called Morrison; now helpless, and in pain from a broken collarbone. Once more required the Captain's aid, to drag him back aboard (and later, to set the fracture!). He had been on the deckhouse, by the mainmast some 80 feet away, when the freak wave struck, and for a second time narrowly escaped a watery grave.

Mercifully there were no more heavy seas; but with the ship seriously damaged – her sails shredded, her cabins half-full of water and much of the stores destroyed – all hands set to, to repair the wreckage of her gear and to bail out the cabins and saloons with buckets. Fortunately, the hatches to the lower decks had remained watertight, so the cargo was largely undamaged and the pumps were not needed to clear the holds. For three days the "Eden Holme" hove to, drifting in the gale while the captain and crew attempted to construct a new steering wheel, and to set up a makeshift arrangement of compasses. In an iron vessel compass readings could be inaccurate, but this would normally be corrected for by setting compensating magnets into the binnacle close to the ship's fixed compasses: however, the "Eden Holme"'s compasses and binnacle had been destroyed by the wave, leaving only the captain's and officers' own instruments for navigation.

By October 11th the ship was able to resume her journey, but more trouble – of a different sort – was to come. Three days later, the second mate was suddenly seized with violent stomach pains; and despite Captain Wyrill's best efforts (the limited medicines and hot fomentations at his disposal were of no avail) he died after two days. The following day, in a howling wind and drizzling rain, the body of Herbert Edgar was committed to the deep: *"a mournful duty"* the Captain observes; *"a fine young fellow, and a splendid officer"* who had been the captain's chief helper in the task of making the new wheel.

Capt. Wyrill considered making for the first port she could attain for repairs – probably one of the South American ports – but decided to struggle on: it took the "Eden Holme" nearly five weeks more to reach Hobart. The *West Cumberland Times* report of the voyage two months later concluded with the words *"The many friends of Captain Wyrill will be glad to know that he looks none the worse for his sensational experience."* This was not entirely true: in his memoir the Captain himself relates:

There were other difficulties through damage aloft, and the crew reduced by three; also my nervous system was so shaken with the shock off the Cape and subsequent continuous strain of gale after gale that... all the charm and romance of the sea that had meant so much to me, left me, and only dread and hatred of it remained. It was as if an old and trusted friend had played me a foul and treacherous trick.

After temporary repairs the "Eden Holme" sailed on to Launceston to deliver the rest of her cargo. Then, with the support of his son (also a sea captain, and in Sydney at the time), Capt. Wyrill sailed his vessel to Melbourne – again, in terrible weather – to load a cargo for London, but all was not well:

During the loading of the ship my friends, noticing my nervous condition, urged me to give up the ship and remain behind. I felt this was the right course but struggled against the feeling, hoping that when I got to sea I should feel better. I got the ship loaded and put out into the bay – tug and pilot ordered for sea next morning – I remaining in town for my papers and to settle accounts. The extra strain, and getting wet through from a tropical downpour whilst getting the ship out of the dock, was the last straw, and the morning found me unable to rise, so I had to give in.

A stand-in master, Captain Lloyd, was found for the return voyage and Capt. Wyrill, relieved of the worry and responsibilities, returned to Launceston to recuperate. There he made a critical decision; important not only to himself, as the *Tasmanian Daily Telegraph* of 4th February 1904 reports:

A large gathering assembled in the Mechanics Institute class room last night, consisting of many friends of Captain J. Wyrill, to bid farewell to one of the most popular of the men who have ever been connected with the shipping of Launceston. Captain J. Wyrill has decided to retire from the sea on his return to England, and as this is, in all probability, the last opportunity they will have of seeing him in this port, it was decided to make a presentation. The room was appropriately decorated with bunting. The mayor (Alderman J.W. Pepper) presided, and included in the gathering were several leading shipping representatives, all of whom have been acquainted with Captain Wyrill for some years.

The mayor made the presentation, and the following address:

Dear sir, We, a few of your many friends in Tasmania, have heard with regret that it is not your intention to make another voyage to our port. For over 40 years past yourself and the different good ships under your command have been household words amongst us. Your arrivals and departures have been occasions of public interest throughout all these long years, during which you have contributed in no inconsiderable degree to the advancement of the commercial, social, and religious life of our city. We have learned to value and esteem you as a skilful mariner, an honourable man of business, a warm hearted friend and sincere Christian. We cannot therefore, permit you to finally leave us without publicly expressing our sentiments and assuring you it will afford us the liveliest satisfaction to hear that retirement from your strenuous sea life is followed such quiet eventide as will be altogether satisfactory to yourself and family. We beg your acceptance of the accompanying small purse of sovereigns.

...A musical evening followed, and their proceedings terminated with the singing of "Auld Lang Syne" and "God save the King."

The Captain then returned to England in an Orient Line steamer, but although recovered and rested he nevertheless declined Wilfrid's offer to resume his old command of the "Eden Holme"; however, professional to the last, he concludes:

I met the ship on arrival in London, put her through Lloyd's survey, made her ready for her next loading, and then gave her over to her new captain.

Captain J.H. Rich

DURING THIS TIME Capt. Wyrill was able to meet up with his colleague and old friend Captain John Rich, also a veteran of the Tasmanian run, who was in London preparing the "Brier Holme" for her annual trip to Hobart. He too was due to retire the following year after a lifetime at sea – beginning as an apprentice at the age of 14 – and with more than 20 years as the master of Holme Line clippers. Many times during these decades his wife accompanied him on the voyages, but Mrs. Rich's health had latterly begun to deteriorate somewhat and she remained in their home in Maryport; so Captain Rich kept in touch with her and their family by post from the West India Dock where the barque was loading. A letter to his son, dated 9th July 1904 – the last before the "Brier Holme" sailed – survives, giving a revealing picture of this experienced, businesslike yet humorous, affectionate and very human seafarer. He complains good-naturedly about having no first mate aboard to supervise the stowage of the cargo, to save expense, yet admits that although:

the owners should not like to see me with my sleeves rolled up, but dear son I am in my element when I have something to do, and 'bossing' men around just suits me.

He comments that he will not have many 'greenhorns' in his crew, as his old steward, carpenter, sailmaker and cabin boy are going with him again; as is his second officer Mr. Millett, whom he describes as a

splendid young fellow. This young man served his apprenticeship under me, was second in command last voyage and is going another voyage in the good old "Brier".

Capt. Rich is less enthusiastic about having a larger than usual complement of apprentices aboard for the journey. Four had been transferred to Hine Bros' care by Messrs. Devitt and Moore when their vessel the "Derwent" was put up for sale, and were allocated to the "Brier Holme" along with two of their own apprentices. One of these, he remarks,

Captain J.H. Rich
(Photograph courtesy of Mr. K. Rich)

...will be very useful to polish off plenty of grub, and do his 'whack' of sleeping... however, I am used to this, having one or two new apprentices every voyage, so must put up with the inevitable....

(Coincidentally, one of the apprentices was Philip Dulling, the younger brother of George H. Dulling, the new Captain of the "Eden Holme".)

Even less happy is the Captain at the requirement to ship a prize bull to Tasmania on the vessel. The animal was destined for the breeding stock of a gentleman farmer who *"is a large shipper of wool in the "Brier", so I see 'wheels within wheels', and the bull must arrive there safely."*

The final straw, however, is that there are passengers booked too: a doctor and – horror of horrors – his wife! *"I would not mind the doctor"* writes Captain Rich to his son,

but a woman, without it's your dear mother, I hate to have on board; they want so much waiting on, and there should be a special steward to attend to their 101 fanciful requirements which cannot be given to them on board an ordinary 'Windjammer', for I only carry a cabin boy, who wants stirring up every five minutes of the day... as a rule lady passengers are never contented with their rations and the cooking on board a sailing vessel.

(The doctor and his wife seem to have changed their minds about enduring the privations of a long sea journey in "Brier Holme", and are not mentioned in any documents or records of the voyage.)

The ship departed on 21 July, 1904, and the "Eden Holme" followed her on September 11th under the command of her new skipper. However, although the "Eden Holme" arrived in Hobart on December 10th after a creditable 93-day debut for Capt. Dulling, nothing had been heard from "Brier Holme" for over 150 days. By the year's end concern had gradually turned to alarm, but trust in the seaworthiness of the barque and the skill of her master kept hope alive that perhaps a dismasted

and crippled "Brier Holme" might be limping towards a port somewhere. Then on January 6th 1905 a telegraph from Lloyd's Agent in Hobart arrived, with the news that all had begun to dread:

The "Brier Holme" is supposed to have been lost. All on board supposed lost. The cargo which has been washed up ten miles from South West Cape has been recognised as belonging to her. Little prospect of salvage.

Two days before, a Tasmanian fisherman called Henry Glover had spotted a considerable amount of wreckage washed ashore between Elliot Cove, a wide bay on the south-western coast, and Port Davey, a natural inlet about twelve miles north of the Cape which forms the south-western tip of the island. He found all sorts of goods – cases, kegs and drums of various kinds, and even part of a piano. In particular he collected a roll of linoleum wrapped in canvas and bearing a characteristic identifying mark and brought this to the authorities in Hobart. Comparison of this detail with the ship's manifest, which was sent by telegraph from Hine's London office to their agents there, confirmed that it was part of a large consignment shipped in the "Brier Holme".

The news caused great sadness in Launceston and flags were flown at half mast in the town, for the barque had been a regular visitor for many years and Capt. Rich, like Capt. Wyrill, was a well-known and popular figure with the citizens. Henry Glover and a deputation of local citizens in Hobart called on the Tasmanian Prime Minister and gave him full details of the situation, but on hearing Glover's opinion that the goods had probably been on the shore for up to six weeks the Premier decided there was no point in sending a rescue party as there was little likelihood of anyone surviving the shipwreck. This decision caused some indignation among the seagoing communities, and the local press opened a subscription fund to pay for a steamer to be sent to search the area.

In fact a search had already been instituted: on January 14th 1905 the steamer "Seabird" had set out to try to locate the wreckage: also two other fishermen from Port Davey, Captains Noye and

Morris, had set off overland with a party of local Customs officers. This was in response to further information from Henry Glover that he had seen the body of a sailor on the shore; and what looked like a camp, lately vacated, on the beach at the mouth of the Davey River The two groups met at the site, buried the unidentified mariner and sailed round to examine the site of the camp Glover had reported. They found clearly discernible footprints, and a number of empty food tins similar to the ones among the flotsam and jetsam on the shore, but no sign of living castaways: unable to do anything more, they returned to Hobart.

The report of these findings renewed the public pressure on the authorities to despatch a properly-equipped steamer to examine the coast, and the following week a Government surveyor, Mr. Crisp, was deputed to lead a party of five men on the steamer "Breone" to conduct a search for survivors. North of Port Davey the searchers found yet more wreckage, including large spars, yards and hatches, and final confirmation of the fate of the "Brier Holme" was a broken wooden board bearing the vessel's name: but the wreckage all seemed undisturbed, with no sign of anyone having been along the shoreline. Turning his attention to the camp Crisp came to the conclusion that whoever had built it – and opened the food cans from the wreck – might have tried to cross the river and drowned, but there was no evidence to believe that it had been a wrecked seafarer. The coast south of the inlet had been searched without result: fires were lit to make smoke, and shots were fired: fishing boats had been in the vicinity frequently and must have been visible to any marooned sailor keeping a watch for rescuers. As no definite evidence of survivors could be found, Crisp sent off a message to the Prime Minister (by carrier pigeon!)

and he and his men also returned to Hobart.

Imagine the public astonishment therefore when a month later the news broke that the fishing ketch "Britannia" was approaching Hobart carrying a survivor of the "Brier Holme", a Norwegian seaman named Oscar Larsen! Excitement was intense, and wild rumours abounded, but everyone – in Tasmania and Maryport alike – awaited the information the rescued man – described in the *Launceston Examiner* as *"none the worse for his experience"*, but who *"had naturally grown shaggy whiskers"* – could supply.

"Britannia" arrives at Hobart

By the time the "Britannia" docked on the evening of February 20th, 2,000 people thronged the dockside to welcome the 'hero' back to civilisation: an official launch, bearing the Port Warden and press representatives set out to tow the fishing boat in and meet Larsen before his arrival.

They were accompanied by no less than the Tasmanian Prime Minister himself, Captain the Hon. J.W. Evans, and it was noticed that the crowd still felt annoyed by his apparent apathy earlier in the rescue attempts: as the *Launceston Examiner* quotes,

At this juncture there was decided evidence that the Premier's action, or inaction, in

connection with the wrecked vessel was not approved of by the people, for Captain Evans, who is usually popular with the crowd, on this occasion was greeted with groans – quite a new experience for him.

Oscar Larson (left) with Capt. Noye of "Britannia"

At subsequent Courts of Inquiry held over the next few days, eagerly reported by the local Press, Oscar Larsen was able to fill in many of the missing pieces of the jigsaw in the mystery of the loss of the "Brier Holme". He recounted that early in November of 1904, as the barque approached the end of its journey, they encountered extremely bad weather: driving rain, fogbanks and strong westerly and north-westerly gales. (This latitude falls within the 'roaring forties' and even in the antipodean summer such conditions, together with mountainous seas, are common.) On November 4th the Captain and the officers had taken their bearings and calculated they the ship was about 100 miles from the mouth of the river on which Hobart lies, but by the following day the conditions were so bad that no observations could be made.

Sailing by 'dead reckoning' the "Brier Holme" turned north-east, and at about six o'clock changed to a northerly course and 'hove to' with only her topsails set. Larsen notes that when he came on watch that evening the second mate was in charge, and the barque was shipping heavy seas from the south. Later that night – between ten and midnight – he was in the forecastle when the cry was heard "All hands on deck!", and within seconds the vessel struck the rocks. Within a very short time the doomed "Brier Holme" filled with water to the rails, her bottom torn open by the reef, and the sea was breaking over the deck. Seven of the crew managed to reach the foremast and clung to the rigging until the pounding of the waves carried it, and them, away. Larsen himself managed to grab some floating spars and was washed ashore alive, but saw only one of his shipmates, a seaman named Muller who was clinging to the jibboom: he too attempted to make for the land, but was swept out to sea (it was presumed that his was the body washed up on the beach later and buried there by the searchers). The fierce breakers and the hungry rocks made short work of the "Brier Holme": her back broke, the mainmast toppled and the stern separated as the ship went down in two pieces.

There is considerable variation between the reports of Oscar Larsen's testimony in the newspapers of Tasmania, mainland Australia, and England as the story broke, causing confusion that in some cases persists to this day. In one report, Larsen tells of seeing a 'flash' or a 'flame' in the after part of the ship as she struck (though he does not say he heard an explosion): from this, the suggestion arose that the ship was blown apart on impact with the rocks by the detonation of the large consignment of dynamite in the cargo. As the Court of Inquiry made clear, this was inaccurate: there was no dynamite aboard the "Brier Holme" at all. The manifest shows that there were kegs of gunpowder, shells for field artillery and primers; not a spontaneously-exploding combination, especially in a hull already completely flooded with seawater. (The ship was carrying quantities of gelatine – is it possible that an enthusiastic but misguided observer misread this as gelignite?) The Court came to the unsurprising conclusion that *"the ship's reckoning was in error"*, but that there was *"no evidence to enable them to determine who was responsible for the loss of the vessel"* and that *"the evidence taken does not support the idea put forward by Larsen that the vessel was blown up as soon as she struck the rocks."*

Oscar Larsen's narrative allowed those concerned to piece together the various strands of the story to explain why neither the wreck nor the castaway was discovered sooner, given that he was only about 14 miles from Port Davey, a commonly-used anchorage for local fishing boats. Armed with Larsen's directions a party found the "Brier Holme", but only with great difficulty: she was almost invisible from land or sea, wedged into a rocky gulch and with only about seven feet of the bow above water. The searching steamers had not been able to approach the shore closely enough to distinguish the wreck because of the reefs and the constant swell, while the dense coastal vegetation hid the site so effectively from inland that Larsen himself had been obliged to mark the track with a piece of red cloth to find his way back to it.

Larsen seems to have missed early rescue by sheer coincidence and bad luck. On a couple of occasions he spotted the search vessels but could not reach the shore quickly enough to attract their attention: when the search party found his camp he was elsewhere, trying to find a track towards civilisation; and although he saw the signal fires lit by Mr. Crisp's group he assumed they were bush fires and took refuge on the beach some distance away for safety! He remained in good condition both mentally and physically (apart from a little scurvy), declaring that he always had confidence that he would be found, and that he had been able to salvage enough food from the cargo that had floated ashore to keep himself well nourished. He existed on a diet of tinned herrings and cans of Neave's Food (a dietary supplement popular at the time, widely advertised for *"Infants, Growing Children, Invalids and the Aged"* and *"Used in the Russian Imperial Nursery"*). Although several cases of liquor were washed up onto the strand Larsen maintained he had not drunk any alcohol – except *"to put in some bad water that he got now and then"*!

It was commented both officially and unofficially that Larsen might well have been rescued much earlier if he had had the initiative to leave some message or trace of his existence at his camp; or to have used an ember from the signal fires to light a beacon of his own; or if he had flown a signal on the foreshore, or kept a better watch. This may have been the basis for the groundless and unworthy rumour circulating at the time that he had been colluding with some of the local fishermen to loot the wreck and had not wanted to be rescued: it may also have accounted for the myth – still perpetuated in some quarters even today – that the "Brier Holme" was carrying gold and jewels worth many thousands of pounds when she went down.

Apart from the single body, presumed to be Seaman Muller, no trace of Capt. Rich, his officers, apprentices or any of the rest of the crew was ever found. A marble memorial to the victims was erected in October 1905 in St. Paul's Church, Dock Street, London: at the unveiling service a large congregation included many of the relatives of the lost seamen and representatives of the Sailors' Home, where many of the crew of the "Brier Holme" had been based when in port. This is not the only memorial: 'Brier Holme Head', just south of Elliott Cove, still features on the maps of the Tasmanian coast marking the scene of the tragedy.

(Incidentally, the body of the prize shorthorn bull – valued at £500 at the time – was washed up: Larsen reported that during the voyage the animal had been so quiet it used to eat biscuits out of his hand.)

Captain J.H. Ritchie

CAPTAIN JAMES RITCHIE, before he retired from the sea for the sake of his health, had been closely connected with Hine Bros. for more than 30 years: since his days in the "Cereal" in 1872, he had captained no less than seven Holme Line vessels – "Hazel Holme", "Myrtle Holme", "Dent Holme", "Fern Holme", "Nether Holme", "Greta Holme" and "Isel Holme" – before taking up the post of Superintendent of Steamships for the Company in 1901. Born in County Down in 1844, he was widely respected and warmly regarded both locally and among his fellow mariners, and was a staunch Presbyterian and teetotaller. Sadly, Captain Ritchie died in September 1905, having collapsed with a stroke on his way home from a lecture at the Presbyterian church. Large numbers attended his funeral, and the *West Cumberland Times* reported that a special carriage was needed to transport all the wreaths sent in his memory.

Captain J.H. Ritchie
Photo courtesy of Mr. D. Ritchie

Chapter Ten
The Gathering Storm: 1906-

THE DEATHS OF CAPTAINS RICH AND RITCHIE in 1905 were followed in the first quarter of 1906 by two further losses. The first was Captain John G. Turney, who had also been in the service of Hine Bros. for many years. Back in 1876 he commanded the "John Norman", and then the ill-fated "Aline". Moving to steamships, he became the master of the "Esk Holme" between 1880 and 1892: then to the "Alne Holme" until 1895 and finally the "Ardmore" until she was sold in 1898 and Capt. Turney retired.

The second death, however, was of a master still in active service, completely unexpected, and even 'closer to home' for the family. The "Forest Holme" had been employed to carry a cargo of phosphates to a French port from Rio de Janiero, and while there Captain Alexander Beaton contracted a malarial fever. He remained acutely ill throughout the return voyage, and although the ship put in to the nearest port (Pauillac on the French Atlantic coast) Captain Beaton's condition did not improve and he died a week later on March 31st 1906. He was only 45 years of age, and only seven years previously had married Mary Hine's daughter, Jane Leighton: they had two little daughters, one of whom was disabled. Capt. Beaton was described as a "capable navigator" and "a cool and resourceful commander, in the wildest of weather": before entering Holme Line service in 1900 he had commanded sail and steam vessels for other companies and was experienced in the Indian and eastern trades. He was well known and liked in the town, and his passing came as a genuine shock to the people of Maryport. A funeral service was held at the port of Boucau, north of Biarritz, and Captain Myles Kirkpatrick was dispatched to supervise the unloading of the "Forest Holme" and to bring her home.

Further changes were to come, as Captain Johnstone announced his retirement in April 1906.

Like Captains Ritchie and Turney, he too had more than 30 years' close association with the Hine brothers, starting in 1872 when he and Alfred became co-owners of the "Jane Harrison". He next commanded the "Glenfalloch", and for 15 years the "Brier Holme". In 1891 he exchanged sail for steam as master of the "Forest Holme" for nine years. After a period on shore due to indifferent health he was able to take to the sea again, taking over the "Loughrigg Holme" for a year in 1901 and as master of the "Isel Holme" since 1902 since Capt. Ritchie's retirement. Capt. Gorley, late of the "Nether Holme", took over the "Isel Holme".

In a different sphere, Wilfrid Hine suffered setbacks too, the first being the death at the end of June of Sir Wilfrid Lawson. Though they had been political adversaries for some years the two men shared a mutual respect and affection spanning decades, and the loss of his friend, together with that of his brother and also of Mr. H.P. Senhouse, affected Wilfrid strongly. The second was another bitter disappointment; his latest attempt to persuade Parliament to approve a Dock Bill was rejected by the House of Lords that month.

The operational problems that had dogged the Holme Line steamers in 1905 also spilled over into this period, when in March the "Abbey Holme" once again found herself in mechanical difficulties. Leaving Maryport on February 24th she had already had to call at Bahia for running repairs on her outward journey, and then had to put into Pernambuco with engine trouble. Her crankshaft had become loose again, piston rods had bent and her main steam pipe had burst, which resulted in a two-month delay (and a hefty £800 bill for repairs). Setting out again in mid-May, the "Abbey Holme" rounded the Horn and reached Iquique, Chile, by mid-August.

After taking on cargo there and in Valparaiso she set off for the homeward journey. In the Straits of Magellan Captain William Brown did not encounter savage natives, as Capt. George Brown had done 25 years before in the "Robert Hine": instead, the "Abbey Holme" encountered Satellite Rock, which holed the ship so seriously that it was judged necessary to beach her on a nearby island to prevent her sinking. Stranded on an exposed shore with two of her holds full of water, the ship summoned urgent assistance from the nearby port of Punta Arenas: a salvage tug responded, bringing steam pumps to keep the "Abbey Holme" afloat while she was towed in for survey and repairs.

The diver's report was encouraging. The holes in the hull could be patched and the ship would then be safe to sail for Buenos Aires where a full examination could be carried out, but the escapade had cost a further ten days' delay for this work to be done, plus the loss of 2,000 tons of cargo. Lloyd's Register of shipping lists the "Abbey Holme"'s movements, and shows that she did not finally reach her destination in New York until December 5th!

The "Loughrigg Holme" was not so lucky. From the records at Lloyd's it seems that this was the first time the vessel had visited the Italian port of Bari, and it was to be the last. Arriving from Swansea with a hold full of coal on April 5th she ran aground on the approaches to the harbour, severely damaging her hull and filling with water. Several attempts were made to refloat her without success, and the Company sent Superintendent of Steamships George Brown to Bari to oversee the salvage attempts. Nothing could be done for the stricken ship, however, and in August the underwriters sold the "Loughrigg Holme" off for scrap: she was purchased by a local company, refloated, towed to Palermo and broken up. Captain Chadwick moved to become master of the "Forest Holme" to replace Capt. Beaton, and left with his new command for Philadelphia. A disgruntled Capt. Brown later reported that he had found the water in Bari undrinkable and the inhabitants dirty, but his grumpiness may have had something to do with being away from home on his silver wedding anniversary!

The "Isel Holme" also made news in March 1906: as she left the Senhouse Dock it was discovered that one of the dock gates could not be closed behind her! This was a potential disaster: as the tide ebbed the drop in sea level could cause ships still inside the basin to ground on the floor of the dock. Despite attempts to close the gate using a tow-rope pulled by the harbour tug the gate remained stuck fast and the dock had to be left to run dry. At low tide a gang of workmen were able to go down into the dock, and discovered that a large rock and an iron bar had become lodged in the channel carrying the gate: these had probably been disturbed by the turbulence from the propeller of the "Isel Holme". The obstruction was removed, and the gates closed again without difficulty at the next high tide. The "Isel Holme" herself was destined to be away from her home port for the next nine months, returning just before Christmas with a cargo of 5,800 tons of iron ore for Messrs. Cammell Laird: the largest single cargo of ore ever shipped into Maryport at the time.

As the "Isel Holme" arrived, the "Forest Holme" was preparing to depart for Baltimore. The ship's company were quoted in the local press as being *"awfully sick"* at the prospect of spending Christmas in the North Atlantic instead of at home ashore, but *"to assuage their disappointment they anticipated Christmas and had a little celebration before sailing"*! The "Greta Holme" (Capt. Millican) was not seen at all in home waters during 1906, as she continued to shuttle across the South Atlantic between the River Plate and Swakopmunde, Namibia.

The "Nether Holme", under Capt. James Roberts, had been engaged on more local trade between Britain and various Mediterranean ports, and her movements as the year ended are well documented. Early in October the ship was bound from Maryport to Swansea to load a cargo of coal destined for the bunkers of the Royal Navy's dockyard in Bermuda, and then to Cape Tormentine to load lumber to bring to Glasgow. The day before departure Captain Roberts discovered his First Officer in a drunken state and fired him, leaving the Company's Liverpool agents with the task of finding a last-minute replacement. As luck would have it, they heard of a young Scottish seaman with a First

Mate's 'ticket' who needed only two more months of seagoing experience in order to be eligible to sit for his Master's Certificate; he was engaged at once (at a salary of £8 per month) and he rushed to Maryport by train to join the ship late the same evening. His name was James Bisset, and he was destined for an illustrious career culminating in becoming the Captain of the "Queen Mary" and "Queen Elizabeth" and Commodore of the Cunard Line.

In his autobiography "Tramps and Ladies", written in 1959, Sir James Bisset, C.B.E., R.D., R.N.R., LL.D. (Cantab.) describes in full and often humorous detail the exploits of the "Nether Holme", her captain and crew, and the vagaries of life aboard a tramp steamer at the time. It was an eventful journey: by the end of the year he had experienced the warmth of Bermuda and the snows of Newfoundland; hurricane-force winds and banks of fog; he had dived into freezing waters to free a hawser that had entwined itself round the propeller; he had set the fractured thighbone of an injured sailor, and arrested a stoker who had gone murderously berserk in the engine room! On the vessel's return he discovered to his consternation that he was still two days short of his target, so he remained with the ship as she continued to Swansea, where he was paid off and discharged. The "Nether Holme" loaded more coal and set off for the Mediterranean while James Bisset, with the absolute minimum permitted experience, went on to study for his 'ticket' (which, needless to say, he obtained without difficulty).

And what of the Hine "Clipper Barques"? News of the Hine ships during 1905 was mixed: the remaining clipper barques had performed well, re-establishing 'normal service' in the wake of the "Brier Holme" tragedy. The "Castle Holme", commanded by Capt. Holman, made a remarkably rapid passage across the Pacific (only 47 days from Newcastle, NSW to Callao in Peru). The "Eden Holme" turned in a sprightly 94 days for the journey from London to Tasmania under her new master Captain George Dulling. The "Myrtle Holme", under Capt. Cobb, encountered severe gales off the coast of Australia and sustained much damage to her bulwarks, rails and stanchions. Despite this she was able to complete the run to Launceston without further mishap or loss of life, and in fact made the journey in only 80 days! She fared better on their return voyage, but lighter winds resulted in a relatively leisurely 117- day run. Such was the reduction in demand for sail, however, that it was over two months before she set out again on July 14th, bound as usual for Tasmania and making landfall in Launceston in 103 days.

In 1906 it was the turn of the "Castle Holme" to suffer a buffeting from the elements, having left London on May 8th with a general cargo of merchandise – including gunpowder – for Launceston and Hobart. At first she enjoyed fine weather and made good times, 'crossing the line' in 44 days, but as she moved southwards and entered the region of the 'Roaring Forties' the picture changed abruptly. Storms reached their height on July 12th, when the "Castle Holme" was rounding the Cape of Good Hope, rolling in a violent wind and repeatedly flooded by towering waves which caused considerable damage to the ship's superstructure, smashing skylights and portholes and filling the saloons, cabins and storerooms with water. At one point Capt. Holman himself was washed from the bridge into the scuppers, and had to be rescued by the courageous Chief Officer, Mr. Weech: fortunately his injuries were confined to severe cuts to the head and damage to his ribs, though the two officers considered themselves very lucky not to have been swept overboard. The tempest continued for another four weeks without respite, blowing the battered barque across the Southern Ocean, but eased as she neared the Tasmanian coast and an exhausted crew brought the "Castle Holme" to anchorage on August 17th after exactly 100 days at sea. The first call was to Launceston's powder wharf to unload the gunpowder; then back to the harbour to discharge just under 1,000 tons of goods, before moving on to Hobart to deliver a further 600 tons.

The third of the remaining barques, the "Eden Holme", was the last to leave. She had left Launceston on February 25th 1906, arriving in London on June 19th, 115 days later. Again, there was a lengthy wait for a cargo and she did not depart until September 16th. As well as goods, the "Eden Holme" carried two passengers on this occasion – a Mr. Haythornthwaite of Carlisle, travelling for the benefit of his health, and his wife. The voyage was uneventful and just before Christmas the ship arrived in Hobart to unload the part of the cargo consigned there: on the 4th January 1907 the "Eden Holme" – still with her passengers aboard – set out for Launceston. Reaching the approaches to the Tamar River late in the evening of the 6th, Capt. Dulling decided to heave to for the night and make for the harbour the next day.

The 7th January dawned fine, with a calm sea and a light east-north-easterly breeze, so at half past five the "Eden Holme" began her approach: the barque's sails had been furled for the night, and only enough canvas had been set to allow her to move at a gentle 3-4 knots towards the channel where she would pick up the harbour pilot. Just after eight o'clock that morning, in response to the Captain's signal, the pilot boarded the "Eden Holme". Peter Mullay was 70 years old and had been the harbour pilot for 20 years, navigating vessels of all sorts into and out of Launceston harbour in all weathers without incident. What happened in the next two hours, however, was about to bring his career to a disastrous end.

Noticing that the "Eden Holme" was using only her mizzen sail, two lower topsails and staysails, the pilot asked Capt. Dulling whether this would be sufficient to 'stay' the vessel; that is, to provide her with enough power to tack or change course if necessary: the captain replied that it would not, so the pilot decided to 'wear ship', or change course in the opposite way from tacking, and go out to sea to wait for a tug which would arrive later that morning. The pilot is in charge of the vessel during this period so Capt. Dulling left the bridge to Mr. Mullay, who set about his plan.

At this point circumstances conspired to produce a catastrophic situation. The wind, which had been light and ENE, veered to the SE and dropped to a light breeze. The "Eden Holme", on an unfavourable tack and relatively unable to make way or respond, was suddenly at the mercy of the ebb tide which at this stage was running strongly at about four knots. Immediately Mr. Mullay called for more sail to be set, ordering the rest of the topsails to be run out:

Capt. Dulling, who had returned to the bridge, pointed out that the topsails were still furled and in their gaskets, and it would take an hour to release them: he suggested loosening the main courses, which would be the quickest way to get sail on. This was done in only about five minutes, but despite this there was insufficient wind to alter the trajectory of the ship in time. Minutes later, with a gentle bump, the "Eden Holme" struck the south-east margin of the Hebe Reef, a submerged rock marked with a buoy, and stuck fast.

Immediate action was vital, and the crew set about trying to save the ship. The sails were rapidly clewed and the ship's boats carried out kedge anchors, by which the "Eden Holme" could be pulled off the reef. In the first half-hour not much seawater had entered the hold and it appeared that little damage had been sustained, but as the minutes went by the water levels began to rise inexorably.

As the tide ebbed so did hope for the stricken barque. The "Eden Holme" was firmly impacted on the rock, listing to starboard, with her hull irrevocably holed and her plates springing open as the level of the sea fell and the current caused more movement of the vessel. The tug arrived arrived about three hours later, but by then it was obvious that the situation was beyond recall. Nothing more could be done except retrieve whatever could be preserved from the wreck. First to leave were the passengers, with their luggage, in one of the ship's lifeboats. Fortunately there had been no casualties, though what effect this had on Mr. Haythornthwaite's health is not recorded.

Over the succeeding few days a concerted effort was made by the authorities to salvage as much of the cargo – and the fittings of the barque herself – as possible. A local steamer moored alongside the wreck, teams of men proceeded to unload the undamaged portion of the contents into barges, and many of the inhabitants and traders of Launceston were eventually able to take delivery of the consignments they had ordered from England. The official sale of the material salvaged raised nearly £1,000: a huge list of items were on offer: everything from the ship's boats and *"one nearly new suit suils"*; *"large quantity cabin fittings and*

Eden Holme" wrecked: cargo salvage in progress

furnishings" and *"about 195 fathoms certified chain cable"* through to *"1 medicine chest (fully stocked)"*, *"10 cwt. prime salt pork"* and *"Quantity butter, tinned meats, treacle, pickles, curry powder, etc."* The "Eden Holme" herself had been insured in London with a book value of £5,000, and Capt. Dulling formally abandoned her to the underwriters the day after the calamity. They were able to sell the corpse of the "Eden Holme" for £265 as scrap iron, but the wind and tides did their work swiftly and mercilessly: within days the vessel parted amidships and she became a total wreck.

The Court of Inquiry into the wreck was held in Launceston on January 23rd 1907 before the Principal Magistrate and two sea captains, and the transcript of the proceedings shows that the matter was scrupulously investigated: both the Captain and the Pilot were legally represented and gave evidence on oath. There was little dispute over the facts of the case – the crux of the matter was the

judgement of Mr. Mullay in firstly, not requesting more 'canvas' at an earlier stage; secondly, not 'wearing away' sooner; and thirdly, not putting down the anchor to prevent the ship drifting into danger. The pilot gave his reasons for his decisions, and maintained that had it not been for the sudden loss of the wind the "Eden Holme" would have passed the reef safely under his charge. Moreover, he called two witnesses in support of his case: Alfred Rockwell, the lighthouse keeper at Low Head, who had watched the whole manoeuvre from the land, and Captain Bradley, the Launceston Harbourmaster, who had 30 years' experience of navigating ships up the Tamar. Both these gentlemen declared that the pilot had acted entirely correctly, and that they would have done exactly the same themselves: Capt. Bradley went on to say that the barque should have been carrying more sail from the outset, *"even before the pilot got on board"*; and that he would have protested to Capt.

Dulling that the upper topsails had not been set. He also averred that he would not have anchored *"except as a last resource"*.

Not surprisingly these arguments failed to impress the tribunal, who found that the casualty was *"due to the want of proper judgement on the part of Pilot Mullay."*. They suspended his certificate for six months; ordered that that he should pay the costs of the inquiry, and formally announced that no blame was attachable to Capt. Dulling.

This calamity marked the 'end of the road' in many ways. Captain Dulling himself, at the age of 27, found himself without a ship, and after only three years as a Captain unlikely to find another command in an already contracted industry. He may also have borne in mind the fate of his younger brother in the "Brier Holme", but in any event he did not return to sea again: he remained in Tasmania and became a farmer. For Pilot Peter Mullay, who had been deeply upset by the "Eden Holme" catastrophe, the suspension marked the end of his working life. The Tribunal had acknowledged his *"long and honourable career without a previous mishap"* and had judged their decision to be *"not too hard on him"*, while his employers declared him *"a most faithful and reliable officer who throughout his long and responsible service had maintained a perfect record without a blot of any kind on his reputation either as regards character or nautical skill and judgement"*. But for a pilot, one mistake is one too many: the Launceston Marine Board awarded him a year's salary, and he retired immediately. Lastly, the final comment upon the whole tragic business comes again from the memoir of Captain John Wyrill:

> *This disaster, following so soon upon the loss of the "Brier Holme", practically rang the knell of the Tasmanian wool clippers.*

Such considerations did not seem to be concerning the Hine family in Maryport, however, and as 1907 dawned Wilfrid was in the news again, promoting yet another new dock scheme for the port – a million-pound project. The *Maryport News* marvelled:

> *Truly Mr. Hine is a wonderful man. Knocked out by the Lords at Westminster midsummer, he comes up smiling at Maryport in the New Year.... He is a Napoleon of business who regards obstacles merely as things to be overcome.*

But while going on to praise Wilfrid's persistence and determination, the report sounds two notes of warning. The local public, after the chequered financial history of the harbour in the past and the disputes over the various schemes put forward in the preceding decade, might well be less than totally enthusiastic about this one either.

Furthermore, the report continues

> *...it is no use shutting our eyes to the fact that now Messrs. Cammell Laird have acquired Workington Harbour they will endeavour to to divert to it the traffic which formerly went there but which during recent years has been coming here owing to the silting up of the Workington channel.*

Nonetheless, the piece concludes:

> *On the other hand the prospect of a new deep-water dock attracting work here must not be lost sight of. Cheap sites and cheap water carriage are becoming of more value... where it becomes necessary to produce on the most economical lines if a hold of the market is to be retained.*

For the Holme Line and Hine Bros., internal changes were beginning to manifest themselves. For some time Alfred Ernest Hine, Wilfrid's son, had been in charge of the London office of the Company, while Alfred Hine Junior was increasingly assuming the role his late father had taken. Living at Park Hill, he was working with his uncle at the head of the Maryport Office, and had been elected unopposed as a Harbour Commissioner. He was elected to the local committee of the National Lifeboat Institute in March (as was Mr. Guy P. Senhouse, also stepping into his deceased father's shoes) and as Captain Hine he still remained an active army reservist with the local Volunteer Company. He was also the Captain of the Golf Club. For some time, he had been the proud owner of one of the first motor cars in the area – and indeed had also committed one of the first motoring offences in the area, being 'booked' and fined one shilling in 1904 for the technical offence of "neglecting to stop when requested to do so by the driver of a restive horse". He was in trouble again in 1906, when his car collided with a cart on a corner. Alfred wrote to the newspaper complaining about their version of the incident, making the point that he had made a wide turn, was on the correct side of the road and was not travelling 'swiftly', as the paper had reported: this prompted the ever-acid 'Ewanrigg' to comment that what may not be swift to a motorist is swift to a horse driver!

His brother John McLennan Hine had also begun to make his name known in the town. He was involved in various sporting activities, and had founded the Maryport branch of the Boys' Brigade. He had trained as a marine engineer, and after being involved with the Holme Line ships directly for some time he decided in 1906 to set up the independent 'Solway Engineering and Ship Repair Company Ltd.' in Maryport. The press welcomed the project, which had established itself in a yard in Irish Street, but commented that *"the town loses heavily each year by the absence of a dry dock in the port"* – a point Wilfrid had made repeatedly in his campaigns for the dock schemes he championed over the years.

Wilfrid himself continued to feature in the town's life as he had done for over 40 years: the dock scheme; church affairs; the coffee tavern; the lifeboat committee; the hospital committee; the British School, the district council. In March 1907 he topped the poll and was returned as Councillor for the north ward of the town, and all seemed set for another routine, busy year.

Then, in July, the thunderbolt struck. On Saturday July 6th 1907 everyone who had financial connections with Hine Bros. received a letter from Lightfoot and Lightfoot, the Company's lawyers. It informed them that they had called in Messrs. Lewis and Mounsey (a well-known firm of accountants specialising in shipping matters, practising in Liverpool and London)

...to investigate the affairs of the firm, with a view to preparing a statement for submission to creditors.

Ominously, the letter went on:

We had hoped that the meeting of creditors might have been delayed until Messrs. Lewis and Mounsey were able to make a complete investigation, but having regards to circumstances which have arisen since we were consulted we have thought it desirable in the interests of the creditors that the meeting should be called without delay, and the accountants will submit the result of their investigation so far as it has proceeded.

The meeting was scheduled for the following Wednesday at a hotel in Carlisle, and anyone with claims against the Company was asked to submit them straightaway.

Given the numbers of people in West Cumberland affected by this situation – chandlers and suppliers provisioning the vessels; tradesmen and artisans servicing them; the workers in the docks who loaded and unloaded them; the staff employed by Hine Bros. in its various offices in Maryport, Workington and Whitehaven; the ships' captains, officers and seamen and their families, and of course the significant body of local citizens who had invested their capital to buy shares in the ships themselves – this announcement caused a sensation throughout the region. The Crown and Mitre Hotel was packed to the doors with the worried and the curious when the meeting got under way: several companies and businesses sent their legal representatives. The press was in attendance, too: the *Whitehaven News* carried a full – almost verbatim – report of the proceedings in its next edition, while the Maryport press carried wide-ranging coverage and comment. The meeting was chaired by a Mr. McCartney, a shipowner from Newcastle, who opened proceedings by calling on Mr. Lightfoot, the solicitor, to outline the situation.

The picture as it unfolded looked more and more serious. The trigger for these events was that the week before, the shipowners and insurers

C.F. Bowring of Liverpool had presented the Company with a bill for £7,000 and it was found that there were no funds to pay it. In the scale of Hine Brothers' normal commercial dealings this was a relatively minor sum, but the accountants' investigations revealed an alarming state of affairs in the firm's finances overall. The steamships had not been paying their way for years (stagnation in shipping freight rates and the cost of repairs to the ageing vessels being the main factors) and the shares that Hine Bros. owned in the ships had been used as security for huge mortgage loans to prop up the business. The sailing vessels had been losing money regularly with each voyage, as they became less and less competitive in the modern transport era. The likelihood of the creditors recouping their outlay – or the other part-owners of the ships seeing a return of their investment – was small, they were told, though if the ships and other assets of the company could be liquidated on favourable terms there might be some nominal repayment. To the dismay of those who had attended the meeting hoping that the problem was temporary and that arrangements could be made whereby things went on as before, Mr. Lightfoot, and after him the accountant Mr. Mounsey, made it very plain that the Company was insolvent.

The major sensation, however, then came from Mr. Lightfoot, who announced that the overall shortfall in the Hine Bros. account amounted to around £20,000 – (over £1.5 million in present terms) and that they had discovered that there had been 'serious irregularities' in the London end of the business, which accounted for most if not all of the deficit. He made it clear that, to quote the press report:

> There had been a considerable amount of conduct that could not be supported. Mr. Hine and Mr. Alfred Hine were in no way responsible for that, though they might be legally as regards a civil remedy. There had been wrong dealings, as he had made clear..., and that the sum would not be recoverable. There were certain assets connected to the London office, but although these had been valued ut £7,700 they were likely to prove of doubtful value.

In answer to a question from a creditor Mr. Lightfoot admitted that Wilfrid and Alfred themselves had not been aware of the position until very recently, when they had called him in; but Mr. Mounsey revealed that there had been no balance sheet produced for the firm's books since 1902. He also told the meeting that the whole situation was complicated by the fact that the company did not hold separate accounts for the different departments of the business, but all moneys – including, for example, the insurance repayment for the "Eden Holme" – went into one bank account and were thus untraceable in audit terms. (He did add, however, that this was by no means uncommon in the shipping world.)

The meeting then went on to consider what was to be done, if anything, and at this point the expert knowledge of the lawyer, the accountant and the Chairman came into its own. They explained that the creditors could vote to declare the Company bankrupt and call in the Official Receiver, but this would incur much higher legal costs – with less funds left over for creditors – and probably considerable delay, given the complexities of maritime law and commerce. The alternative resolution, which Messrs. McCartney, Mounsey and Lightfoot spent a long time urging the anxious, confused and angry meeting to adopt, was to agree a Deed of Assignment, whereby the estate would be administered by Trustees and a Committee of Inspection. This could deal with the Company's affairs in order to wind up the business on the best terms possible: for instance, it was pointed out that if the steamships were to be sold they would fetch better prices in home ports than abroad. The Committee would have the experience of the shipping business that was needed at this time, and indeed Mr. McCartney revealed that:

> he and others had been carrying on an undertaking for £100,000 for years and kept paying their way, and had saved many thousands that would have been lost had it gone into bankruptcy.

He went on to advise the gathering bluntly that:

They might save money by this resolution, but otherwise it was hopeless.

He also pointed out that the agreement of the owners of the principal mortgages had to be obtained – not all had attended the meeting – but it was generally assumed that they too would wish to salvage as much as possible from the wreckage of the Company. (A series of hasty consultations took place over the following few hours, and this turned out to be the case.) One of these, Messrs. Chance and Service of Glasgow, held mortgages for nearly £50,000 on various Holme Line steamers.

On this gloomy note the creditors finally agreed the resolution, recognising that only by these means could there be any hope at all of repaying the Company's debts and the co-owners' investments. Mr. Mounsey was appointed the Trustee of the Estate, and Mr. McCartney agreed to serve on the Committee. The other members of the Committee were Mr. Bowring of Liverpool and Mr. John Dowthwaite, a Maryport man who had previously been a manager for Hine Bros., but was present at the meeting as a creditor – to the tune of £3,000! It was then decided that separate meetings of the shareholders of each of the ships would be held the following week, and the meeting broke up.

The following week's sessions were a lot more rancorous. As Mr. Mounsey and Mr. Lightfoot were the only ones dealing with the totality of the business the creditors of the various individual ships found themselves in a queue to have their matters dealt with, and invariably tempers shortened as the early meetings overran their time. Eventually they decided to combine the steamship meetings and then deal with the sailing ships; but what the shareholders heard did not improve their mood at all. The sailing ships' accounts had been audited regularly, but ran at a loss: of the steamers only the "Greta Holme" (on charter delivering livestock from South America to South Africa) had made any money at all: the steamers netted a profit of only £1,000 in all, in five years. Mr. Mounsey agreed with one of the lawyers present that the only asset was the difference between the mortgages and the steamers' value. He also agreed that the Company's

London office books were *"a complete mess"*, and that no-one from the local office knew anything about this. Mr. Leighton of the Maryport office was summoned to the "Castle Holme" meeting and suffered a very uncomfortable few minutes of interrogation, but as charters for the barque were all handled in London (interestingly, at this point Mr. Lightfoot is reported to have interjected *"By Mr. A.E. Hine"*) he couldn't answer the creditors' queries. Feelings obviously began to run high, and at one point Mr. Lightfoot is reported to have indignantly refuted a suggestion that he and Mr. Mounsey were concealing matters from the shareholders!

After five hours the meetings finally drew to a close. On a lighter note the Maryport press noted *"under these circumstances it is not surprising that Mr. Lightfoot, who was on his legs a goodly proportion of the time, found it necessary to send out for a refresher in the shape of a cup of tea!"* It was agreed that the principal mortgagees would take over the running of the various vessels until they could be returned to home ports and sold at advantageous prices, while the two remaining clipper barques would be sold off as soon as possible.

At the first meeting there had been expressions of sympathy for Wilfrid in his misfortune, and the usually critical 'Ewanrigg' commented:

It is a heavy blow for one of Mr. Hine's age to see the fruits of a lifetime of hard work and often at times of perplexing worry, swept away at one stroke of cruel fortune.

He went on to commiserate with Wilfrid's wife and sister-in-law Mary, who

...have won the respect and goodwill of the Maryport people by their readiness to help others. There has been no movement having for its object the betterment of any section of Maryport but has had their cordial support and oftimes practical aid.

By the following week, however, the feelings of the townspeople had apparently changed: Ewanrigg writes:

The calamity that has befallen the Holme Line is a bad thing for Maryport and for the shareholders. Some of the latter are sorely tried about it, and no doubt it is difficult when a man loses money to accept the loss philosophically. Yet it is no use crying over spilt milk, no use a man wearing himself out by fuming and fretting....

He also reminds them of the risky nature of their investment, with the salutary words:

But with shipping it is generally a case of 'enjoy the fat years', and some of the shareholders in the Holme Line have had their good years: they have in the past opened letters at their breakfast tables containing fat cheques....

How much good these no doubt well-meaning observations did is not clear, but there is no indication of any sympathy or good will expressed locally in response at any time thereafter.

For Wilfrid, the position could hardly be worse: financial ruin stared him in the face. Hine Bros. was not a Limited Company (it was revealed later that Wilfrid had investigated the possibility of forming a limited company some years before, but because of various legal and other complications – and possibly Alfred's death – he had not proceeded with the matter). Thus his personal fortune, his house and possessions were included in the assets of the company and were vulnerable to the demands of the administrators. Moreover the revelations about the disorganised state of the business and his own unawareness of it; the true state of the finances of the ships and the Company itself, and the obvious implication that his own son Alfred E. Hine was responsible for serious irregularities in the conduct of business in London which basically had brought down the whole edifice around him, must have added deep humiliation to his woes. A potent indication of the depth of his reaction came the following week, when the *Maryport News* reported that Wilfrid had resigned all his appointments at his beloved Trinity Baptist Church: he subsequently gave up every public office and committee position he held, and never attended another meeting of the district or county councils.

Within a month, advertisements appeared offering Park Hill and Camp Hill for sale by auction in September. The prospectus for the sale makes it clear that the brothers had spared no expense in the past to equip the houses to a high standard, and the adjoining outhouses – a conservatory, stables and 'motor shed with inspection pit' , plus a gardener's cottage – made them, in the words of the auctioneer, Mr. Joseph Kendall, *"the most valuable residential property ever offered in the history of Maryport"*. Despite this, and despite what he described as the "give-away price" of £2,000 for the two houses together (they had cost £4-5,000 each to build, he said) Mr. Kendall failed to attract a single bid for the houses, even offering them separately and at the nominal price of £500 – as he put it *"less than for a Curzon Street house"*. The houses were withdrawn from the sale, the auctioneer commenting that there was obviously no demand for them – not a helpful conclusion for the committee of administrators!

The dismantling of the Holme Line continued, however, with the sale of the vessels: the first to go was the "Nether Holme", for £7,500 in October, to a Welsh company. This was somewhat less than the £9,000 'book value' quoted at the shareholders' meeting, but the mortgages on the vessel amounted only to £1,100. (Incidentally, while in transit to Cardiff under her new owners and the command of a new captain the "Nether Holme" ran aground and was wrecked on the rocks of the Pembrokeshire coast.)

In November the "Isel Holme" went under the hammer and was sold for £20,000: this was the largest and most modern ship of the fleet and she went to the Nautilus Steam Shipping Company, Ltd. of Sunderland, who renamed her the "Myrtle Branch". Her sale did not benefit Hine Bros., however: she had been valued at £30,000, and the mortgages accounted for the whole of the proceeds of the sale. Next to go was the "Greta Holme", sold abroad by auction the same month for a reported £13,000 – again, not reaching her valuation of £16,000, and mortgaged by £4,000 (plus another £3,000 owed to a Mr. Constantine of

Wreck of "Nether Holme", December 1907

two clipper barques "Myrtle Holme" and "Castle Holme" were sold to foreign buyers, the "Castle Holme" raising only £2,000 from a Norwegian firm. This left only the "Forest Holme" (Capt. Chadwick), in the nominal ownership of the Company but managed by the mortgagees until she too was sold in 1911.

The family too began to disperse. In January 1908 the press recorded the Boys' Brigade's farewell to its C.O., John McLennan Hine, who it noted had *"secured an appointment in Luton"*. In February it was Alfred Hine who was leaving, receiving *"a smoker's cabinet and other smoker's requirements"* from his fellows in the Cricket Club, of which he had been captain for some time. At the presentation it is recorded that

> *...Mr. Hine replied in an admirable speech in which he said that he was glad to find that his were not fair weather friends, but friends who stood by him in the storm as in the sunshine.*

Their cousin William Leighton, who had been a senior clerk in the Maryport office, had departed three months earlier for Hull, where he had found a post with a large shipping firm.

George and Barbara Brown remained in Maryport, but tragedy struck their family as the year ended. Barbara's son by her first marriage, Alfred Robinson, was 33 years old (it was he who had been born in Australia after the maiden voyage of the "Eden Holme" in 1875). He served in several of the Holme Line steamers, and at the time of the firm's collapse was Chief Engineer of the "Isel Holme". Returning from Workington on his motorcycle one afternoon in November 1908, he met a caravan on the wrong side of the road at a bend: swerving to avoid it, Alfred 'ran out of road' and collided with the wall and parapet of a bridge. He sustained severe head injuries and died shortly after. (He had been due to travel with his stepfather to Glasgow the next day: Capt. Brown was taking charge of a new ship launched there, and Alfred would have sailed with him as Chief Engineer to deliver her to her owners at le Havre.)

Middlesborough and awarded by the Court of Appeal in 1908). This litigation, together with an unsuccessful attempt by the shareholders to have the "Isel Holme" seized in America, was widely believed to have discouraged potential buyers of the ships, resulting in the disappointing returns.

In 1908 the dispersal of the Holme Line was complete. The steamship "Abbey Holme" and the

Wilfrid himself remained in Maryport with Jane and his daughters, and in October had had to suffer the indignity of seeing their house sold in circumstances bordering on the bizarre. At another auction, this time held at the Golden Lion Hotel by a different auctioneer, the property once again failed to attract any bids at all at the starting price of £1,000: and when the owner of the Hotel offered £100 for the two houses – the lot having been offered for sale with no reserve – she found herself the new chatelaine of the £10,000 'Hine Mansions'! Quite what the administrators of the estate thought of this outcome is not recorded, but it was another massive blow to hopes of salvaging the situation for Hine Bros.

So at the age of 70 Wilfrid faced up to the prospect of earning the money to make ends meet for his family. He went back into business as a shipbroker, working from an office on the North Quay (the premises at Custom House Buildings were up for sale) and set to work. In January 1909 he was mentioned in the *Maryport News* again, for almost the first time since the collapse of the firm. On his way down Shipping Brow to his office he slipped on an icy path and fell, knocking himself out. The report goes on to mention that:

> although he has suffered pain he has not been incapacitated for work. Mentally, it may be noted, Mr. Hine has lost none of the cheerful optimism and strenuous energy that have characterised him throughout life. He has been instrumental in shipping a cargo of coal to Tunis, where Cumberland coal has never been shipped before, in the hope of opening up a new trade.

Kelly's Directory for 1910 lists *"Hine Bros., Shipowners and Coal Exporters"* at North Quay; but in the following year the "Forest Holme" was sold and the Maryport office closed down.

The 1911 Census returns show that Wilfrid, Jane and three of their unmarried daughters had left Maryport and were living in a Private Hotel in Bayswater, London. Their youngest son, Robert Wilfrid, listed as an "Actor and Vocalist", and his wife Marion – also an "Actress" in the census – were living with her mother in Mitcham, London. Of the eldest son, Alfred E. Hine, the former head of the office of Hine Bros. and Willis in London, there is no sign.

Mary, Alfred's widow, still lived in Maryport but on the day of the Census she was recorded as a 'Visitor' with her married daughter Ethel Pye-Smith in Sheffield. John McLennan Hine, his wife and their four children lived in West Bridgford, Nottingham, where he declared he was working for an Insurance company as a marine engineer.

Alfred Hine was living in Lewes, Sussex, with his younger brother Wilfrid and his sister Mary. Alfred is listed as a 'Motor Engineer' and 'Employer', with Wilfrid as 'Assisting in the Business' and 'Worker'.

So, with another Alfred and another Wilfrid Hine embarking on another venture, the story closes: ...or does it?

Chapter Eleven
The End of the Line?

THERE HAS ALWAYS BEEN UNCERTAINTY about the 'End of the Line' for Hine Bros. and the Holme Line fleet. From a purely commercial standpoint the end came in mid-1907, when the Company went into administration with huge debts and inadequate assets. As a 'fleet' the end must be counted as 1908, when all but two of the ships were sold to other owners. It was 1911 when the last steamer, the "Forest Holme", was finally disposed of; when the office of Hine Bros. in Maryport closed for the last time, and when Wilfrid (now living in genteel poverty in London) described himself in the Census as 'Merchant' and not 'Shipowner and Broker' as he had done before. It is also the year determined by John McLennan Hine's son Alfred in his account of the Holme Line in "Sea Breezes" in 1959. Yet there is a strange footnote to the story, still unexplained a century later.

At the end of 1912 the Prince Steam Shipping Company of Newcastle put up one of their steamers for sale: this was the "Imperial Prince", a 2,500-tonner built in 1890 by Short Bros. of Sunderland and resembling in many ways the ships J.L. Thompson & Sons had built for Hine Bros. in the past:

Lloyd's Register for December 1912 records the change of ownership in an entry added in ink, declaring the new owners to be the *"Holme Line S.S. Co. Lim."* : but who the owners of this company were, or the address of its offices, remains a mystery (no further details are given in the Register, except that the company owned all 64 shares). This new title was not one Hine Bros. had used in the past; they had never been a Limited Company, and neither Wilfrid, his family or the Administrators were apparently in any position to raise the cash to buy a steamer! The ship had been trading around the Mediterranean ports and North Africa for the Prince Line and seems to have been at Constantza, in the Black Sea, at the time of the sale: by March 1913 she had returned to the Tyne to load a cargo of coal for Dakar, West Africa. From there she steamed to Gambia and collected a shipload of peanuts for Marseilles: having delivered these on May 1st, she moved to Carthagena and loaded up with iron ore, ready for her first visit to her new home port.

The "Imperial Prince" not only looked like a Hine Bros. steamer, with a high stem and a clipper stern, but had other similarities: in particular, the lines necessary to enter Maryport docks. According to the register she was 40 feet in breadth, and had a shallow draught of only 18 feet and 5 inches.

Loaded with iron ore, however, she drew 27 feet, and so had to coordinate her arrival with the spring high tide – which she managed to miss because of rough weather. After lying at anchor outside the harbour for a fortnight waiting for the next opportunity she attempted to enter on June 4th 1913 and promptly ran aground in the channel, just outside the harbour entrance! Fortunately she could be refloated at the next high tide, and was towed into dock by the harbour tug the following day. After this singularly inglorious arrival the cargo of ore was discharged and a load of bunkering coal loaded, whereupon Mrs. Barbara Brown – sister of Wilfrid and wife of Captain George Brown – appeared at the dock and in a short ceremony renamed the ship the **"Myrtle Holme"**! The day following the ceremony, June 14th 1913, the latest 'Holme Line' vessel set sail for Canada.

The role of the Hine family in this whole affair is not clear, but involvement there certainly was: in the *Whitehaven News* of July 24th 1913, the following appeared:

Mr. Hine, of the Holme Line Steam Ship Company who left Maryport last week for London was taken ill on the journey, and collapsed on arrival. He is now lying seriously ill in a nursing home.

Apart from this cryptic item, however, no further details are known: not even which of the three possible Mr. Hine's (Wilfrid, Alfred Ernest or Alfred Junior) was the patient!

The ship's schedule was to deliver the bunkering coal to various ports on the eastern seaboard, then collect a load of timber and return to Garston, on the Mersey. After leaving Canada problems arose: whether due to poor loading of the cargo or other factors the "Myrtle Holme" started to list alarmingly to port. The list became so pronounced that it was necessary to call 'all hands on deck!' and the crew had to spend one night frantically dumping the timber loaded on the deck overboard, and shovelling coal from one bunker to another, to right the vessel. On a more or less even keel once more the ship limped into Liverpool, unloaded what was left of the timber and spent the next three weeks in dry dock at Birkenhead for repairs.

On August 23rd, the "Myrtle Holme" set off again, having loaded coal at Newport for Santos in Brazil. Fortunately this leg of the voyage was trouble-free, as the cargo also included 1,000 tons of explosives for Rio de Janiero! Lloyd's list notes her arrival on October 3rd, leaving three days later with holds full of manganese ore. She was bound for Baltimore, U.S.A., but again trouble was brewing: a serious leak on the port side below the waterline meant she had to put in to Pernambuco (now Recife). Repairs took a whole month, so the ship did not arrive in Baltimore until December 3rd. The next call was Tampa, Florida, where the "Myrtle Holme" took on board a cargo of phosphate rock to be delivered to Cette (now Sète) in France, and on January 1st 1914 she set sail.

Once again misfortune dogged the voyage: a few days out the Master, Captain J. Roberts, became seriously ill. (He probably suffered a stroke: Nanson Holm, the mess room steward, described that he "had to be fed like a child".) The Chief Officer took over and the ship diverted its course to put in at

Gibraltar. Capt. Roberts was taken ashore to hospital, but died the next day.

The "Myrtle Holme" reached Cette on February 3rd at five in the morning, and the steward was astonished to see Capt. George Brown on the dockside. (In his account the steward referred to him as "The Company's Marine Superintendent", though in the 1911 Census return Capt. Brown had declared himself 'Out of Employment'). He had been alerted by telegraph from Gibraltar and had travelled down immediately to supervise matters – a major undertaking for one in his mid-sixties, in mid-winter in pre-WW1 Europe. The ship was unloaded, and under a replacement captain took on a consignment of iron ore for Barrow-in-Furness, where once again Captain Brown awaited their arrival. As Nanson Holm put it, years later, *"...it had been a voyage of misfortune and loss..."*, and Captain Brown brought it to a conclusion on March 14th 1914 when he paid off the crew for the last time. A new crew moved the ship to Liverpool, where she was sold – ironically, to Thompsons of Sunderland, the very company who built the ships that had been the foundation of the Holme Line's success. However, to confuse the picture further, an entry in Lloyd's List on September 17th 1914 refers to the luckless steamer being aground again – this time, near Suez – and when a report of this appeared in the Maryport press the following week the ship was still described as being *"owned by Messrs. Hine Bros. of Maryport"*.

Far from reviving the fortunes of the Holme Line (if that was indeed the aim) the "Myrtle Holme" must have returned a huge financial loss during her short but ill-fated career. Loss of part of her cargo; two protracted delays in deliveries, and extensive, expensive repairs in foreign yards all add up to disappearing profits at a time of slump in the shipping trade. She does not feature in the Lloyd's Register thereafter, and nor does the 'Holme Line Steam Ship Company'.

In December 1914 the affairs of the Company were finally wound up. The Committee of Inspection and the Trustee – appointed by the creditors over seven years previously – produced their report, which included the following excerpt:

The realisation of the estate has presented great difficulties and involved a large amount of litigation. At the time of the execution of the Deed of Assignment it was anticipated that a substantial dividend would be paid, a large surplus over the amount of the mortgages being anticipated from the sale of the shares in the steamers. This anticipation has not been realised as the action of certain creditors in seizing one of the steamers in America (though finally unsuccessful) made buyers chary of purchasing the vessels, with the result the mortgagees had to hold the steamers for a considerable time and the amount ultimately realised was insufficient to meet their claim...

...The accounts show a balance in hand of £4,302 – 7s – 11d. (£4,302.39), which sum is equivalent to one shilling and one and fifteen sixteenths of a penny (approximately 6p.) in the pound.

By this time, however, history had moved on, and events on a worldwide scale consigned the affairs of Hine Bros. and the Holme Line to obscurity; while with the collapse of the Company Maryport sank into a decline from which it has not since recovered. As far back as January 1909 'Ewanrigg' had described the situation as

...a blow from which Maryport has not yet recovered. It shook confidence, impaired credit, lessened the amount of money spent in the town, caused not a few families to seek fresh fields and pastures new, to the detriment of local trade and the value of local property because others have not come to take their place.

The original colliery at Ellenborough had closed in 1912, adding to the economic troubles of the town; and although another mine opened at Risinghow after 1914 the damage was done. The plan for a new deep water dock had long been abandoned, and as 'Ewanrigg' had

predicted Workington soon took over what remained of the shipping business in the area. As late as 1965 the *West Cumberland News* commented

...It is, however, nostalgic to think, and the older inhabitants will do so, that had the Ellenborough Colliery lasted another two years, and the "Myrtle Holme" made a profit on those two last voyages, the outbreak of war would have made both colliery and shipping line a nationally necessary asset. ...it could have grown again under the needs of war. Against this, it would have had to move its trade, if not its headquarters, away from Maryport with the trend for ships to get bigger and bigger and carry vastly more tonnage....

Time, and global conflict, hastened the passing of the family too. By this time, of course, the Great War had begun: Captain Alfred Hine re-enlisted at the age of 46 and went to war in France. So did his younger brother Wilfrid, who joined the Royal Sussex Regiment as Alfred had done in the Boer War: he was made a Lieutenant, was wounded at Arras but survived the war. John McLennan Hine did not: at 42 years old he joined the Royal Navy and was an Engineer Lieutenant aboard H.M.S. "Invincible".

H.M.S. "Invincible", 1916

Lt J McLennan Hine, 1916

grievous loss for Wilfrid after nearly 60 years of marriage: and when his daughter Jane Fletcher Hine died on February 2nd 1921 it must have seemed another crushing blow to him. Three weeks later Wilfrid too passed on, 83 years old and far from his Cumbrian roots, and was buried in Hampstead Cemetery,.

The *West Cumberland News* devoted extensive coverage to Wilfrid in its edition of February 26th 1921, although it was more than a decade since he had left Maryport and the Holme Line had folded. As well as an obituary which enumerated all his activities in support of church, politics, education, the courts and civic administration, there was a lengthy commentary article which after opening by recognising Wilfrid's vigour, energy and capacity for sustained hard work went on to a trenchant appraisal of his aspirations and the missed opportunities:

He lost his life, as did all but six of the ship's company of over 1,000 men, when the battleship was sunk by enemy gunfire at the Battle of Jutland on May 31st 1916.

Joseph Jackson Hine died following surgery at the Cumberland Infirmary, Carlisle in June 1915, and his obituary notes that four of his surviving children now lived abroad (including Ernest and Myrtle, née Millican, in Buenos Aires; and Joseph, the younger son, who had enlisted in the Canadian Brigade).

The family of Wilfrid and Jane Hine now centred round London. It has not been possible to trace the whereabouts of Alfred Ernest Hine, but Robert Wilfrid 'Bob' Hine was in Mitcham, while Anne Hine had become Mrs. Martin Moser and was living in Beckenham. The other four daughters, all still single, lived close to their parents in West London. Mary Christina worked as a secretary, Isabella was a teacher and Elfrida, the youngest, a milliner, sharing Wilfrid and Jane's address and possibly supporting them financially too: Jane Fletcher Hine, the eldest daughter, lived nearby in Leinster Square.

Jane Hine died in the summer of 1920, a

...In him we saw a rare combination of mind, determination and will that, had it been united with a command of capital, would have made Maryport a second Middlesborough. He was a man of big ideas... Wilfrid Hine thought in fleets, in deep water docks. And now the host of weak-eyed men in Maryport living must recognise that Wilfrid Hine was a man of vision. He fought strenuously, but unfortunately without success, for a new deep water dock at Maryport, and the Workington project proves how truely he read the riddle of the future. An optimist of optimists, he was just the man wanted in a cautious community that looks so long before it leaps that it never leaps at all. Unfortunately, Maryport only gave birth to one Wilfrid Hine. Had it produced a score the town would today have ranked as a first class port.

The piece continues

...and no man loved his native place with more sincere affection than Wilfrid Hine... (He) would fain have followed in the footsteps of that other energetic, strong-minded son of

Maryport Thomas Ismay, and had his ambitions been realised it would have been Maryport not Liverpool that would have reaped the benefit.

It is easy – perhaps too easy – in hindsight to categorise the factors involved in the collapse of the Holme Line. Following the death of his brother Alfred, Wilfrid may well have found the sheer amount of work involved in running the business too much: he may have overestimated the capacity of Alfred Hine junior to match his father's skills, or misplaced his confidence in his own son to cope with the London office. He may have allowed himself to 'take his eye off the ball' while attending to the affairs of the church, the coffee tavern, the Harbour Commission, the district council and his campaigns for a new dock. He may have given insufficient consideration to external factors – the era of the merchant sailing ship was long gone; the trend towards bigger cargo steamers had overtaken the Hine fleet, and the passenger trade (as Ismay and the White Star Line had shown) had passed the smaller ports by. His age and his own failing health may also have affected Wilfrid's judgement and performance at this crucial period. However, none of this should detract from the value of Wilfrid and Alfred's 40 years of commitment, enterprise and hard work, plus the courage, loyalty and calibre of those who supported them in their endeavour – shipbuilders; captains, officers and crews; wives, children and families; townspeople, colleagues and neighbours – all combining to paint an impressive picture of what could be achieved from a small town on the windy Cumberland coast.

Alfred Hine, 1841-1902

Wilfrid Hine, 1838-1921

Mary Hine née Eaglesfield

Jane Hine

Appendix
Hine Bros. Fleet List

"ABBEY HOLME"
Iron Barque
Built Blumer & Co., Sunderland
Launched 16/9/1869
Length 157ft 7in Breadth 28ft 2in Depth 17ft
587 tons gross 522 tons NNR
Owners: Nicholson & Co., Liverpool (Wilfrid Hine,
manager) 1869-73: then Hine Bros.
Captains: 1869-73 W. Robinson; 1874-6 Randall;
1876-81 Bryce; 1882-90 Rich
Wrecked South Shields, 8/4/1890

S.S. "ABBEY HOLME"
Steel Screw Steamer
Built J.L. Thompson & Sons, Sunderland
Engines by G. Clark of Sunderland
Launched 1899
Length 342ft Breadth 45ft 2in depth 16ft 1in
3105 tons gross 2861 under decks, 1996 net
Captains: 1899-1908 W. Brown
Sold foreign, 1908; re-named "Rigel"; scrapped
1927

"AIKSHAW"
Iron Barque
Built Doxford & Co., Sunderland
Launched 1873
Length 171ft Breadth 28ft 9in Depth 18ft
596 tons gross 573 net
Part-owned by Hine Bros. 1875-7 then wholly-
owned
Captains: 1875-8 Tyson (part-owner); 1879-88
Tate; 1889 Humphreys; 1890 Dawson; 1891
Cobb
Wrecked S. America, Dec. 1891

"ALINE"
Iron Barque
Built Hardie, Sunderland
Launched 1867
Length 141ft 3in Breadth 29ft 7in Depth 18ft 2in
474 tons gross
Owners: Ord & Co., Sunderland 1867-72 then
    Hine Bros. 1872-80
Captains: 1872-80 J.G. Turney
Wrecked S. America, 13/9/1880

"ALNE HOLME"
Iron Screw Steamer
Built J.L. Thompson & Sons Sunderland
Engines J. Dickinson, Sunderland
Launched 6/7/1876
Length 220ft 3in Breadth 31ft Depth 16ft 9in
1036 tons gross 658 net
Captains: 1876 J. Wilkinson; 1877-8 R.A. Turney;
    1879-89 C. Markham; 1890-1 T. Morwick;
    1891-5 J.G. Turney
Wrecked 5/5/1895, Burriana, Spain

"ARDMORE"
Iron Screw Steamer
Built Bartram, Sunderland
Engines Fowler & McCollin, Hull
Launched 1872
Length 215ft 8in Breadth 30ft Depth 15ft 2in
928 tons gross 597 net
Owners: 1872-4 Ross & Co., Liverpool; 1875-8 St.
    Andrews S.S. Co., L'pool; 1878-9 W. Johnston
    & Co., L'pool; 1880-92 Hine Bros.
Captains: 1880-5 M. Kirkpatrick; 1886 Capt.
    Smith; 1887 M. Kirkpatrick; 1888-98 P.J.
    Greggans
Sold 1898; stranded Pentland Firth, 20/8/99

"BAVINGTON"
Iron Screw Steamer
Built Hope, Newcastle
Engines Wilson & Hall, Dunstonl
Launched 1873
Length 81ft Breadth 19ft 5in Depth 8ft 6in
79 tons gross 47 net
Owners: 1873-9 various; 1880-3 Hine Bros.
Captains: 1880-2 Connell; 1883 Tully
Wrecked Maryport, Sept. 1883

(no photograph available)

"BRIER HOLME"
Iron Barque
Built J.L. Thompson & Sons, Sunderland
Launched 1876
Length 206ft 1in Breadth 33ft 6in Depth 19ft
921 tons gross 894 net
Owners: Hine Bros.
Captains: 1876-89 J. Johnstone; 1890-1904 J. Rich
Wrecked near Port Davey, Tasmania, 5/11/1904

"CASTLE HOLME"
Iron Ship
Built Bartram, Haswell & Co., Sunderland
Launched 16/9/1875 (reduced to Barque 1880)
Length 213ft 9in Breadth 34ft 5in Depth 20ft 7in
1042 tons gross 996 net
Captains: 1875-6 W. Robinson; 1877-82 J.
    Williamson; 1882-94 W. Bryce; 1895-1901
    Hurst; 1902-8 E.J. Holman
Sold foreign 1908; re-named "Ester" in 1912,
    "Ternan" in 1916 and "Tarnan" in 1922;
    wrecked 18/12/1924, Hovs Hallar, Sweden

"CEREAL"
Wooden Barque
Built Denniston, Sunderland
Launched August 1859
Length 112ft Breadth 25ft Depth 16ft 2in
298 tons gross
Owners: various to 1871; then Wilfrid Hine &
    others inc. Capt. James Ritchie
Captains: various to 1870 then 1871-2 J. Wilson;
    1872 J. Ritchie
Burned at sea (fire in cargo) abandoned
    28/9/1872

"CLARA"
Wooden Brigantine
Built Nova Scotia
Launched 1865
Length 90ft Breadth 23ft 2in Depth 11ft 2in
145 tons gross 145 net
Owners: various to 1876; 1876-83 Hine Bros.;
    1883-6 Capt. W. Shilton; 1887-90 Capt. B.
    Sheffield
Captains: various to 1870 then 1876-82 G.
    McLeod; then owners
Dismantled to a hulk 1891

(no photograph available)

"DENT HOLME"
Steel Screw Steamer
Built J.L. Thompson & Sons, Sunderland
Engines by J. Dickinson of Sunderland
Launched May 1883
Length 230ft 5in Breadth 33ft 3in depth 15ft 5in
1221 tons gross 932 under decks 791 net
Owners: Hine Bros.
Captains: 1883-4 J. Ritchie; 1884-5 J.N. Hurst
Lost 6/7/1885 collision in Gulf of St. Lawrence

(no photograph available)

"DENTON HOLME"
Iron Ship (reduced to Barque 12/5/1877)
Built Harland & Wolff, Belfast
Launched 19/6/1863 as "Star of Denmark"
Length 214ft 5in Breadth 32ft 1in Depth 21ft 7in
998 tons gross
Owners: 1863-90 J.P. Corry & Co.; Hine Bros. from
    10/5/1890 & re-named
Captains: 1890 J.H. Rich
Stranded & wrecked 25/9/90, nr Fremantle, W.
    Australia

(no photograph available)

"DERWENT HOLME"
Steel Screw Steamer
Built J.L. Thompson & Sons, Engines J. Dickinson,
   Sunderland
Launched May 1888 as "Crest"
Length 284ft Breadth 38ft 2in Depth 19ft 4in
2107 tons gross 1565 net
Owners: 1888-90 Crest Shipping Co.; Hine Bros.
   from 1890 & re-named
Captains: 1890-96 W. Holmes; 1896 J.G. Turney;
   !897-1901 W. Holmes
Sold foriegn 1901; re-named "Flandres";
   foundered off French coast, 13/12/1911

"EARL OF CARRICK"
Iron Screw Steamer
Built Abercorn Shipbuilding Co., Paisley
Engines J. & T. Young, Ayr
Launched May 1875
Length 137ft 1in Breadth 21ft 1in Depth 11ft
258 tons gross 151 net
Owners: 1875-6 G. Clark, Ayr; Hine Bros. from
   1876
Captains: 1877-8 W. Holmes
Wrecked Oban, Sept. 1878

(no photograph available)

"EDEN HOLME"
Iron Barque
Built Bartram, Haswell & Co., Sunderland
Launched 9/1/1875
Owners: Hine Bros.
Length 201ft 8in Breadth 32ft 2in Depth 18ft 5in
827 tons gross 794 net
Captains: 1875-6 J. Robinson; 1877-96 J.H.
   Randall; 1896-1904 J. Wyrill; 1904-7 G.H.
   Dulling
Wrecked Hebe Reef, Tasmania, 7/1/1907

"ELIZABETH AND ANN"
Wooden Screw Steamer
Built North Shields
Engines Wardhaugh & Bulmer
Launched November 1875
Length 78ft 2in Breadth 19ft 6in Depth 8ft 6in
84 tons gross 41 net
Owners: 1875-81: Robson & Renwick, Newcastle;
    1882 W.H. Poole & Co.; 1883-9 Hine Bros.
Captains: 1875 A. Renwick; 1883-9 R. Tully; 1890
    A. Gardner
Sold 1890 to R. Mason, Maryport

"ESK HOLME"
Iron Screw Steamer
Built J.L. Thompson & Sons, Sunderland
Engines by J. Dickinson, Sunderland
Launched 1877
Length 206ft 2in Breadth 30ft 5in Depth 16ft
925 tons gross 739 under decks 595 net
Captains: 1877-9 G. Brown; 1880 W. Brown; 1881-
    92 J.G. Turney (1889 W. Halliday; J.G.T.
    suspended)
Wrecked 31/1/1892, Wolves Rocks, Wales

"FERN HOLME"
Iron Screw Steamer
Built J.L. Thompson & Sons, Sunderland
Engines by J. Dickinson, Sunderland
Launched 1883
Length 310ft 6in Breadth 40ft 2in Depth 24ft 5in
2610 tons gross 2410 under decks 1715 net
Captains: 1883 G. Brown; 1884-7 J. Ritchie; 1887-
    8 C. Markham
Wrecked 9/7/1888 Newfoundland Canada

"FLORENCE RICHARDS"
Iron Screw Steamer
Built J.L. Thompson & Sons, Sunderland Engines
    by J. Dickinson, Sunderland
Launched 1874
Length 231ft 5in Breadth 30ft 1in Depth 16ft 8in
1051 tons gross 823 under decks 667 net
Owners: 1873-5 S. Richards; 1876-80 Hine Bros.;
    1881-90 R. Nicholson, Liverpool
Captains: 1874-6 J. Wilkinson; 1876-8 J. Kay; 1879
    Capt. McLeod; 1880-6 J. Asplett; 1887-8 J.
    Goodall; 1889-90 T. Winder
Foundered 10/3/1890, Portugal

(no photograph available)

"FOREST HOLME"
Steel Screw Steamer
Built J.L. Thompson & Sons, Sunderland
Engines by J. Dickinson, Sunderland
Launched July 1890
Length 295ft 6in Breadth 39ft 1in Depth 20ft 2in
2407 tons gross 1544 under decks 1763 net
Captains: 1890 G. Brown; 1891-99 J. Johnstone;
    1899-1904 A.R. Beaton; 1904 J.Roberts; 1905-8
    J.Chadwick then various to 1911
Sold 1911; resold in 1912 and 1913, re-named
    "Kardamila"; sold and renamed "Begonia
    No.4" in 1916; sold again 1917 and re-named
    "Camphill"; sunk by torpedo 26/6/1917

"GLASTRY"
Wooden Brigantine
Built Prussia (?)
Launched 1861
Length 87ft 7in Breadth 24ft Depth 12ft 6in
167 tons gross 148 net
Owners: various to 1876; 1876-8 Hine Bros.; 1878-
    80 J. Davidson, Maryport
Captains: various to 1875 then 1876-8 Capt. Saul;
    then R. Shepherd
Sold 1878; not in Lloyd's Register after 1880

(no photograph available)

"GLEN HOLME"
Iron Screw Steamer
Built Denton Grey & Co., W. Hartlepool
Engines by T.P. Richardson & Sons, Hartlepool
Launched 1870 (ex "Margaret Banks")
Length 213ft 6in Breadth 29ft 2in Depth 16ft 2in
826 tons gross 738 under decks 532 net
Owners: W. Banks, London; 1882-93 Hine Bros.
Captains: 1884 W. Spruce; 1885-9 T. Morwick;
   1890-3 W. Wilson
Lost May 1893 collision in Sound of Islay, Scotland

(no photograph available)

"GLENFALLOCH"
Iron Barque

Built Troon
Launched 1861
Length 140ft Breadth 28ft 1in Depth 17ft 5in
449 tons gross
Owners: various to 1869 then W. Grieve,
   Greenock; 1872-83 Hine Bros.
Captains: various to 1869 then Capt. Skinner;
   1873-7 J. Johnstone; 1878-83 Saul
Condemned 1883 & Sold Foreign (Chile); renamed
   "Natalia"

"GRETA HOLME"
Steel Screw Steamer
(picture courtesy of Mr. Anderson)
Built J.L. Thompson & Sons, Sunderland Engines
   by J. Dickinson, Sunderland
Launched July 1893
Length ft in Breadth ft in Depth ft in
2626 tons gross under decks 1678 net
Captains: 1893 G. Brown; 1894-1900 J. Ritchie;
   1901-7 J. Millican
Sold 1908; sold foreign, 1911 and re-named
   "Antonios"; lost with all hands, Scilly Isles, 1912

"HAZEL HOLME"
Composition Barque (iron beams)
Built Turnbull, Whitby
Launched May, 1870 as "King Arthur"
Length 138ft 9in Breadth 28ft 5in Depth 17ft 5in
422 tons gross 399 net
Owners: 1870-2 T. Turnbull, Whitby; 1872-87 Hine
    Bros. (W. Hine from 1872); 1887-8 H. Battle,
    Valparaiso
Captains: 1872-3 J. Pearson; 1874-5 W. Clark;
    1876-8 W. Holmes; 1879-83 J. Millican; 1884-7
    Capt. Austin; 1887-8 Capt. Marsh
Sold Foreign 1887; wrecked 1898

S.S. "HAZEL HOLME"
Steel Screw Steamer
Built J.L. Thompson & Sons, Sunderland
Engines by G. Clark of Sunderland
Launched 1/5/1900 and named "Hazel Holme"
Length 358ft Breadth 45ft 3in depth 26ft 7in
3107 tons gross
Sold while fitting out, December 1900 and re-
    named "Hughenden"; foundered 22/12/1911
    in Bay of Biscay, only two survivors

(no photograph available)

"HENRY SCHOLEFIELD"
Iron Screw Steamer
Built J.L. Thompson & Sons, Sunderland
Engines by J. Dickinson, Sunderland
Launched April 1872
Length 220ft 4in Breadth 30ft 2in Depth 16ft 7in
963 tons gross 842 under decks 622 net
Owners: 1872-8 Tully & Co.; 1878-81 Hine Bros.
Captains: 1878-81 Capt. Clark
Wrecked 24/12/1881 Nethertown

"HORATIO"
Iron Screw Steamer
Built Lindsay, Newcastle
Engines by Bowden Bros., Newcastle
Launched October 1873
Length 156ft 2in Breadth 23ft 7in Depth 13ft 9in
418 tons gross 387 under decks 262 net
Owners: 1873-6 R. Fell; 1877-89 Hine Bros.
Captains: 1877-81 Morwick; 1881 Turney; 1882-8
   Greggans; 1889 Brough
Stranded and wrecked 1889, Texel

(no photograph available)

"ISEL HOLME"
Steel Screw Steamer
Built J.L. Thompson & Sons, Sunderland
Engines G. Clark of Sunderland
Launched 24/8/1899
Length 397ft 6in Breadth 45ft 10in Depth 28ft 3in
3650 tons gross 2380 net
Captains: 1899 G. Brown; 1900-2 J. Ritchie; 1903-
   6 J. Johnstone; 1906-7 W. Gorley
Sold November 1907 and re-named "Myrtle
   Branch"; sunk by torpedo, 11/4/1918

"IVY HOLME (1)"
Iron Screw Steamer
Built J.L. Thompson & Sons, Sunderland
Engines by J. & F. Wilson, Sunderland
Launched April 1881
Length 110ft Breadth 21ft Depth 8ft 1in
170 tons gross 98 net 148 under decks
Captains: 1881 J. Connell
Foundered 1881 maiden voyage

(no photograph available)

"IVY HOLME (2)"
Iron Screw Steamer
Built J.L. Thompson & Sons, Sunderland
Engines by J. & F. Wilson, Sunderland
Launched April 1883
Length 120ft Breadth 22ft 1in Depth 9ft 5in
247 tons gross 156 net 193 under decks
Captains: 1883 J. Connell; 1884 J. Williams; 1885-7 Brough; 1888 W. Gorley; 1889 W. Wilson; 1890 D.B. Scott; 1892-4 E. Hall
Sold foreign 1894 and re-named "Chindor"; resold 1903, re-named "Kontzesi"; wrecked 1929, Spanish coast

(no photograph available)

"JOHN NORMAN"
Wooden Ship (Reduced to Barque)
Built Barnstaple, Devon
Launched 1855
Length 153ft 8in Breadth 27ft 6in Depth 17ft 5in
513 tons gross.
Owners: various to 1870; 1870-2 Redway & Co., Exeter; 1872-82 Hine Bros. (W. Hine 1872-6).
Captains: 1872 J. Hurst; 1874-6 W. Bryce; 1877-9 J.G. Turney; 1879-82 Nicholson
Abandoned at sea, 21/6/1882

(no photograph available)

"LOUGHRIGG HOLME"
Steel Screw Steamer
(picture courtesy of Mr. & Mrs. D. Ritchie)
Built J.L. Thompson & Sons, Sunderland
Engines by G. Clark of Sunderland
Launched 6/6/1891
Length 283ft Breadth 37ft 7in Depth 19ft 2in
2069 tons gross 1503 net
Captains: 1891 G. Brown; 1892-7 J. Millican; 1898-1900 D.S. Turney; 1901 J. Johnstone; 1902-6 Chadwick
Grounded & Wrecked Bari, Italy 2/4/1906

"MAGGIE GROSS"
Wooden Brigantine
Built New Brunswick
Launched 1865
Length 101ft 8in Breadth 25ft 9in Depth 11ft 4in
185 tons gross 179 net
Owners: various to 1876; 1876-8 Hine Bros.; 1879-
    80 S. Morrison; not in Register after 1880
Captains: various to 1874 then 1874-6 Holmes;
    1876-7 Wedgewood

(no photograph available)

"MAITLAND"
Iron Screw Steamer
Built Duncan, Port Glasgow Engines by Rankin &
    Blackmore, Greenock
Launched 1872
Length 190ft Breadth 27ft 6in Depth 14ft 6in
660 tons gross 550 under decks 422 net
Owners: various to 1877; Hine Bros. 1876-80
Captains: various to 1876; 1876 J. Wilkinson; 1876
    W. Brown; 1876-9 Capt. McLeod; 1879-80 M.
    Kirkpatrick
Sunk by collision, Feb. 1880

"MERSEY"
Iron Screw Steamer
Built Sunderland
Launched 1868 approx date (no details known)
Owners: 1868-75 Powell & Co.; 1875-6 Hine Bros.
Captains: 1875-6 Wilkinson; 1876 J. Robinson
Wrecked off Skomer Island, Wales 11/8/76

(no photograph available)

"MYRTLE HOLME"
Iron Ship (reduced to Barque 1878)
(picture courtesy of State Library of S. Australia)
Built Bartram, Haswell & Co., Sunderland
Launched 19/6/1875
Length 211ft Breadth 32ft 9in Depth 19ft 7in
945 tons gross 902 net
Owners: 1875-1908 Hine Bros.
Captains: 1875-81 J. Ritchie; 1882 Austin; 1883-90
    J.W. Millican; 1891-8 W. Cobb
Sold Foreign 1908; re-named "Glimt"; sunk by
    submarine, 4/9/1915, North Sea

S.S. "MYRTLE HOLME"
Steel Screw Steamer
Built Short Bros., Sunderland

Launched July 1890 and named "Imperial Prince"

Length 293ft 5in Breadth 40ft 2in depth 18ft 5in

2525 tons gross 2398 net

Owners: 1890-1912 Prince Shipping Co. Ltd. (J. Knott); Dec. 1912-June 1914 "Holme Line S.S. Co. Ltd."

Captains: various to 1912; 1912-14 J. Roberts; 1914 J.W. Clark

Renamed "Myrtle Holme" June 1913; sold 1914; acquired by Goshi Kaisha Kishimoto Shokai of Kishimoto in February 1915 and renamed *Yeirako Maru*; wrecked on Amherst Rocks in the China Sea on 11th April 1915

"NETHER HOLME"
Steel Screw Steamer
Built J.L. Thompson & Sons

Engines by G. Clark of Sunderland

Launched September 1888

Length 277ft Breadth 37ft 2in Depth 19ft 5in

1969 tons gross 1285 net

Captains: 1888 J. Ritchie; 1890-5 C. Markham; 1896-1900 Wilson; 1901-3 Gorley; 1904-7 J. Roberts

Sold October 1907; stranded Pembrokeshire Coast, 3/11/1907; refloated and scrapped 1908

"OVINGTON"
Iron Screw Steamer
Built Osbourne Graham, Sunderland

Engines by Christie, Gutch & Co., N. Shields
Launched 1873

Length 187ft Breadth 28ft 3in Depth 14ft 3in

687 tons gross 536 under decks 444 net

Owners: 1873-5 Humble & Thompson, Newcastle; 1875-81 Huntley & Bulmer; 1881-9 Hine Bros.

Captains: various to 1881; 1881-7 J. Winterhoff; 1888-9 W. Gorley

Lost in collision, 29/12/1889

(no photograph available)

"QUEEN OF THE FLEET"
Wooden Barque
Built Nova Scotia
Launched 1857 details not known
Owners: various to 1874; 1874-5 Hine Bros.
   (Managing owners)
Captains: 1874-5 Capt. Tierney
Abandoned at sea, 1875

(no photograph available)

"ROBERT HINE"
Wooden Barque, Copper-bottomed
Built Taylor & Scouler,Sunderland
Launched 21/5/1868
Length 119ft 8in Breadth 27ft 3in Depth 16ft 4in
327 tons gross
Owners: Nicholson & Co., Liverpool (Wilfrid Hine,
   manager) 1869-73; then Hine Bros.
Captains: 1968-70 J. Wilkinson; 1871-2 E. Ward;
   1873-6 G. Brown; 1876-84 E. Hall
Sold 1885; wrecked Brazilian coast, 19/8/1891

"RYDAL HOLME"
Steel Screw Steamer
Built J. Blumer & Co., Sunderland
Engines by Amos & Smith, Hull
Launched 13/8/1889
Length 270ft Breadth 36ft 6in depth 20ft 2in
1931 tons gross 1759 under decks, 1265 net
Captains: 1889-99; W. Brown; 1899 W. Gorley
Sold 1900; resold 1902 and re-named "Ronda";
   bought by Admiralty 1914 and sunk as a
   blockship

"SAN DOMINGO"
Iron Screw Steamer
Built Pearse, Stockton
Engines by Blair & Co., Stockton
Launched May 1874
Length 230ft Breadth 31ft 1in Depth 16ft
1079 tons gross 847 under decks 682 net
Owners: 1874-7 Dixon, Harris & Co.; 1878-89 H.
   Bucknell & Sons; 1889-99 Hine Bros.
Captains: various to 1889; 1889-99 W. Gorley
Sold foreign 1899; re-named "Blenda"; sunk by
   mine 21/11/1920, Baltic Sea

(no photograph available)

"THOMAS VAUGHAN"
Iron Screw Steamer
Built Middlesborough: Engines:by Black &
    Hawthorn, Gateshead Launched August, 1871
Length 190ft Breadth 26ft 8in Depth 15ft
645 tons gross 575 under decks 419 net
Owners: 1871-5 C.E. Muller; 1876-81 Hine Bros.
Captains: 1871-5 J. Walker; 1876-8 W. Brown;
    1879-82 J. Branthwaite
Foundered 7/1/1882, Jack Sound, Wales

(no photograph available)

"THORN HOLME"
Iron Screw Steamer
(picture courtesy Maryport Maritime Museum)
Built J.L. Thompson & Sons, Engines by J.
    Dickinson, Sunderland
Launched February 1881
Length 260ft Breadth 36ft Depth 18ft 5in
1697 tons gross 1376 under decks 1101 net
Captains: 1881-2 G. Brown; 1883-90 W. Holmes
Stranded St. Lawrence River, July 1890; sold,
    refloated & renamed "Louisburg" 1891;
    wrecked 1911

"TOM ROBERTS"
Wooden Schooner
Built Milford
Launched 1838
Length 76ft 9in Breadth 21ft 3in Depth 11ft 8in
122 tons gross 103 net 118 under decks
Owners: unknown to 1869; 1869-74 Richards &
    Co.; 1874-84 Hine Bros.; 1884 W. Walker
Captains: 1838-69 J. Samuel; 1869-74 D. Williams;
    1874-6 E. Hall; 1877-84 R. Carswell
Sold 1884; wrecked 16/11/1887, Isle of Man

"WEST CUMBERLAND"
Iron Screw Steamer
Built J.L. Thompson & Sons
Engines by J. Dickinson, Sunderland
Launched 21/2/1879
Length 240ft 5in Breadth 34ft Depth 18ft 3in
1387 tons gross 1123 under decks 898 net
Captains: 1879-81 G. Brown; 1882-8 W. Brown;
    1889 Markham; 1890 M. Kirkpatrick
Sunk in collision, Finisterre, 11/6/1890

Bibliography

Ashmore, Lt.Cdr. B.G.
  Maryport Harbour, 1978: Allerdale District Council.
Bennett, Tom
  Shipwrecks around Wales, Vol. 2, 1992: Happy Fish.
Bissett, Sir James
  Tramps and Ladies, 1960: Angus & Robertson, London.
Evers, Henry
  Navigation in Theory and Practice, 1850: Collins, London
Falkus, Hugh
  Master of Cape Horn, 1982: Gollancz, London.
Greenhill, Basil and Giffard, Ann
  Edwardian and Victorian Ships and Harbours, 1978: and
  Edwardian and Victorian Merchant Steamships, 1979: Batsford.
Jackson, Herbert and Mary
  West Cumberland, 1991, and
  Holme Shipping Line, 1991: Firpress, Workington.
Lubbock, Basil
  The Colonial Clippers, 3rd. Edition, 1924: James Brown & Son, Glasgow.
  The Last of the Windjammers, Vols I & II, 1929: Brown, Son & Ferguson.
MacGregor, David R
  Merchant Sailing Ships 1850-1875, 1984: Conways, London.
  Clipper Ships, 1979: Argus.
  Square Rigged Sailing Ships, 1977: Argus
Osler, A. & Barrow, A
  Tall Ships Two Rivers, 1993: Keepgate Publishing.
Rothwell, Catherine
  Ports of the North West, 1991: Printwise Publications, Ltd.
Sawyers, William
  A List of the Cumberland Shipping, 1840: Crosthwaite & Co., Whitehaven.
Wilmore, Graham
  Steel's Shipmaster's Assistant, 1846: Longman, London.

N.M.M. Monograph No. 5, 1972
  Problems of Ship Management and Operation 1870 – 1900
Various Authors
  The Ship, National Maritime Museum Series, 1980: HMSO.
  Admiralty Manual of Seamanship, Vol 1, 1937: HMSO.
  Lloyds' Maritime Atlas, Eleventh Edition, 1977: Lloyd's of London.
  The Admiralty, and the U.S. Hydrographic Office: Pilot Manuals - UK and Australian coasts.